Frank Kermode

has been Lord Northcliffe Professor of Modern English Literature at University College, London, King Edward VII Professor of English Literature at Cambridge and Charles Eliot Norton Professor of Poetry at Harvard. He is the General Editor of the Fontana Modern Masters and Masterguides series, and of the Oxford Authors. His previous books include *The Genesis of Secrecy*, *The Classic*, *The Art of Telling*, *Forms of Attention*, *An Appetite for Poetry* and *The Sense of an Ending*. He was knighted in 1991 and lives in Cambridge.

From the reviews of *Not Entitled*:

'Delightful and engrossing'   JOHN BAYLEY, *The Times*

'The most original and entertaining new book I've read has been Frank Kermode's memoir . . . wry, self-doubting, beautifully written, it's full of well-judged gloomy hilarity.'
      ANTHONY THWAITE, *Sunday Telegraph* Summer Reading

'[A] gentle, honest, well-mannered, almost holy book.'
      DESMOND CHRISTY, *Guardian*

'Full of musing and wonderfully mellow . . . The war opens out into a long and wonderful chapter of actual memoirs, but he was a naval officer, mostly the captain's secretary, so life is observed in others, and a more brilliantly described series of mad captains I have never read. These pages are written with loving attention and deep bitterness, which humour never quite overcomes: they are for connoisseurs, better than the novels of Larkin or the poems of practically anybody. It looks as if this genius, lugubrious and unsung, will plod his way through life undiscovered.'
      PETER LEVI, *Spectator*

Further reviews overleaf

'Very few, if any, books published this year, or indeed any other, will carry the same sharp but generous insights into the human condition as this quiet ramble round the borders of his own life . . . a privileged glimpse into a finely tuned mind.'

ANTHONY HOLDEN, *Literary Review*

'Marvellously witty and vivid . . . Kermode is a writer of rare stylishness and subtlety.' IAN HAMILTON, *Sunday Telegraph*

'Wonderful . . . an elegant, often very moving, piece of writing . . . the book glows beautifully with characters from the author's solid, low Anglican childhood.'

IAN THOMPSON, *Independent on Sunday*

'[Kermode] writes a sensitive English, sometimes superbly. His mood has its own private elegance, candour and humour . . . Could become a classic.' STEPHEN TUMMIN, *Daily Telegraph*

'[An] elegantly and shrewdly paced memoir.'

ALAN ROSS, *Times Literary Supplement*

'Compulsive . . . Kermode is a fearless memoirist, not at all afraid of the ridiculous at the heart of the sublime.' *Economist*

'There is wit, there is satire, there is outright comedy, and at the same time running through the book a strain of sadness, of ironic yet amused discontent with the human condition. All this gives the book a very special texture.' DAVID DAICHES, *Scotsman*

'*Not Entitled* is graced with the qualities we associate with Kermode's style – clarity, concision, fluency. Like a mountain stream it flows over varied ground; hilariously comic passages alternating with poetic descriptions and clever character analysis. . . . A terrific read.' SHUSHA GUPPY, *Times Higher*

FRANK KERMODE

Not Entitled

A Memoir

Flamingo
An Imprint of HarperCollins*Publishers*

Flamingo
An Imprint of HarperCollins*Publishers*
77–85 Fulham Palace Road
Hammersmith, London, W6 8JB

Published by Flamingo 1997
1 3 5 7 9 8 6 4 2

First published in the UK by
HarperCollins*Publishers*, 1996

First published in the USA by
Farrar, Strauss and Giroux, 1995

A catalogue entry for this book is
available from the British Library

ISBN 0 00 686329 9

Set in Caledonia

Printed and bound in Great Britain by
Caledonian International Book Manufacturing Ltd, Glasgow

CONTENTS

He was a kind of nothing, titleless.

—SHAKESPEARE, *Coriolanus*

NOT
ENTITLED

Man to Man

Frank returns to Douglas (3,2,3)
—Times *crossword puzzle clue*

Between these origins and that ending is where the weather is, fair or foul: the climate of a life. Not, as some have said, a dream, but a climate, a microclimate, *le temps qu'il fait.*

There can have been no salting of herring at our place during the autumn of 1919; my mother was pregnant and pregnant women cannot put down herring, it will simply disintegrate and leave you with a barrel of smelly slush. Taken with boiled potatoes and with buttermilk or water—Adam's ale—or, on rare occasions, real ale for Father, herring was a staple. Having to forfeit it was the first of many disappointments or privations imposed on a struggling young couple by their first child. They began even before he was born. That event took place at the end of November, in a tenement bedroom, neither place nor season propitious. Clearly he survived, and they lived through a herringless winter to ensure that he did, well enough to be writing this seventy-five wild Decembers later, dotage fended off, for the moment, by the thin roof of sanity.

Part of the difficulty these kind people experienced in rearing me was that I was generally unable, with my best efforts, to do things that other children seemed to manage without much thought, certainly without the terror that immobilised me at the prospect of failing in tasks where success was the norm, such as tying shoelaces. The other day my garden was invaded by rabbits. I wasn't in the least terrified, after all I have seen worse in my time, though I notice that by way of excusing my failure to act I have just said "rabbits" when in fact I saw only one, and there may have been only one—a large one, however—which nevertheless ran away when challenged by a territorially outraged squirrel. If there had been a plague of rabbits I doubt if I'd have done anything about it except hurry slowly to the telephone. The dripping tap, the puncture, the broken lock, the rat in the yard, even the light bulb that burns out in a fairly inaccessible socket, I take these problems under consideration and do nothing. Here, alone in a house with more rooms than I can use, I can close a door on broken chairs, bury my blank tax return deep in a chaotic filing cabinet, easily lose my keys or my diary. All this may be attended to, with much shouting, groaning, and cursing, another day, when it has become obvious that it must be, and that nobody else is going to do it.

My mother was quick to notice this trait. *"Traa dy lioaur,"* she would say, time enough is your motto. Always at the heel of the hunt. The Manx expression, though variously spelt, is understandable, for she had been a farm girl and some Manx still lingered in the countryside at the beginning of the century; as late as when I was around you might be given good-day in Manx on country roads and were expected to answer accordingly. But I've never heard "the heel of the hunt" anywhere else, and wonder where she can have picked it up; there are. no foxes on the Isle of Man, and no word for fox in Manx, which puzzled the Bible translators when they came to the little foxes of the Song of Songs and several others as well. Samson alone needed three hundred of them, three hundred of what shall we say, they must have asked themselves, surely not rabbits? Here was a clear indication that to be Manx was to be, in an admittedly not deeply wounding way, exiled from the life and language of the English. Moreover, gentry were scanty on this island, and can only have hunted other beasts, rabbits perhaps, but they could conceivably have used this teasing expression of those who arrived late at the paltry kill. My mother's early life was not something she said much about, her origins were fascinatingly obscure, but phrases of this sort are unlikely to have derived from her own experience. I suppose she may, as a girl, have collided with some mini-squire and picked up this and other exogenously lively terms.

One such I remember because it certainly came from a world of which she can't have been anything but entirely innocent. Somehow she had made the acquaintance of a Mr. MacNulty, a commercial traveller no doubt, Irish obviously. I see his bow tie and spats, and his jolly red face, his bright little blue eyes and bristling red hair. I now recognise him as a serious drinker, but to me as I then was he was only a most courteous jolly red man, out to charm us all with his kind knowingness and all the good things he would say in his phlegmy voice. How he formed the habit of calling on us, and how she formed the habit of encouraging him to do so, I have no idea, except that she often referred to him as her notion of a gentleman. She placed a high value on gentlemen, often urging me to become one, and told of specimens she had met when she was a waitress—people who had spent time in England and even been to London, there acquiring the needed polish. On this particular evening MacNulty knocked and entered as usual; she was welcoming but embarrassed because the house was unusually untidy. "Oh, Mr. MacNulty," she said, "do come in. I'm sorry you find me in this state, the place is like a whore's garret." MacNulty's face, against all precedent, grew solemn, and he replied, "You must promise me never to say that again. It means something very bad." Of course she never did say it again. Like the heel of the hunt, it had blown in from some alien scene and settled on her word-hoard. She liked the sound of words. As we discovered only after her death, she had in her youth won prizes and certificates as a reciter of dialect poetry. To love words, whatever they meant—even without knowing what they meant—more than the world, which you can't properly handle unless you have some understanding how its things work, was part of my inheritance.

I think MacNulty kept on coming because he admired her readiness to be ecstatically impressed by his blarney, but also because he was intrigued by her innocence. Hogarthian whores' garrets may well have been a familiar element of his world, but so was the idea of a young woman who had nothing to do with such a world and ought not to make even ignorant allusion to it. I still wonder where the banned expression came from, and where she can have heard it. I have never come across it since.

The big war was not long over, a destroyer of innocence, one might have supposed; it must have been so for those who, like my father, survived several years in France. But apart from some incidental hardships, those who escaped death, mutilation, or premature bereavement were probably not much changed by it. A town of about twenty thousand people is just small enough to sustain relationships of blood or acquaintance which, simply because they are tenuous, are frequently and in pleasurable disputation researched and rehearsed, so that Douglas had quite enough complexity to satisfy its inhabitants' desire for security in a world interesting enough in itself, without their having to bother about Britain, which they simply called "away" or "across." Its ways of life, its ways of earning, its ways of talking, its preferences in wickedness were alien and a bit menacing. The occasional incursion of an exotic like MacNulty was enough to satisfy our curiosity about "away." As far as I could tell, my father's military service, which must have set him among the English, Welsh, and Scottish daily for several years, had not the slightest effect on his assumptions and prejudices or his speech, which remained a slow and cautious Manx, to him of course the norm from which the fuss of the Welsh, the whining of Liverpool, the apparent gormlessness of northern English, and the suspiciously smart foreign clatter of the southern dialects were simply aberrations, as, in a way, their speakers themselves were.

There was no strong need to join such people. You left the island if a war made it necessary, or—rarest of exigencies—to go to college or university, and were expected in any case to come back as soon as you could. Indeed, it was close to unthinkable that you might think of not coming back. Yet the mesh of family and social relationships was so fine that any tear, whether caused by death or disgrace, including the disgrace of emigration, was soon mended. The idea of living anywhere else can never have occurred to my parents. I'm not sure when I first entertained it, though after my own war was over I had long been quite sure that I had to choose exile. It was, to the Manx of the time, a perverse and inexplicable choice. For a while when I was over on a visit people would stop me in the street, a man of thirty or so, and express surprise that I should still be a student. What other reason could there now be for my long absences? Then as time passed and my visits grew less frequent, the mesh was mended and nobody knew me at all.

So the town, considering the odds against the enterprise—time, sin, poverty, death—made a good attempt at seeming changeless. The new gossip was really only the old recycled. The names on the war memorial began by repre-

senting loss but became part of a reassuring permanence, like
the missing leg of the butcher or the presence always of children wearing clogs, hilarious girls, and white-moustached old
men, each behaving as beclogged children, jolly girls, and
sourly amused old men on bowling greens always do behave.

Yet there were harbingers of change, intimations of mut-
ability, like the foreign-sounding voices of Savoy Hill, barely
audible through a large gramophone horn attached to the wireless my father built around 1924. From that horn there had
previously emerged only the sounds of my father's favourite
records, ranging from comic songs like "When Father Painted
the Parlour You Couldn't See Pa for Paint" to the pure tenors
of Joseph Hislop and Heddle Nash. Now it transmitted whis-
pers, in accents we hardly recognised, which sought to make
more actual a world elsewhere that was grander than ours,
though ours had its own gradations of grandness. Remote as
these voices were, they were soon more immediate to us than
the English newspapers, received late in the day and in any
case lacking for us both the miraculous immediacy of broadcasting and the authoritative gossip of the local journals. One
of those local journals was the sage and serious *Mona's Herald*,
Mona being the Roman name for the island; the editor was
the father of my schoolfellow Nigel Kneale, whose *Quatermass
Experiment* was to introduce supernatural horror into the tradition of television drama. Perhaps Kneale, his head full of the
tales of wicked Manx fairies, also crouched over his father's
wireless and heard strange, distant foreign voices, as from another planet.

We were much too far from any transmitter to use a crystal
set, and the wireless was large and cumbersome, the first thing
you noticed when you went into the room. It required batteries
both wet and dry. Every week I would take the wet battery
to a garage in Athol Street, where they would recharge it for
sixpence. These errands took me into the intellectual and ad-

ministrative centre of the town. That Athol Street had a few small garages and shops did not seem to harm its dignity. It represented, among other things, the Inns of Court of our world. The courts themselves were nearby, and so was the House of Keys, the parliament of that world. The police station was just round the corner. The advocates, as we called them, practised their own peculiar Manx brand of law in their offices in Athol Street. Nowadays the street is also occupied—infested, as some might say—by offshore banks and companies whose operations occasionally transcend the ordinary limits of just conduct as implied by almost any system of law; but in my day Athol Street still marked a frontier between respectability and disgrace. "If he doesn't change his ways he'll find himself in Athol Street" was a dire prediction, of bankruptcy if you were well off, of worse if you weren't.

The young and the poor heard a great many such warnings, but the lawyers and businessmen who actually found themselves daily in Athol Street were naturally exempt. They were among those on whom my mother had founded her conception of the gentleman. This was not entirely a matter of giving women the wall rather than the gutter, or of confidently reacting to certain social stimuli, for example the approach of a lady or a funeral, by raising the hat or cap. It had also to do with the way important people addressed their inferiors or, in the good old sense of the word, condescended to them. But it was hardly conceivable that such displays of chivalrous conduct could be consistent with irregular dress. The clothes worn by the gentlemen of Athol Street, rich, ample, watch-chained, confirmed their status, too high for envy but not for emulation. I had no inferiors but could practise with my cap. My father, a workingman, had a rich array of hats, including a bowler for Sunday walks, the main object of which was to offer opportunities for its courteous removal. I even remember a top hat, held close to the spout of a steaming kettle to freshen the nap, but I may be borrowing this hat from someone else's father, or someone else's memory.

Much later, his morale destroyed, he wore detachable collars, which to my priggish annoyance he would tear off as soon as he got home. Modern men who work as he did would never dream of wearing collars, ties, and suits, but at that time open-necked shirts were either not invented or considered suitable only for strolling on seaside promenades. Once in his own house, and no longer needing to be respectable, he was entirely indifferent to his appearance, at any rate between the neck and the calf. In spite of his impatience with collars he was strangely obsessed with extremities and their decorous covering, and placed what seemed to me a fanatical emphasis on the care and cleaning of shoes. This was a permanent cause of friction between me and an otherwise quite good-natured parent. Gentlemen had gleaming, perfectly formed shoes, not scuffed on the toe caps by kicking stones or crumpled at the back by the lazy habit of stuffing the foot in without undoing the laces.

It was an important consideration that many of my contemporaries had no shoes at all, and understandably lacked aspirations to gentility. In the 1930s, when almost everybody was out of work for at least forty weeks a year, poor children were issued with clogs at the public expense. Showers of sparks followed them as they tore round the streets and the school playground. They didn't seem to mind, but I knew very well how I'd have suffered. If I failed to clean my shoes, or if my dissolute ways drove my father to such despair that he was bankrupted or took to drink and lost his job, I would be compelled to wear clogs. Here was a threat, but it came to nothing, like so many others. It is interesting for an old man to reflect that few of the very dreadful retributions that threatened him in youth were ever exacted, even when deserved. So far, anyway.

Perhaps bringing up children was done in a more threatening way in those days, especially among the lower classes, and since the threats were so frequent and various, many would never be realised, and one came to assume, perhaps too easily, that they were just forms of words, their disciplinary work done there and then rather than in some blighted future. But the shadows of such threats, even if mostly lacking the power to inflict real harm, capable at best of creating an atavistic unease, can persist throughout life; now that I am perfectly free to neglect my shoes entirely if I want to, I still feel unhappy when I notice that I have used them roughly and neglected to polish them. I take every opportunity, when in America, of having my shoes cleaned by professionals, whose skill I greatly admire. It is a confessional experience: one steps down from the dais glowing with restored virtue. But even now my shoes could never, after the first weeks, survive a paternal inspection. Every crack in the uppers reminds me of the sudden transformation of my father, spotting a scuffed toe cap or a trace of mud on the heel, into a loud, bitter enemy, he who was ordinarily quite gentle and affectionate, the more remarkably in that he had so inexplicably begotten a son who resembled him in no way whatsoever, being fat, plain, shortsighted, clumsy, idle, dirty (not only as to footwear), and very unlikely to add to the family store of sporting cups and medals, tributes to his skills in football, swimming, and, later, bowls, at which he was a champion. I am glad to say I have a son, and a brother-in-law, who are able to win cups and medals as he did.

An even more troublesome survival of my early training is, or was, a habit of deference, acquired to please an insistent mother, and now hardly a bother at all, cancelled by the insouciance of old age. Formerly, though, it was very irksome, and got me into difficulties at important moments in my life. It was a tendency to irrational and premature compliance with the expectations of anybody who assumed the right to demand it. This was partly a consequence of having been born poor, but to reliable people who trusted one another without question and rarely imagined they were being imposed upon, even though they very often were. In a way you could trust even the boss or a policeman, trust them to do their office. After all, there is no doubting the reality of an authority that can give you the sack or, even if you are on first-name terms, as you very well might be with the local constable, lock you up. But this trust could also extend to people who had no such sanctions at their disposal. In short, I have been much too ready to assume in all acquaintances an innocence of motive, as if it were impossible that they should be deceivers, slanderers, cheats, without pity for anybody who made such an absurd assumption. But that is not the end of it; having found out my mistake I might well react excessively, for to break such a habit may call for a violent effort.

Such reactions have sometimes got me into trouble, and then I blame that early training in politeness and motiveless civility, mostly, as I've said, at the hands of my mother. Why was she so keen on it? Partly, no doubt, because of *her* early training. Just what form this took it is impossible to say. Information about her childhood lay under a permanent ban. It seems certain, though barely credible, that her parents emigrated to the United States when she was no more than a few days old, leaving her behind. We know little about her fostering, though it has been established that in her second year a fifteen-year-old girl carried her on foot from Douglas to Braddan church, a long walk with such a burden, and there had her christened by a certain Canon Kermode (no known connection with the family she later married into). It is not known how she came to spend her youth at Kewaigue, a hamlet two or three miles out of Douglas, in the parish of Braddan. She must have gone to school somewhere, very likely one of those tiny village schools with only one classroom that were still to be seen in the villages when I was walking about the island.

And perhaps it was a good school, for she was not ignorant, only innocent.

After that she went to work in a Douglas café, the very place where those well-shod and courtly advocates and businessmen gathered for coffee or light lunches. It still stands where it stood eighty-odd years ago, though somewhat changed. The girls no longer live above the shop as they did then. My mother always spoke of this time (the earliest time she ever did speak of) with affection. Her memory was not only of the impressive customers but of the gaiety of the girls. They wrote facetious rhymes in one another's albums, and probably went in for a little gentle flirtation. Lively girls, they did not mind looking alike in their white blouses and long black skirts. They had left school at fourteen unconvinced of the sadness of their lives. Given as she was to little bursts of giggling, it was easier than you might expect to think of my mother being gay, even a little wild, though the fun was associated with a condition of servitude, however benignly imposed. Later her memories of the shop were always of fun and giggling, which would make her giggle again and, as she grew old, laugh more hugely, gulping for breath and laughing on. In her last years she wept a good deal but giggled still, sometimes imagining herself to be a girl in a teashop, weeping on her visits to the empty present. So she never wholly lost her gaiety, though she did lose her mind.

On the day she was told of my father's death, a brilliant cold day in late March with the wind rattling the hospital windows, she understood what we were telling her; her face crumpled and her eyes poured tears. But the matron, passing briskly through the ward, called out, "What's this? What's this? Tears on Easter morning?" and she giggled and said, "Oh no, matron, that won't do, will it?" Authority, ignorant of her real wants, was ordering her to be cheerful, and she obeyed.

Still, there may have been a moment in her life when she herself had been capricious, officious, demanding deference, as was the right of pretty young women. After my father's death she mistook me for him as he had been long ago. Once she demanded the present of a scarf she had seen in a draper's window in the town, I suppose fifty-odd years before. Having no idea how to deal with this command, I foolishly rushed off to the town and bought a scarf that was in that same shop window. When I got back to her, she had returned to the desolate present and scolded me for this absurdity, asking what possible use such a frippery could be to her.

Somehow the gaiety was dependent on the vulnerability, it derived from the threat of desolation, it was a carnival escape from fear; it might even have been a fear of hell, a terror long in decline in the thoughts of the educated classes though not in the pulpits of our town. But she was obedient rather than religious, and what she feared most was the capacity of other human beings, especially those close to her, to threaten, cheat, and betray, after all a very reasonable fear, though her having to deal with it as she did was probably a reason for my discounting it.

I reflect often on this association of gaiety with terror, giggling with desolation. It had nothing to do with the well-known comic defiances of the poor, the boldness of the music hall, the naughtiness of Marie Lloyd and her imitators, with some of whom I was early acquainted. Large and ornate women and beery male comics from Lancashire would, in summer, pack the huge halls of my native town and tell off-colour jokes about the Rector of Stiffkey, who was defrocked for some sexual offence and later, doubtless driven by extreme poverty, had exploited his notoriety by allowing himself to be exhibited in a barrel at Blackpool, where, I seem to remember, he was attacked by a lion; or Gandhi, his diet described as consisting of a glass of water and a caraway seed; or posh London girls caught taking cocaine. They made a world, blowsy, bawdy, and wicked, which their holiday audiences could inhabit for a carnival hour, for it contained images not only of the absurdities and miseries of a la-di-da upper class that wasn't, in the 1930s, feeling much of the real pinch. This pleasure they could have in Douglas, as in Blackpool, another favourite summer resort, without needing to abandon their own tripe-and-cowheel world, and their own reassuring, saving kinds of coarseness and sentimentality. The singer Florrie Ford came year after year for a generation, fat, loud, rich, fantastically overdressed, but certainly in touch and offering the audience a hugely magnified image of their own Cockaignes. It's said that when a man threw a banana at her she caught it, ate it, and invited him to come back afterwards and get his skin back. I once met Miss Ford; it must have been in the summer of 1939, when I was working at a summer job collecting tickets on the Fleetwood or Liverpool ferries. Reclining, vast and perfumed, in her private cabin, she handed me two tickets, one for herself and one for her dog. She wanted me to ask where the dog was, so I did. "Dead!" she cried, exploding with grief.

Although they were arranged for the benefit of the inhabitants of Lancashire mill towns emptied by their annual holidays or "wakes," and for the vast armies of Scottish shipyard workers, we natives got some good from these mildly libertine summer shows, and we could dance to the big bands, Jack Hjlton, Roy Fox, and the rest, picking up girls in the vast ballrooms, pretending to be carefree "visitors" with wealthy parents living in some part of England that sounded remote and posh, say, Sussex, or any other place not in the north, enjoying exceptional liberties to which we were certainly not entitled, exploiting our superior knowledge of the place, its glens, beaches, pubs.

But Douglas did not, in those hectic summer weeks, really belong to us. It reverted to us only in mid-September, when we settled down to the severity of winter manners and, for many of us, the struggle to survive the long months of un-employment. The only release came at the end of the year, especially on New Year's Eve, still for Celts in those days the more important winter festival, though there might, from time to time, be a wedding, at which some relaxation was permitted, and when the gaiety of all had been fuelled by port or, on the grandest occasions, whisky, the lights might go out and the house ring with squeals and giggles as the young did, or came near to doing, what was never spoken of. To people who did their normal courting in cold doorways, bundled up in over-coats, these moments of licensed excess, this freedom to giggle, touch, and unbutton, must have been almost unimaginably precious. In the ordinary way there was little licence on offer to the young, who were then younger than now, though I feel the young of my mother's youth must have been younger still, and still more strictly inhibited. All the same, they found their way to be occasionally happy, the wild giggling above the shop consistent with maidenly propriety, though not, when inop-portunely remembered, with the end-time of senility.

SEEKING A RELIGION appropriate to our condition, we were, at any rate in winter, solid low Anglicans in a town otherwise devoted to Protestant dissent or Irish Catholicism. We chose the church, or rather the branch of the church, that suited best our social station and aspirations. We were not in trade, or we might have preferred the Methodists, inaccurately classed along with the other nonconformists as Ranters, but said to have a spiritual and commercial grip on the world of shopkeepers. We were contemptuous of the Irish, with their inherited habits of poverty and large families, of bowing and scraping before graven images, of hanging pictures of the Pope in their parlours and allowing themselves to be bullied by priests. Sometimes, though, it seemed they had more fun than we did, especially after Mass on Sundays, when they did as they pleased while we had no liberty at all.

Sunday was, and since the shadow persists, still is, the day of tedium. You couldn't play cards (the devil's books) or read anything except the Bible and a conscientiously vacuous paper called *The Sunday Companion*. There were no Sunday newspapers and of course no movies. For me, the choirboy, there were three sessions at church, and a boring afternoon family walk, gloves in hand, cap at the ready for raising, followed usually by tea with ancient relatives or pseudo-relatives (I had no real ones). Yet these privations were seen as the price one willingly paid for not being Catholic. We were not subtle about doctrine but could recognise and resist with enjoyable indignation Romish tendencies in our own church. Once a new vicar called the Reverend Talbot Easter, which sounded so bogus that only the worst could be expected, made the choir turn to the east for the recitation of the Creed and bow the head at the mention of the Second Person of the Trinity. This little bit of ritual, observed in hundreds of Anglican churches, was amongst us an impudent and outrageous innovation; it set the fires of revolt, which went out of control when Mr. Easter began to introduce fancy-dress vestments and *candles*. Next stop Rome, we cried; we might as well give up now and join the micks, join the queues that, to our bewilderment, formed on summer Sundays to get into Mass, as if it were a picture show.

These ignorant idolaters were as alien to us as Jews. Although we never met Jews, they nevertheless had a place in our insular fantasies, figments to be feared and despised. I remember my father coming home from work for his midday dinner and announcing that yet another shop in the main street had sold out to the Jews. I was already suspicious of such claims, and sure enough it turned out that the shop, like many others, had been sold to a non-Jewish English business. What he meant was that the shop was no longer Manx; the English and Jews were alike in being not Manx, and in being too crafty and acquisitive for us to deal with, gentlemen though some of them might superficially seem to be. At any rate, in this context of rapacity and exploitation Father could not be bothered to distinguish between them. Hairsplitting of that sort did not appeal to him, and he was not pleased that I seemed to be developing a taste for it.

For some reason his attitude (shared, I think, by most of the population) was compatible with a reverence for the British royal family, members of which made periodic duty visits to the island, to remind us that the monarch was and is, among so much else, the Lord of Man. The English and the Europeans, the Americans and no doubt the inhabitants of the world at large are generally unaware that Man is not part of the United Kingdom. It is a dependency. From time to time it has even rebelled against this yoke, though never with the indignation or force of the Irish. There was an ancient insurgent called William, or rather Illiam Dhone, Black William, but he didn't last long; they shot him. A few years ago a Home Rule movement protested against all the wicked things the rich English had done and were doing to us. Its members learned Manx, the language of nobody anymore, and formed an association called Aeglegh Vannin, a miniature copy of Sinn Fein. It was said that the Crown owned our foreshores. Certainly it was represented by a governor who had power of veto over the legislation of the House of Keys, the ancient island parliament. He would be a grandee of some sort, sometimes of little fame, though in my time we did have R. A. Butler's father and, once, a blue-blooded Leveson-Gower.

One essential qualification was that the governor should never, on any account, be Manx. This was rightly a cause of resentment, since it was a ceremonial affirmation of the inferiority of the natives. Yet when the British got into a war, the

Manx, who in principle at any rate could probably have shown
a bit of legislative independence or selfishness and stayed out
of it, were quick to introduce conscription (thus, it might be
argued, showing themselves more loyal than the Northern
Irish, who are so emphatic about being part of the U.K.) and
make the right patriotic noises. For despite our natural caution
and historically quite explicable distrust of the English, we
boasted, after all, only a qualified foreignness; our courts are
only up to a point independent, for somebody in the Home
Office keeps an eye on them, indulging them in their paper
severities, such as the law against homosexual conduct between
consenting adults (or indeed anybody else), the sentences of
birching for juveniles and the death penalty for murder. These
laws are now asleep, less because of the Home Secretary's
disapproval than because we are menaced by Europe (of which,
characteristically, we are not a full but merely an associate
member) and the European courts dislike such practices,
which it seems not unlikely that some Home Secretaries, and
great numbers of Tory voters, would favour.

It is not surprising that some of us Manx who have made
our lives in England have had to settle for a permanent condition of mild alienation. When, after Britain went into Europe,
my passport (held since I was seventeen) expired, I was asked
to certify that I had grandparents who were born in the United
Kingdom. I was unable honestly to do so, and for a while it
seemed I might lose my passport, but representations to the
effect that I had served more than five years in the British
Navy, and had, at any rate technically, been appointed to my
current job by the Queen, eventually persuaded the Foreign
Office that I continued to merit its protection when abroad.

UNAVOIDABLY it grew more and more difficult to feel at
home in my homeland. Of course it had not been like that in
my earliest days. I belonged perfectly well in the house where

I was born. Our rooms were off a dark corridor. I had a "cousin," son of the landlady, who was a year older than I, dominant and left-handed, which is probably why I, though not left-handed, do several things with my left hand, shave thus, throw a ball thus, and kick with my left foot. I have a left-handed daughter but cannot here enter into questions of nature and nurture.

There were always people about, most importantly, the "aunt" who was the landlady and my chief consoler when I was out of favour with my parents. Later it turned out that it was she who as a girl had lugged my mother to her christening in 1895 or whenever it was. There were her daughters, and what seemed large numbers of strangers sitting round her kitchen table drinking tea—chorus girls from the shows, travelling salesmen. There was a dog called Barney which occasionally fouled the corridor. Protests about this were dismissed with accusations of oversensitiveness. "It's only good clean shit," she would cry; or, if the coalmen scattered coal dust in the corridor, "It's only clean coal." Carrie was important to me, and was for many years kinder and more forgiving than my mother ever felt it correct to be. So whatever I am is in part her work. She also contributed, in a way I shall have to elucidate later, to the absorbing mystery of my mother's origins.

When I was nine we moved out of this uterine tenement and into a low rental house provided by the town council, not much more than a quarter of a mile away; the contact with Carrie and her tribe, though necessarily less close, was maintained. What kept it alive was probably that web of covert family connections of which I knew and still know nothing and, of course, the other web of talk that kept the initiates in and the outsiders out.

A great deal of this talk concerned sickness and death. Even the boisterous Carrie suffered from a number of afflic-

tions, all apparently just short of fatal, and all baffling to the
medical profession. This has had the effect of turning me
against illness. I have myself reached an age greater than either
of my parents achieved, and of course I have survived many
friends, so that the last and necessary sickness is often in my
thoughts, and sometimes it seems I am following Prospero's
retirement plan: he promised that every third thought should
be of his grave. But that is quite another matter from being
obsessed with sickness as a normal condition of life. And it
isn't my impression that my coevals are thus obsessed. In this
respect the society of my childhood was quite different. The
flashes of carnival gaiety I have mentioned were the more
brilliant against the everyday background of Lenten morbidity.
It was a world in which everybody was more or less ill. Heart,
stomach, nerves were the ground bass of conversation, the tune
specifying a tumour or a stroke of unprecedented severity, a
disaster in what were called the waterworks. Cold houses, hard
work, toothlessness made rheumatism and indigestion seem
inevitable conditions of life.

Fastidious without the least right to be, I quite early
loathed all this talk, though it seems to me now that to be thus
obsessed with sickness is not the worst evil; it provided people
with surrogate terrors they partly knew how to manage. The
local doctors figured in conversation as regularly as the diseases
they fought against, each subject to passionate support or opposition. The hospital, visible from our house, was both terrible
and familiar, crowded at visiting hours and, like all hospitals
in those times, stinking of ether. At any given time somebody
of my father's large acquaintance would be in there. Their
symptoms and sufferings constituted almost his favourite topic,
with marginal commentary on the kindness or brutality of the
nurses. I remember a Christmas visit, when I was in my late
twenties and long uprooted. Full of morose self-disgust, and
feeling myself being driven crazy by the incessant talk of illness,

I exclaimed, almost involuntarily, that I was sick of the malady monologue and requested a change of subject.

There followed such an explosion of rage that within minutes I was packing my bag to leave. This disaster was prevented by a dramatic apology, a handshake unavoidably offered across a room, though my reluctance to accept it arose as much from my sense of having done something unforgivable as from irritation at my father's behaviour. He had, after all, earned the right to be tedious in his own way, which was acceptable as part of the conversation I had long ago dropped out of. He knew well enough that I was bored, which only made it more repulsive of me to say so, especially since I knew how disappointment, hard labour, and diabetes had conspired to destroy the patient good humour for which all, including myself, had earlier admired him. If I had not taken that hand, the rest of my life would probably have been quite a bit more miserable than numerous other defections and follies have made it.

When I think intently about him, as I now oblige myself to do, I think not of a cantankerous old fellow but of cheerful, manly, conscientious Jack, whom everybody he passed seemed happy to greet. I see him rolling along the street swinging a bag of fish picked up fresh on the quayside—in the mind's eye at least still wriggling—pleased to be bringing home this surprise, glad that I am coming to meet him. He called me John (or rather Jawn) for my mother and he had never agreed about my Christian name. Although he won the argument on the way to the christening, and his choice came first, everybody else knew me by my mother's choice. Still, I was thus nominally identified with him.

He could do some things well, like playing games, and imagined he could do everything else that a proper, handy man might undertake; it took me years to find out that he was really almost as clumsy as he said I was, almost as much what he called a *phynodderee*, a Manx word for a clumsy fairy. I still think some of my own hopelessness at handyman tasks was caused by his constantly mocking me for being stupid with my hands, though I have to admit that his view was shared by the woodwork master at school, who could not believe my ineptitude could be due to anything but insolence, so he beat me and snapped my pathetic work over his knee.

But I won't exonerate my father altogether. On reflection I take the view that his sneering at my attempts to use a screwdriver or change a washer were really expressions of an otherwise hidden sense that I wasn't the kind of son he would have preferred to have fathered. I miserably sympathised with this disappointment. When I was, briefly and ineptly, a Boy Scout, he came to train us for the Fireman's Badge, or whatever it was called. I shamed him by being the only boy who lacked the nerve to drop from a quite low attic trapdoor into a sheet held below. He wanted me to be more like other men's sons. I don't of course mean that he didn't love me; loving people you know intimately has to be consistent with your finding them infuriating in all sorts of ways, short, perhaps, of conscienceless betrayal; this was something he knew, something it took me a long time to find out.

During the war he had been a driver in France, and later drove a van and cars for many years, but he was the worst driver I have ever known. He had never had to take a test, and would almost certainly not have passed one. He behaved as if there were still very few other cars on the road, swinging into the left gutter before turning right. But he never had an accident and no one ever supposed he would. Well known to be sober, reliable, and practised, he was continually in demand to serve on inquest juries, and enjoyed telling of the cunning with which he sometimes evaded the local coroner, Herbie Green, who, when a suspicious or an accidental death was reported, would prowl around the streets looking for trusted acquaintances. This bowler-hatted predator would leave Fa-

ther alone in the busy summer months but pursue him
doggedly in the winter, knowing that work was slack because
there was only one boat a day to and from Liverpool. Despite
the lack of work he was always kept on through the winter—
that was what made it worthwhile to soldier on in the job—
and an inquest might be a relief from sitting alone on a fifty-
six-pound butter crate under the bacon flitches that hung from
the roof of his big storeroom, drinking tea with condensed
milk or toasting cheese for the mousetraps.

His life in the summer months was far too frantic for him
to allow me to visit him at work, but out of season he would
sometimes let me hang out with him in his place of work. We
would sit there in the storeroom surrounded by the smells,
drinking tea with condensed milk. The store was on the first
floor (on the British calculus, the second floor on the American), and goods for delivery, such as the heavy butter crates,
would hurtle down a greasy plank laid beside the stairway, to
be stayed at the bottom by other hands. In the busier months
these would be the hands of an assistant, a dwarfish grey-haired
figure known only as What-you-tink, from his habit of saying
very little except that. In the most taxing part of the summer
season, or in emergencies, he would be joined by Peter, a fat
drunk with almost imperceptible eyes in his swollen face, who
turned up late and at intervals through the day fell asleep.
What-you-tink wasn't much use, but he was a cut above Peter,
whose share of the work normally fell to my father. Out of
season I was sometimes allowed to take their place, to stand
at the bottom of the stairs and catch the crates.

On these rare visits we'd walk or drive together the four
or five hundred yards to the steamers at the pier, stopping to
pick up linen at the laundry, where women peering through
the steam would call out greetings. I was popular because he
was: "So you're Jack's boy! He's a fine lad, isn't he?" Less
often we'd call on the upholsterer, a tall, witty, philosophical

fellow who would meditatively tease me and give me sweets. The people who worked in this rather dingy maritime centre were more humorous and more various than might be supposed. Harry comes to mind, a bespectacled and learned railway clerk, who died young of some catastrophic illness my father could not or anyway did not specify. He would ask me riddles and conundrums, to be answered next time we met. There were others, solemn teasers, expert in this or that, liking to amuse or confuse a child.

Arriving at the steamers, Father would summon stewards to help him transfer the crates, the meat, the laundry. I was proud to note that they behaved as if they liked him. I seriously needed him to be liked. There was much banter, mostly directed at me and kindly meant, so that I didn't mind it. But the moment I most dreaded on these excursions was approaching, and I must retreat to the deepest attainable part of the ship in order to muffle the noise of the siren, five minutes before departure. Even the puny hooter of the little ferry that carried holidaymakers across the harbour made me panic. I greatly admired the long-haired violinist who performed on this boat, not only because of his abandoned playing and the rate at which he snapped the hairs of his bow, but for the calm, almost the indifference, with which, a hundred times a day, he bore the noise of the siren. Of course the big bellow of the larger steamer, which made one's body vibrate, was altogether more appalling. Once it had sounded, I left my hiding place and rushed ashore before it could issue the further blasts that signified its being under way. I enjoyed all this, despite my panic, because I liked my father to be liked and trusted, and also because he never reproached me for my phobia about the siren, though he must have envied fathers whose boys could be depended upon to behave more normally. I was well aware of this, but like the stewards, I felt I could trust him.

As the persistence of the coroner showed, this trust was

general, but not all Father's dealings with the law demonstrated the same correctness and civic spirit. He liked what he called a flutter, not at the racecourse near our house, where he was sure all the races were fixed, but in the street or in the barber's shop, where of course betting was illegal. Once, when he failed to come home at his usual time, we discovered that he had been arrested while placing a bet at the barber's, and was being held in the police station. I expected my mother to be horrified at the news, but she knew her town well enough to take it fairly calmly, giggling a little. I don't remember if he spent the night in a cell, but probably not; he was on good terms—"well in," he'd have said—with the police; they were neighbours and he had often worked with them in his capacity as voluntary fireman. I liked to think of the cops bursting into the barber's, grinning at the criminals, and affectionately hailing my father. He came home cheerfully, showing no remorse, and continued to have his flutters at the same shop, escaping further trouble by reason of a greatly improved intelligence service, which made subsequent raids abortive, as, at the critical moment, nothing was going on in the place but innocent shaving, haircutting, and the surreptitious sale of condoms. Wickedness resumed after the police had departed.

I decided I liked this touch of loucheness in my otherwise very honourable father. Now and again he was lucky, and once he won £37 on the football pools—a large sum at a time when you could buy a new Hercules bike for £3.19.9. I got the bike, and the rest, or most of it, went on presents for our extended and admiring pseudo-family.

The people he made less attempt to please were the clerks in the office that adjoined his store, the white collars. When I was sixteen or so, I worked with these men for a summer and saw that their attitude to my father, no doubt given more subdued expression because I was there, was a sort of amiable disdain, amiable when things were going well, much nastier if they weren't. The workers in the store were jocularly called peasants, and we, putting in our forty-four-hour week in the small and often stifling office, were, by implication, gentry; of course there was a small amount of self-deprecating irony in this.

The youngest of the regular office staff was a small, randy, moustached man with an affected bass voice, who liked to fantasise about country fairs and the opportunities they offered for ditch seductions. An older clerk, a Mr. Ganley, strikes me now as epitomizing one mood of the time. Grave, precise in dress and manner, he rarely spoke, but when he did, whether in the office or at a casual meeting in the street—he would be alone, as he always was—he treated me with the same courteous formality he extended to everybody. He was one of those men—probably more common then than now—who seemed, in middle age, to have settled for a perfectly satisfying solitariness. He did whatever he thought it right for him to do, and declined to do anything else, a sort of variant on Bartleby the Scrivener; I prefer not to. Or perhaps a more than usually contented Gissing character.

Later I met others of this type, and they were often people who spent their days looking after money that wasn't theirs; quite lately I recognised as Ganley-like the conduct of a formidably silent and correct college finance officer. When, at the time of the great inflation of the 1970s, he was informed that his salary was to be suitably increased, he rejected the boon with distaste. "I trust I am not living at a time when my remuneration can be altered beyond my needs and without my consent." Of course I never heard Ganley say anything like that, but I can easily imagine him doing so.

He was a character, but so were the others, characters or what used to be called humours. Randy young Johnny was the Card. Mr. Ganley was the Clerk. You couldn't believe there was a Mr. Ganley, a real one, submerged, potentially passionate, with a private face different from the mask he chose to present to the world—the droopy moustache, the celluloid collar, the dark suit on the most sweltering days. A flash of that real self might appear if he thought his inferiors were stepping out of line. In hot weather we were sometimes sent a case of fizzy lemonade to ease us through the day. But Mr. Ganley insisted on a just distribution, one bottle for me, two for Johnny, three for him, and the rest for Mr. Christopher, the office manager or chief clerk. The only thing that made him furiously angry was interference with this scheme, as when, one day, I took two bottles, arguing, correctly but impudently, that Mr. Christopher, who had a passion for pop, also arranged his own private supply.

Mr. Christopher was another memorable figure, having a purple face, scanty grey hair, an enormous parrot nose, and a mad cracked voice. His bit of the office was divided from ours by a partition about five feet high, and all day long you could not see him, but you could hear him singing and chanting obscene runes and slogans. When well lubricated with lemonade, conceivably spiked with whisky, he would appear, or rather his head would appear, above the partition and scream like a parrot. He would cry out in what was meant to be a girl's voice, "Take it out or I'll snap it off," and reply, in a deep bass, "No, leave it in and we'll show it to the captain in the morning." Or he would remain hidden and mutter, just audibly, "If the weather was only finer we could see the Wall of China if it wasn't for the houses in between." Or, "As I was saying to me brother, If it's not one thing it's another."

Sometimes this monologue went on all day, accompanied by the tuneless whistling of the non-carbuncular young clerk and, by contagion, mine also. Even the entry of the boss's son, dropping in as he happened to be passing on more important business, expensively dressed, public-school-accented, could not stop the whistling. "This place is like a bloody aviary," he said. He ordered it to cease, but sometimes would himself enter whistling, using it like the rest of us to get through the day, and immune to his own discipline. "This place is like a gory birdhouse," somebody murmured; and when the coast was clear, the whistling would begin again, music appropriate to our almost unbearable boredom.

That summer I at least learned something about the importance of hierarchical arrangements in business. My father was *ex officio* quite near the bottom of the list, though with What-you-tink and Peter below him. At the top, above even the boss's son, was the boss, a hard old Scotsman who never, for all his meanness, lost my father's respect. There was something patriarchal or familial about this attitude of his. He was often called to the old man's residence, and had contributed, in their youth, to the practical education of his sons. They had a passion, easily developed on that island, for fast motorbikes and cars. One of the sons was sent off to the colonies and died of blackwater fever. The other we have encountered, now in the business, deferred to but not respected: He'll never be the man his father was.

When the old man died, his preservative regime of Scotch whisky having finally let him down, my father's tirades against the son, now the boss, grew more frequent and intemperate. He now bitterly detested the gentry in the office, though there was some kind of bond, quite tenacious, between him and Christopher. Whatever it was, it was something that I never understood—like so much in my parents' world.

It seems reasonable, considering all this, to say that my father was short of what might be called structural luck. Indeed, his life was plagued by misfortune; but in certain less important matters he did quite well. He attracted presents: his position in the stores made him a favourite of victuallers, whom he could oblige in various ways throughout the year, and every Christmas there would be delivered to us geese and turkeys, legs of pork and lamb, bottles of whisky, rum, sherry, and port, large tins of Jacobs' biscuits. This bounty could be embarrassing; these were the days before we even dreamed of having refrigerators and freezers, and even in a cold pantry it was impossible to hoard the meat, so he gave much of it away; it would not have occurred to him to sell it.

The drink was useful at New Year's, when there would be callers you never saw at any other season. They came for the drink, and were rather grudgingly welcomed; it seemed they had some kind of hold over us, but chose to exact only this price. Or perhaps they had places on the kinship diagram, so carefully hidden from me. They would sit in silence, hardly pretending to be there for any other reason than the booze. The women would be served ginger wine and mince pies; unlike the men, they would do some polite conversation. On the whole my father, who greatly enjoyed the holiday except for New Year's Day, remained civil under these provocations, though with an occasional burst of temper, as when he ordered one particularly awful man out of the house with terrible threats about what would happen if he ever returned. Rages of this sort were rare until, much later, they were fuelled by diabetes. These rows were upsetting; even the Christmas bounty turned out to be less fortunate, and less virtuously applied, than he would have liked.

I muse upon my father's wreck, and wonder if mine will in any way resemble it. Probably not; the difference will be maintained. He had qualities I totally lack, a different sense of mutually beneficial relationships, a different, less cautious estimate of pleasure. He valued pleasure and had, in the good years, the years when he could work like a dog all day and take my mother dancing at night, an equanimity I have lacked. As her only son, and for many years her only child, I was my mother's, by right and by temperament. Montaigne said that he was different persons at different times, not merely double but multiple, and that is likely to be true of everybody, but there is doubtless some genetic constraint on the multiplicity, and also constraints of nurture. I wasn't entitled to be my father's boy, but in all my actions, good and evil, I am either pleasing or rejecting my mother.

Of such constraints it is virtually impossible for the individual (who of course isn't, in any case, strictly individual) to speak sensibly. However, I wonder about the character of my inheritance. Is there a gene for luck, perhaps recessive? I have been luckier than my parents. When I was still very young I found, browsing in the public library, a book of quotations, one of which—hackneyed, but then new to me—particularly impressed me: "There, but for the grace of God, go I." I might have used it on many occasions. My parents might never have needed to say it. They had their quarrels but had the grace to mend them; they had constancy, were never even tempted by the thought that in difficult times desertion was an option. They were in the end unlucky, and as even Machiavelli knew, you need luck. I've had my share of it, and now I don't know whether it has run out, though I notice that my grip on the theory that one ought properly to live as if lucky enough to live for ever is slackening, or at times seems to be. There, but for the grace of God, go I is a thought that crosses the mind as friend after friend fails to live for ever.

In seasons of calm weather it can still seem a good enough fate to be old, alone, and yet still pretty industrious, still listening, but now without the old anxiety, to the promptings of the puritan conscience, deaf to the seductions of "well-earned" leisure, and not much troubled by the consideration that these good days, like all the others, are included in the countdown. It must be remembered that these good days are intermittent; on most others the whole notion seems spurious and affected, dying is a disagreeable prospect, no grace will intervene to prevent it or make it agreeable, or even to stop me worrying about the humiliation of lying around being a slightly sinister nuisance to whoever has the job of tidying up after me. But meditations of this sort—banal, otiose, self-pitying—are among the causes why I think that I am not the sort of person I should choose to know if I had any choice in the matter.

THERE WAS SOME POINT in preparing for death by saving the burial money as one saved for everything, by means of jars and boxes on the mantelpiece. There money was stored for death as for life, for burial as well as for clothing and food. The friendly collectors would arrive on their bicycles, collect the cash, enter the tiny premiums in their books. They would chat with the housewife and the children, pat the dogs. I remember best the clothing man, who was called Mr. Cain and came from a shop named R. C. CAIN, D.C.F.C.S. We never found out what these initials meant, though the boys would say they stood for "Do Come For Christ's Sake." The shop was grand enough without them, festooned by wires down which cartridges full of cash whizzed along to the cashier and back to the customer. It was so impressive that I couldn't help wondering why one of the Cain family should have to pedal around in all weathers, a man always genial, always as up-to-date on the medical condition of his customers as on their paltry arrears, always playing an informed part in the communication system of this society. He was as much a symbol of its social order as the curate.

Without death the insurance men would have been out of a job, but their weekly visit—as the poet Philip Larkin, thinking of ambulances, noticed, no street was missed—was somehow cheering. The premiums were paid so that one wouldn't be too much of a posthumous nuisance, or perhaps to give somebody else a small start in the world. When I was twenty-five and deeply estranged from her, my mother tried to hand me what was then a good lump of cash, fifty-five pounds, representing the maturity of a policy she had taken

out for me when I was born and for quarter of a century paid
for out of a jar.

The worst aspect of death was widowhood. It was so
normal a condition that nobody seemed to regard it as de-
serving of special attention, but it was hard. Widows were left
to get on with their lives as best they could, often by scrubbing
or taking in washing. I knew one such, who lived in fanatically
tidy privacy, in a single room of our tenemented house. It was
a privilege, by me unsought, to enter her room. Her husband
had died young, around the time of the Boer War, from, I was
told, the kick of a horse. She had a way of clearing her throat
which maddened me (my famous fastidiousness) and spoke
incessantly of her employers, owners of a cake shop and models
of gentility. I went to see her when, in her late eighties, she
was dying of some abdominal obstruction. "Look after yourself," she advised me. "If I'd looked after myself this wouldn't
have happened." So this woman, who had always been a bit
of a scold, ended by reproaching herself and, I couldn't help
thinking, me, for omissions or slovenlinesses which in my case
had certainly occurred already but had as yet no visible consequences. Death, for her, was a result of human error, an
excellent religious attitude; disobedience brought death into
the world and all our woe.

A more important widow in my life, and in my mother's,
was Carrie, our landlady in the tenement house, the woman
who carried my mother to Braddan church, who cosseted me
when I was in disgrace, befriended chorus girls, and talked
about good clean shit and good clean coal. She had four children, all older than I, and might have thought of me as a
welcome extra child. So far as I know—this was part of the
general mystery of my mother's birth—we had no blood connection, but as I had no grandparents, no uncles or aunts, no
cousins, she was much more to me than a casual titular aunt,
being a refuge, a confidante, the one to count on.

Her husband had died at forty, a wild man who never

wore socks or a shirt and had worked in the South African goldfields. He was, for no obvious reason, a dedicated Orange man, and, in an almost wholly soccer culture, a fierce rugby player. He once stood, tumultuously but unsuccessfully, for the House of Keys. He did so many things that I can't remember what was his main way of making a living—something tells me he was a stonemason—but I do remember that when I was about five he died of tuberculosis, and that his widow shrieked as she ran past me down the stairs.

Carrie worked as caretaker and cleaner of a Mission Hall just down our street. We called it the Mishy, and were allowed to play there on wet days, thumping the piano, sometimes smoking and playing wicked games. The Mishy was used for Sunday-school Christmas parties, and the contrast between the sedate gaiety of those occasions, usually presided over by a virtuous and indefatigable church worker known as Fat Annie, and the wild private goings-on of the rest of the year gave one some insight into the character of civilisation and its discontents.

Carrie must have been poor but never allowed us to think so. On Saturday nights she would meet another plump widow called Ginny, and they would drink in a favourite snug. Throughout my childhood, and in later years when I was home on leave or on a visit, she would exclaim with delight at the sight of me, and lead me into her little kitchen, where, fumbling and cursing, she would light the two gas jets over her mantelpiece and retreat into the even smaller back kitchen to find whatever it was she kept there on purpose to give her visitor a treat—sweets in the early years, and later Scotch.

Despite her good nature, she was always involved in obscure family feudings, especially with her mother-in-law, a woman known to all, including me, as Granny, who tried hard to resemble Queen Victoria in dress and manner; and with a sister-in-law who kept a wool shop in Athol Street and was, though virtuous, full of anger at the life she'd had forced on her—virginity, and the care of a tyrannical invalid mother. These people lived by the church where Granny's husband had been the verger, and the house had at all times a sort of churchyard piety. With its inhabitants it was apparently possible for Carrie to quarrel, but she somehow retained a habit of radiant benevolence to almost everybody else.

During wartime leaves I would take her to the council house my parents had moved into, a house designed by somebody who had a very low opinion of the needs and deserts of the lower classes, and we would drink too much while playing incompetent whist, my mother, a recent learner, giggling furiously and constantly reneging. Then I would walk Carrie, half carry her, home, very slowly, with many halts and much groaning, up the steep hill through the blackout. Now, if I wanted to, I could think of my escort duties on those incredibly slow midnight walks as a recompense for the services she had done us, beginning with that long walk to Braddan. During the war the skies over the island were full of aeroplanes, mostly from RAF training fields, and as we toiled up the hill, an invisible plane might pass overhead, whereupon she would stop, gaze upwards, and call on God to bless and preserve the poor boy up there. Then came the usual cursing and fumbling with the gas, the flask of whisky from the back kitchen. Although I was a favourite I was not the only one to benefit from this generosity; there were those jolly, worried chorus girls, and the commercial travellers, spatted and bow-tied, sharp as knives, yet in those years desperately improvising a living and glad to have their moments with this genial, free-spoken counsellor.

Carrie seemed to belong pretty exclusively to the town, which makes that excursion to Braddan all the more mysterious, and raises unanswerable questions about my mother's association with Kewaigue. Carrie never spoke of this, or of anything else relating to my mother's youth. If I had uncles and aunts and cousins in America she would have known about it. There was certainly an "aunt" who had married a German farmer and lived on a fruit farm in Wisconsin. Every Christmas she sent me a book, usually by James Fenimore Cooper, but later she appears to have developed an interest in Thomas Mann, whose *Doctor Faustus* was the last of the long series. I joined the silent conspiracy and never even asked about this American Aunt Ollie.

All this shadowy business gave a particular flavour to my version of the family romance. What we have found out about the whole kinship problem, and it isn't a lot, has been the work of my sister, many years younger than I; born when I was twelve, she was at first to me an interloper, though one for whom I felt much tenderness, and I bore, and still bear, all the marks of an only child, in my sister's nonage cruelly deprived of the excessive maternal care I had once felt myself entitled to for ever. That made Carrie even more important, but it was part of the tacit agreement that I should never ask her about Kewaigue, nor would she have told me, though my mother's rare and scanty reminiscences of early life nearly always included it.

Sometimes my mother and I would walk quite near that village, in the autumn blackberrying in the hedges, or, even more memorably, strolling in spring through fields that were in those days full of primroses. I remember her agile over stiles, running in her tight skirt, evidently happy, perhaps a little too happy, happier than sensible people will allow themselves to be. She would point across the fields to Kewaigue, where, before moving into the teashop, she had led the life of a farm girl, a life she partly relived in her last days. But we never went into Kewaigue itself.

There were reminders of that place which did not make her happy. Strange, even sinister, figures would come to our house. The worst of them was Pegleg Caley, a tramp of sorts, who seemingly had some claim on her attention. Finding him at the door she would be horribly but civilly nervous, offering him food and drink, perhaps money. Still upset when my father came home, she would cry out as he came through the door: "Pegleg came, Pegleg was here this morning." Other rustic callers turned up, less menacing but still feared. Dark figures such as these may lurk in everybody's memory of childhood, but I think there were more such visitations in mine than in less reticent families; most children have a clearer idea of their kin and the associates of their kin than I had. Pegleg had something to do with the mystery of my mother's parentage, I was sure of that.

Complementary, though less frightening, obscurities existed on my father's side. Such information as dribbled down to me had an unreal quality, and the adult intelligence cannot trust it. However, he certainly had a Welsh grandfather, said indeed to be Welsh-speaking, a sea captain from whom he derived his middle name, Pritchard. There was a photograph of this ancestor (as of no other) in which his face is obscured by a cap and a full beard. He seemed heroic, and was said to have had commands under sail. Memory further insists, or imagination constructs, another photograph of a fine schooner he commanded. His daughter married a Kermode who played the organ in some church or chapel, begot my father, and died of tuberculosis at twenty-eight, so of course I never met him. He owned a small grocery store with an off-licence, which my grandmother inherited. I don't remember her, though I was assured that I was at least once taken to see her in her retirement, in the derelict silver mining village of Foxdale, in the middle of the island.

Why she decided to live in that gloomy spot I can't say, though it may have had something to do with a wartime scandal. She had remarried while my father was serving in France, and the second husband turned out to be a crook. He is said to have stolen the liquor from what was now, by marriage, his own shop, inventing evidence of a break-in. He was found out, and it suggests that the family still had some influential friends in the community, for my father was able to keep reports of police proceedings out of the local papers. But the business was ruined, and the house they lived in had to be sold, so by the time my father got back to civilian life, his patrimony was gone.

This may not be exactly what happened, but there is some truth in it, and it accounts for the fact that in certain moods my father dwelt on the fact that he had, through no fault of his own, come down in the world. There were two adjacent districts of the quite small town that he always avoided, the street where the shop was (and until recently remained) and, nearby, the rather handsome square containing his mother's house. He had married in 1918 and, needing a job, took what he regarded as a temporary one as a storekeeper. He stayed in that job, which I described earlier, until a year or so before he died, in 1966. At first, and indeed for a long time, there was nothing for it but to carry the butter, cheese, bacon, and meat down the pier on a handcart, in the summer making many such trips every day and masochistically clocking up the miles on a pedometer. He was a strong, fit man, but often close to exhaustion. Later the boss bought him a battered van, and he drove it or its successors for many years. I have called him a terrible driver, but now I remember that he manoeuvred many times a day through the chaotic traffic on the narrow pier, and drove fast and safely across the island to Peel on the west coast when the fierce east and northeast winds that struck the Irish Sea three or four times each winter prevented the steamers from docking at Douglas.

That was about as far as his luck went. I have on my chest of drawers a photograph, perhaps a wedding photograph, showing him in a private's uniform, a good-looking young fellow, with my mother, demurely pretty, her hair short and slightly untidy, both of them looking quite pleased but somehow wary. Whether this was taken before or after the loss of the shop I don't know, but have decided that he has the air of a young man with prospects, a future in a town where he had been well known from birth. A scion of a respected family and himself already respected, he cannot have foreseen that he would have to spend his whole life in a menial job, and to give thanks that he managed to keep it through the long depression. He never joined a union, because his boss would not allow it; he treated my father as the kind of friend a faithful retainer can be allowed to be, and answered worries about, for example, lack of provision for a pension, by undertaking to take care of that himself when the time came. I believe this promise was not kept. My father retired, as fit as diabetes allowed, but not happy. My mother's illness left him much alone, and I remember finding him one January day staring at the wall in a freezing room, absolutely immobile. His health suddenly deserted him. I remember him in hospital, stuck all over with tubes, and very cross with a nurse who, he alleged, had handled him roughly. I asked a young houseman what his prospects were, and for answer he asked me snappishly whether it wasn't obvious that the old man was worn out. He was seventy-two.

ONE OF THE POINTS on which my father and mother entirely agreed was that I should not be a peasant. That is why my summer job was not in the stores, where it might have done me good to replace greasy drunken Peter as the lesser of my father's assistants, but with the gentry in the office. He was always capable of finding me gentlemanly summer work. One summer I worked in another, darker office, belonging to an associated company that supplied the steamers with liquor. The clerks stood all day from eight to six at high

Dickensian desks, with an hour for lunch and Saturday afternoon off. My workmates were genial men of my father's age
who had served in France, one lacking a left arm. They treated
me nicely, perhaps because they had sons of my age, perhaps
because, like so many other people, they liked my father.

My job, at the foot of the ladder, was ullage clerk. I kept
a ledger, recording, in as clerkly a hand as I could manage,
but to no useful end that I could see, the tally of returned
empty beer bottles, which ran to many thousands. At ten-
thirty in the morning there came a pleasant break from this
inconceivably tedious routine, when I was sent out to a nearby
café to buy what my seniors called their char and wads, hot
sticky buns soaked in butter, and lovely milky coffee.

Working in bad light on the ullages hurt my eyes, and I
was at an age to be afflicted by styes. Some of these were cured
miraculously by having an old lady's wedding ring passed over
them, but at one point this treatment failed, and as I could
hardly open my eyes, I took a couple of days off work. On my
return the boss, one of those severe, rich men who did very
well out of the poor drinkers of Lancashire, came in and remarked that he hadn't seen me for a while. I explained that I
had been having trouble with my eyes. "You're here to have
trouble with those ullages," he replied. He was paying me
thirty shillings a week, and when he died he left a great fortune,
to which I suppose my ullages made a small contribution.

My summer jobs always had some connection with the
shipping business. They were all fairly trivial, of course. In
one of them I was able to work out that the money saved by
my spending the day checking tickets to ensure that we got
the right payment from the railway company was less, and
always virtually certain to be less, than the sum they paid me
to do this. The office in which I conducted these researches
was much the most pleasant I had worked in—large and well
lit, it was peopled by calm kind clerks, some of whom had

been there so long that they still talked with animation about the sinking of one of the company's vessels in the Mersey around 1905, and, a more recent event, the use of others for military purposes, including Admiral Keyes's raid on the German submarine base at Zeebrugge in 1918. These interesting men were impressed when I told them of my discoveries, which had involved voluntary research into the records of several previous years and appeared pretty convincing. But they were impressed by my folly even more than by my diligence, for to them it seemed improper to combine the roles of worker and efficiency expert. Anyway, they argued, who could say there might not be, in the future, some gigantic error or swindle that would go undetected if there was nobody to do my job? And since I hadn't checked everything from the beginning of time, how could we be absolutely sure there had been no such catastrophe in the past? What they were really and understandably saying was that it was always a foolish thing, especially in the 1930s, to destroy a job.

The most glorious of my father's achievements in finding me gentlemanly vacation employment occurred when I was nineteen and became an assistant purser in the Steam Packet Company's largest and proudest ship. This was in 1939; but my nautical career extended not only beyond but before this date. As a fourteen-year-old I had sold newspapers and magazines on the boats, a job calling for tireless enterprise and salesmanship, not, as it turned out, my genre, which was a pity, for we were paid by commission on sales. By far the most successful of my mates was a pleasant deaf-mute, whose sales figures were always astonishing and rather shaming to those who, with roughly equal opportunities—though he was naturally given the plum sailings—did far less well. Still, it was an interesting and even an adventurous life. Fortunately I had by this time overcome my terror of the ship's siren and was soon quite at home on the often turbulent Irish Sea. Sometimes

I'd be away overnight, in Liverpool or Fleetwood, eating with the stewards and, when I had read all my wares, sleeping in some lounge. The magazines I sold are now mostly forgotten, with names like *The Passing Show*, *Answers*, *Titbits*, along with movie and mildly girlie magazines whose titles I've mislaid. They were less interesting to me than the stewards, temporary summertime employees, mostly Liverpool Irish, of necessity hardworking but inexpert and sometimes a bit grubby. Often at night they would come aboard slightly drunk and exchanging cheerful insults. If the matter grew very serious one might call another "bastard." This, I discovered, was the ultimate insult because of the slur it cast on one's mother. It was used only when the speaker was looking for a fight. There were many fights.

Ruling over this crowd there would be a crafty chief steward whose main business it was to supervise the almost invariant lunch (soup, fish, lamb or beef, pudding). He was usually on good terms with my father, who supplied the food that was to be ruined under his care. From him I learned some basic rules of menu making: all bacon was Wiltshire, all lamb Welsh (even if it was Manx, at least as good), and so forth. Very occasionally something called sparrowgrass would appear on the menu. It seemed characteristic of the man, possibly of his *métier*, that nothing should be called by its true name. His was a culture based on misrepresentations. He was a shifty self-serving boss, falsely professing to be dedicated to the welfare of passengers, and aided by a team of backstreet boyos dolled up in black ties.

I ought to have found this experience instructive, but I don't think it occurred to me that things in general were rather like that, self-interest dictating all kinds of fraudulence, often quite mild of course, but inconsistent with the high idea of gentility to which, with such persistent encouragement, I aspired. I still had much to learn.

On the other hand, I did find out what it meant to work, however unseasonably, however against the grain. I might get up at five for a 6 a.m. sailing and, on a Saturday, cross the Irish Sea four times, the intervals between crossings occupied in getting fresh stores of magazines to sell to passengers often so packed in that they could hardly get their hands into their pockets for the money to pay for them. I would force a way through, keen to sell, not only for the money but also because when the tray was stacked high with papers the strap bit into my neck.

When I'd got rid of my load, or all of it that I could hope to dispose of, I would try to find a place on deck or in one of the vibrating lounges and think, or survey the seascape, sometimes wickedly spinning halfpennies into the ocean, or counting the Mersey lightships, or watching my native hills fade behind us or come into sharp focus as we approached them: first large and vague familiar shapes, then Douglas Head so close that one could no longer see other hills, only that hill over the harbour, with its lighthouse and its camera oscura, with, to the right, the handsome sweep of the bay and within its arc the Conister rock. Passing that rock and its Tower of Refuge on our right, we were as good as berthed, waiting only for the gangway to be put ashore, then running up the weedy steps and home.

The life of a purser was of course much grander and much better paid, though three-quarters of my earnings went into the family purse. However, I had a pleasant cabin and even enjoyed the work, hard as it often was, especially the checking and collecting of tickets from the weekend crowds. Authoritative in my uniform, I would patrol the saloon accommodation, warning people found there with steerage tickets to remove themselves into the even more crowded accommodation they'd paid for. An hour later I would return and fine any who had failed to move. Sometimes these delinquents would be groups of mill girls who had persuaded themselves they could charm me into letting them stay illicitly where they were. But I was firm, and they had to pay the difference between the two fares. They would slowly extract powdery shillings from their handbags, eventually handing over most of the money they had, for it was common for girls to arrive with very little cash, in the expectation of finding boys who would pay for their pleasures. Now I feel the pathos of all this, and wince a little as I write; but I don't think I felt it then, when I was trying hard to rid myself of the habit of wincing.

Stranded overnight in Fleetwood, the younger officers would dress carefully in their neat cabins and go in search of girls. It was a dull resort compared with Douglas with its perpetual summer carnival, but in youth is pleasure, and I think quite affectionately of Fleetwood. In the morning I would take my place beside the railway clerk in a hut with two guichets. I was capable of being surprised that in what everybody agreed were hard times some people seemed to have money to burn. In those days bank notes for values over a pound were distinguished by their size—they were almost as large as a small handkerchief—and their fine white paper. A £5 note was something to take notice of—it represented a good deal more cash than most people earned in a week. Yet men would come forward opulently waving fives or even tens, and it was not unknown for some to walk away without their change. The railway clerk, an honest and likeable fellow, kept a sponge by his window, so that if somebody left change behind he could conscientiously use this sponge to rap on the glass.

Ours was a big ship, capable of carrying more than two thousand passengers—far too big to be used often for the less important traffic to Dublin and Belfast, ports which I had visited as a paperboy and which I have visited in different capacities since, but my images of them have remained unchanged since I was fourteen: of Belfast, the huge and rancorous anti-Catholic slogans painted on the sea walls; of Dublin, a woman pausing as I passed her in a street outside the dock gate to urinate without pudency in the gutter. Memories of my career as purser are gentler. They include the familiar faces of contract passengers, middle-class people who sailed daily back and forth across the Irish Sea in what they had been persuaded were the interests of health. Some of these stoical figures I came to know, and we might pass the time of day. Half a lifetime later I discovered that one such passenger was the mother of the poet Roy Fuller, and we wondered whether I had ever made her acquaintance and asked after her son the solicitor. Of course this was mere pleasantry, but I'd have liked to come even that close to somebody connected with literature, even though she wasn't a poet but only a poet's mother, indeed merely the mother of a solicitor who would be a poet later.

All this happened in the summer of 1939, which saw the end of the peace and the end of a world, or of many worlds, including one of mine; for I was never again to live on the island, being there only as a transient as, in some ways, I have since that time been wherever I happened to find myself.

I HAVE SAID VERY LITTLE, from my point of view far too little, about my secret life, since I certainly had one apart from all this summer bustle. I began as a philosopher, an eye among the blind, though naturally I did not reveal my vocation to my friends. There was a whole society of children from whom such truths must be kept. These were the friends of the street. With them I led my public life, and of course it was essential—there had to be a shared language before there could be a private one. Much of it was body language. It was still possible for children to play in the street. Their games required chalk, for hopscotch (mostly a pastime for girls), a rope, and an easy acquaintance with every cul-de-sac and lamppost in the area. Lampposts played a livelier part in our lives than in those of the next generation; their attendant was a bit like the sandman. The lamplighter bicycled up to us, his pole topped by a hook which pulled a lever to light the gas, and this was the signal that sent most of us home. Careful fathers would stand at their front doors to count their children in. Others, more indulgent, and to the keen disapproval of more scrupulous neighbours, allowed their young to "roam the streets" as long as they wanted.

This was a breach of the rules, most of which required everyone to accept arbitrary divisions of time, both diurnal and seasonal. For the most part we recognised them quite effortlessly. There were seasons of play, though nobody knew how they had come to know a new season had started; it would just happen that the tops appeared, the slim T-shaped ones that leapt through the air and the solider tops, more stable, turnip-shaped. Then, without consultation or announcement, the hoops came in, hoops of metal or wood begged from brewer's draymen. Summer was heralded by a one-armed Italian ice-cream man, pushing his handcart, skilful with his scoop. On his good days the baker might let you sit beside him, take the reins, and pretend to drive his van round the block.

There were limits to this world beyond which its signs and rules were invalid. Out of bounds was a large open space known as the Tar Patch, inhabited by enemy children wearing clogs. Once at least things got out of hand; stung by some insult or aggression we invaded their territory and set fire to the rubbish dump of an adjacent garage. From a distance I watched my father, in his ornate fireman's helmet, helping to put out the blaze. A more pastoral scene was the area of open fields called The Gooseneck, long since built over, where we might, a bit later, explore little girls behind the hedges.

The first days of June there were the Tourist Trophy races, motorcycle races run over a horribly dangerous thirty-

eight-mile circuit covering the northern half of the island and
involving a mountain climb along with hazards of every conceivable sort. We were unavoidably obsessed with these races,
and would sometimes, early in June, get up at four, the dawn
a mere thread, to watch the riders practising and in the paddock collect famous or exotic autographs—Italian, Spanish,
even Japanese (a name now springs to mind, and I remember
collecting the autograph of one Kenzo Tada)—obligingly written by hands still shaking from the effort of speed. We expertly
discussed the bikes—the still triumphant Nortons, the Velo-
cettes ruined, as all agreed, by the experimental twin cylinders,
the Scotts that buzzed like wasps, and eventually, as British
power declined, the Moto Guzzis and the sinister German
NSUs, gleaming potently in the dawn light.

Such memories must have been, for Manx children, deep
and formative. Here were men whose achievements one could
never hope to equal. All around was good Wordsworthian
material, sea and mountain, the annual delights of gorse and
heather, the dense summer fogs and howling autumn gales.
But they counted for less than the memories of these leathered
heroes, who hurled themselves on their beautifully smelly machines round the dangerous corners, through the mists and
over the mountains; moreover, they quite often killed themselves, or spent months in the local hospital being put together,
wooing the nurses with tenderly expressed obscenities in Spanish or Italian. Much later a friend and I would visit some of
these bored and lonely figures, who would talk incessantly and
fascinatingly about their need of women. This talk had a boldness, an immediacy, a conviction that if the sufferers could only
get about more freely, women would be waiting for them
everywhere. At seventeen we found this confidence exciting
but unconvincing.

When we were very young—I find I can't be more precise
at present—the events that were the most thrilling to watch,

and to imitate, were the sidecar races. At corners the passenger would fling himself almost out of his seat, helmet no more than an inch above the road, fighting gravity as a crewman fights the wind, with leg and stomach muscles. We imitated this trick, linking arms and throwing ourselves around corners. One evening at dusk, on a patch of rubble-strewn ground where a house in the street had been demolished, we fell, my partner and I. He disentangled himself from me and got up, but I did not. Sensing that I had suffered more than the everyday knock or scratch, my partner ran off and, cleaving honourably to our rule that the less adults knew about our affairs the better, said nothing to anybody. This fellow, incidentally, died over Holland in May 1940. He had joined the RAF in peacetime as a regular and was obviously doing rather well, already a sergeant pilot. When he was killed, his mother went around claiming, unanswerably, that her son had joined the peacetime air force, with no desire for wartime service; it was not part of the deal that he should be exposed to hostile action. This line of argument entailed that all regular soldiers, sailors, and airmen should be instantly demobilised as soon as a war began. But anyway, there he was, dead at twenty.

At present I do not remember, but a few years ago I did remember, and am now remembering that memory: the blackness, the pallor of mortar fragments, the blank walls of the houses on either side, the sense, even the acceptance, of desertion. How, I have wondered, did that moment end? Why was I entitled to be rescued? Did I call out and attract the attention of a passerby? Did my mother come looking for me with a torch? Was I there at all, lying still, in pain? How could I have been out so late, after dark in June, at four years of age, I who for years after that went obediently to bed at eight o'clock? The hospital, memory of a memory of a memory, was full of brilliant lights. There was a steel splint full of holes— not very likely in 1924 or 1926, or whenever it was. The doctor was a Dr. Wood, not, I think, Dr. Steel. He told me I was going to be brave, so I was. Later I was much commended. They cut the sleeve of my jersey, if I was wearing a jersey, which is probable. There is an appalling reek of ether, which means that this was a hospital of long ago.

Perhaps I was proud to become for a while an important part of the conversation about people and their sicknesses. Poor Quine is gone, I hear old Quilliam is done for; the doctors, each of whose experience and diagnostic talents were known and weighed against the others, were amazed, had never seen the like of it. The ward sisters were familiar to all, this one an angel, that one a faggot—a word that has changed its meaning lately. Though they were still under thirty, hale and handsome, my parents seemed to think they lived perpetually on the brink of some medical catastrophe, and they fell ill frequently, usually with diseases one nowadays rarely hears mentioned: quinsy, whitlow, neuralgia. My father, still the curly-headed athlete, sat for hours spitting blood into a bowl from his suddenly sunken mouth, the confidence of that wartime photograph gone for good, his youth deserting him early. I had not wanted, though doubtless I deserved, my own experience of desertion among the rubble, but I had borne my wounds more cheerfully. All the same I could sense his loss and it deepened my own forebodings, my fantasies of loss that time confirmed for me, as for everybody. The story of a life must, insofar as it is truthful, be at least in part a story of loss and desertion inflicted and received.

It was the dawn of this understanding that prepared me —at what age I can't even guess—for the great moment of my childhood, the climax of my philosophical career. It was a smoky evening in late autumn, probably not yet five o'clock, but the shops were burning their gaslights and the assistants were beginning to drag in for the night the pavement displays of buckets, stepladders, fruit. It was just the time to go and buy damaged apples or broken biscuits. Perhaps I had been sent out for the newspaper, for the papers, brought by sea from Liverpool, arrived in the shop about this time of day. Or possibly my errand was to buy three of the little cakes called Maids of Honour, to be eaten after the cold meats of the evening meal. Late October, then, and early dark, the most intimately disturbing of times and seasons. The place was Buck's Road, a flattened part of the hill that winds steeply upward from the town centre and the seafront. Cable cars ran up and down this hill and you could see, through the metal slot in the roadway, the quivering cable. The cars were famous for having cut off a boy's leg, and to remember that is to remember also the sight of this boy, much later, playing tennis, wearing a Ronald Colman moustache and stalking keenly round the court, he who had earlier observed all too intently the agitation of the cable, slipped and cried out, to find himself thereafter entitled to only one leg, but bold still and brave, and always cool with the girls.

No cars appeared that evening and I wore no splint or sling. Near Newby's, the paper shop, was the ironmonger's, where Marion, a girl I liked very much, so trim and pretty, with neat black hair and an overall shining white, carried mops and clotheshorses indoors, behind her the bright screen of light of the shop window. But Marion was only a little older than I was and could not have been working at the ironmonger's until years later. Opposite these shops was one of a string of nonconformist churches and chapels on that side of the road, I forget what kind, Primitive Methodists, Wesleyans, Baptists, conventicles we, as good Anglicans, did not attend. The church directly opposite the ironmonger's was certainly Congregational, and in it, if its notice board was to be believed, there preached almost incessantly the minister, a Mr. Shave. It was outside Mr. Shave's church that, as a consequence of my philosophical aspirations, I had a word with God.

This was an experience of unusual fulness and integrity, comprising: the smoke falling from a dense array of chimney-pots into the chilly dark of the street, the lights of Newby's shop brightening from moment to moment, pretty Marion clattering her pails, many possibilities of presence that belong to the word if not to the world. Nor was this fulness, this allness one might almost be permitted to say, a matter of simple undifferentiated good, to be shared by passersby with glowing cigarettes and turned-up coat collars, by Mr. Shave or even by Marion. It included negatives they might want to exclude; it belonged to me alone, blooded by the world as a gambler is flushed by inexplicable certainties, a Pythagorean world arranging itself around a hunch. The faint smudged pink of the sky above the church complied with the noises of the street and the tread of unilluminated persons, who had no notion of the plenitude of which they were part. If there were splints and bowls of bloody water, and there were, and torsos parted from their limbs, and there were, they helped the harmony. Nothing called for further explanation; desertion was a proof of union, loss of gain.

In these unusual circumstances it was needless to ask questions, for the answers could only confirm what was already certain; yet it seemed, for all that, the right time to make one simple enquiry, less for the sake of an answer than to show approval of the whole gigantic system, and gratitude for the privilege bestowed. And so, contemplating among all the rest the numerous busy figures going about their business against the flaring light, considering their planetary distance and difference from myself as well as the indications of close resemblance, I put a question that had been exercising me: Did other persons, when they ate oranges, experience the taste I had of orange?

The orange was chosen, perhaps, for its globality, or its alien origin, but except for that measure of resemblance to a world anything edible would have served as well, the Maids of Honour for instance, or the boiled ham that would precede them at supper. A pomegranate, to be bought for a penny in that very street and eaten with the help of a pin, would have done very well. As examples of persons any persons would have served, the one-legged boy or Marion smiling, a lock of hair escaping from her neat cap, or even Jack Fat, the blind man who cadged in the pubs and was sometimes given a pint of water instead of beer; he would drink it without stopping for breath and then ask for the beer he had been promised; or Pegleg Caley, when, taking a break from terrorising my mother, he accepted some nourishment, perhaps the cakes and ginger wine she tremulously offered.

Why that question? I knew nothing of the epicurean variety of the world, except as it was expressed in boiled ham, Maids of Honour, an occasional orange. Must every other living person taste the orange differently, though experiencing it as the taste proper to orange as each knew it, and so recognising it and, since language was something we certainly shared, being able to make it known to others as orange, just as they might call something, say a sunset, pink or smoky pink, and so convey to others a notion of the shade they had in mind, though having wholly private experience of that colour, experience quite inaccessible to anybody else? It was not by any means the first time God had been asked to comment on problems of this sort. He presumably knows not only the true taste of orange and the colour of pink or smoky pink but also the innumerable fugitive, deviant versions of them as experienced by the merely sensate, every one of these millions of private sensations, dying, it may be, with the mortal sensers. Red and purple, apple and ham, eau de cologne and ether, dwelt essentially in those immaterial eyes, palate, nose. It was clearly a waste of time to trouble oneself with barren problems of multitude. Possibly what I had discovered at that moment was a reason why, with remarkable unanimity, the creatures have hitherto decided they must have gods.

Now, as the smoke dropped onto Mr. Shave's church on that evening of newspapers, buckets, and damaged fruit, the street-long cable-slot still gleaming in the shoplights, I ended my career as best philosopher, seer blest, eye among the blind, and so forth. The next step was, as might be foretold, to enter the prison house of my own incommunicable intuitions, and soon to be committed to the long labour of learning how to pretend to know something a little better than I did, and to know how to say it with apparent clarity to others, all similar in certain respects, all knowing how to use the same language as mine to explain their recognitions of oranges or smoke. It is an acceptable condition, in which we are able to believe that we communicate, that we may be distincts yet not divided.

Long afterwards I began a long poem about the pink smoky dusk and Marion with the buckets, and all other undivided distincts, and about God considered as the perfect smeller, taster, toucher, but it somehow collapsed into rubble and it seemed the honourable or, at any rate, the human course to leave it lying there and say nothing about it to anybody. I once came across a rabbinical midrash which said that when Moses smashed the tablets no blasphemy occurred because God had miraculously erased all that was written on them before they struck the stony mountainside and broke into rubble. My poem was all the purer for being smashed.

AS TO MY MORE formal education, I went to school when just short of four years old and enjoyed the first morning, but at lunchtime walked the short distance home and told my mother I thought that would be enough for the day. But she was not having this. I was either at school or not, she reasoned, and as I had clearly announced that I was, she made me go back. I myself angrily rejected the kindergarten class, with its rocking horse and fingerpaints, and consequently was throughout my school years more than a year, and sometimes two years, younger than my classmates. This circumstance, and my being an only child, gave rise to the illusion, even now not entirely dispelled, that I am always the youngest person in the company.

We had to do needlework, and my clumsiness and bad eyesight, not yet noticed by teachers or parents, combined to make threading the needle a nerve-racking job. So began the trail of terror I had later to negotiate, when my manual incapacity was such that teachers were crossly convinced that I was deliberately producing work beyond the reach of ordinary incompetence. An art master, a man of sarcastic but generally tolerant habit who preferred such subjects as mops standing in a bucket of water, could find no other explanation than insolence for my terrible drawings, my failure to meet this fairly elementary challenge from reality. And I have always had this trouble, remaining without skill at matching the world with my representations.

Since nobody any longer can compel me to carve or draw, or even hang a picture straight, it may be supposed that my incapacity became a trifling problem once the pains of childhood humiliations had faded. But it has persisted, and may be related to some of my difficulties in dealing with other people, especially women. I lack what appears to be in others a perfectly ordinary skill or tact in handling not only things but persons. I notice this ability among children in playgrounds and people in pubs; or when somebody draws a sketch map, peels an orange, assumes an attitude obviously correct but not in my repertoire, or embarks on a seduction. They all seem to know what it takes; where and how they found it out is a mystery to me.

My lack of qualities so natural to others that they never needed even to congratulate themselves on having them was emphasised by my being a fat boy, not just plump or robust but fat. Although all the children in the street might have been assumed to eat much the same kinds of food as I did, a diet of which no good parent would now approve, they stayed thin. But perhaps they were of even poorer families than ours, and I now think that although I probably had a predisposition to be fat, as I had to be clumsy, both conditions were worsened by the treatment I got at home, so that as I owed my clumsiness in part to my father, I owed my obesity to my mother, and especially to her soups. The favourite was a sort of broth made out of cheap bacon bones, bought by me for a few pennies from the grocer. Vegetables called potherbs—also very cheap—were added to the bones. When the soup was finished you fished out the bones, on which there was always plenty of meat. Now such plenty can nowhere be found; God knows what happens to the bones of bacon bought in supermarkets.

We got through quantities of butter, bought in a shop called the Maypole, where the girls slapped away expertly at great heaps of it with their patterned paddles, wrapping it with the speed of conjurors and probably giving you slightly more than you were paying for. And of course there were the cakes, not only the Maids of Honour (the only name I remember at the moment), but pastries of all sorts, each bought at the shop which made it best, and the bags of sweets brought home by Father on Friday night to ease us through the leisurely, tedious siege of Sunday.

Probably it is by reason of such memories—they include the great sacks of flour, oats, and sugar at the grocer's, the rich smells of coffee and tea—that there remains, stubbornly paradoxical, the notion that those were times of plenty, when the fact is they were times of penury. Yet I grew fat, and stayed so until, suddenly, I became a slender adolescent, still of course shortsighted, the victim of various tics, worried about many things, especially girls, for a few years looking, and even contriving to feel, like other youths. Old age, and a mild but inappeasable addiction to alcohol, restores the fat. When to be competitive would now be ridiculous, I still rather envy, among the dwindling company of my contemporaries, those who remain, or seem to remain, slim and clear-eyed, age-defiant, tomb-defiant, as ever easy and bold with women.

THERE WAS ANOTHER notable difference between me and my contemporaries of the early years, almost as marked as the difference in manual skills and figure. As they exceeded me in dexterity with chisel or pencil, so I outclassed them in talking and writing. This endowment was one reason why I spent all my school time with older children, who probably regarded their own skills as normal (and my lack of them as pitiful) but thought of my compensatory gift of the gab as odious, especially as it won the praise of unloved teachers. There was a Miss White, a small, oldish woman—so memory, dependent on stereotypes, dictates—with tied-back hair and pince-nez, dreaded by the other kids as a bit of a fizzer, given to outbursts of bad temper during which you might get slapped, but always energetic, and to me interesting. I remember her showing us the length of a yard, and by way of illustration stretching her short legs in an extravagant stride. It was she who made me sure of unpopularity by commending a brief piece of mine about the delights I hoped to enjoy in a career as a lighthouse keeper (I think it was in the form of a monologue by the lucky man) and, worse, by reading it out to the class. Miss White must have been a good teacher. She taught me, for instance, how to tell if a number was divisible by three and, even more interesting, by eleven; I have asked highly educated literary persons if they know these tricks, which I mastered seventy years ago, and as a rule they don't. She made me skilful in the shortcuts of mental arithmetic, a subject then known for some reason as mensuration and, in those days before calculators, regarded as a very important preparation for life. I still scorn the calculator for all but my most complex or tedious arithmetical needs.

At seven I was moved to another school, which also happened to be near home. I have few memories of this school. One is of jamming my thumb in its iron gate; I noted that it took about a hundred days for the black nail to grow out. Throughout life I have continued, sometimes obsessively, to make such purposeless observations, counting days, hours, yards. Another memory is of a headmaster who stated that if any of us dared to open our eyes during morning prayers God was quite capable of striking us blind. I found that every boy willing to discuss this problem had risked it, as I had, and at least half-opened his eyes. All had escaped blindness, at any rate for the time being.

The offences of adolescents—simple loutishness, as when kids from a nearby school now drop their cola tins and candy wrappers over my garden fence, or habitual lying—are partly the consequence of the lies and fictions and bad faith to which adults have subjected them for years; meanwhile, they are being prepared to do the same to another generation. Or some of them are—not everybody is as wicked—no, stupid—as that headmaster. But we have not yet quite abandoned the idea that terror in one form or another is a good preparation for adult life. It is inflicted at a time when the child is too weak to prefer its own fictions to those imposed from above. Years are wasted on this process of imposing mind-forged manacles, time that might be devoted to the passing on of much perfectly ordinary, useful news about life that we need but are never offered, nor even allowed to suspect we need it. The disinformation later acquired we now pass on in modified form to our successors.

Still under ten, I was allowed to move, with the chosen twelve-year-olds, to the local high school, which served the whole island except for the northern part. Every morning I could watch from my bedroom window the arrival of the small trains bringing pupils from the south and west. It was then time for me to set out for school, a mile or more away, all uphill. On the way I would join the flood of country kids, thought to be much tougher characters than we of the town; certainly they endured the almost daily ordeal of caning with a sort of flushed stoicism, even a quiet impudence, we all admired, though it was likely to earn them even more severe treatment next time round.

I was by a long way the youngest boy in the school and on my first day was singled out for celebrity by the headmaster; I had come first in the scholarship competition, which was based on the examination that later came to be called the eleven-plus. I was made to mount the platform at morning assembly and stand among the gowned teachers to be admired by the whole school. The idea may have been to please me, but the appearance, in the wake of the headmaster's eulogy, of a fat, blinking, bewildered infant caused a great howl of spontaneous laughter from the twelve- to eighteen-year-olds of the captive audience.

This was not a good start, and it marked me as a victim. A large boy would summon me to meet him in the lavatories and beat me up. Once he blackened both my eyes, and—like many before and after me, but for each of us it is the first time in history—I had to invent an impossible accident to explain my condition to my parents. They cannot have believed me, but had no idea what to do about it. For a long time my life was ruled by fear of this boy. I'm fairly sure his motives weren't pervertedly erotic—he could have picked on many prettier and equally vulnerable kids. Schools of the kind I went to had no need to monitor love affairs between pupils. There was no need to forbid them because they never happened; you might as well legislate against levitation. My parents were politely acquainted with the parents of my persecutor, and we were sometimes all together, away from the school setting. Then we behaved civilly to one another, silently agreeing, though with some reluctance on my part, that our relationship was not the business of adults. This wasn't the result of negotiation, or even a conscious decision of mine; it would never even have occurred to me to mention it. In private I was entirely in his power, which he exerted without evident emotion; he wasn't angry with me but seemed to regard his beatings as a duty he was bound to carry out.

In those desperate early years I was a great disappointment to my mother, and to myself. She took a painfully serious interest in the reports of progress, sent by post to the parents at the end of each term. They commented on each subject and gave everybody a place in his form. It must seem strange that I was expected to be top boy in a class of thirty-odd, all by so much my seniors, but my mother was horribly upset when at the end of my first term I was, I think, ninth in the class, falling next term to eleventh. Her distress was unbearable, and mine impaired what power I might have had to improve my performance. The teachers did not help when their reports perfunctorily lamented my unrealised potential, my laziness, my wanton lack of concentration, given visible form by my chaotic appearance, all crumpled clothes and food-stained ties and lapels.

This misery went on for years, though I could convince neither my parents nor myself that I hadn't, in spite of the evidence, preserved a natural superiority over the other boys, which only my wilful indiscipline prevented me from proving. By twelve I was completely incompetent. I suppose we now have specialists who understand without difficulty that a child of twelve or thirteen, overwhelmed by fear and despair, can have what adults think of as a breakdown; perhaps there were such people even then, but I had no access to them. It didn't occur to me that I could look for somebody to give me counsel, and anyway, I had no notion of what it was that I should be counselled about. But I knew that my life was intolerable, each day producing a new variety of torment. My parents worried, but took the measure of my collapse by observing the collapse of my performance in school; I dropped rapidly towards the bottom of the class—a shameful position, though since we were arranged in order, with the top boys at the back of the room, this at least got me a front-row seat where I could see what was written on the blackboard.

It must seem strange that I never spoke to anyone of my semi-blindness, imagining that it was somehow another aspect of my delinquency, and strange also that for so long nobody noticed it. In the end some teacher did, and I was taken to the optician's. He was a Mr. Holmes, and outside his shop there was posted, in appropriately bold letters, the slogan YOU CAN'T BE OPTIMISTIC WITH A MISTY OPTIC. This certainly covered part of my own case. Mr. Holmes made me some spectacles. At first they added to my feeling that the world, in which other people seemed to find themselves quite at home, was to me a foreign country in which I had no bearings. Having to wear glasses seemed a terminal humiliation; now I truly couldn't bear to be where and what I was. I temporarily solved the problem on the way out of the shop by beginning to feel dizzy. I bumped into a glass case and fainted, for the first and only time in my life.

Meanwhile, there was the problem of those reports. The teachers were not all bullies, but the sad puzzlement of the Latin master at the growing ignorance of a once promising pupil was as hard to bear as the anger of the inflexible, cane-waving old man who taught algebra and trigonometry. The headmaster, summing up, expressed his disappointment, but he had no doubt experienced many such, and it cannot have occurred to him that I needed more help than I was getting.

I knew that no allowances would be made at home, not of course because my parents were cruel, but because they had absolutely no understanding of what was happening. The issue was for them, as for me, one of moral responsibility, which I seemed to have altogether renounced.

For me the great need was to conceal from them the extent of my delinquency. There was going to be a report which showed that I was now twenty-eighth in a class of thirty, with only a pair of wanking no-hopers beneath me. I could not live to see the distress of my parents when they discovered this, and imagined that if they should do so, my guilt and misery would be even greater, hard though it might be to increase them.

That I got out of this dilemma by a trick is an indication less of my own naïveté than of my parents'. I am still too ashamed to describe it, partly because it was a lie, partly because it was so transparent a lie. It is close to incredible that they were deceived and I have often wondered whether they really were, whether in fact they saw through my puerile deception, decided to treat it as a symptom rather than a crime, and, after much consultation, agreed that the best course was to let it pass. If that is what happened, they must have known thenceforth that I was, if not a liar, then somebody whose truth was suspect; and they would have been quite right to think so. But I think they lacked the subtlety necessary to such decisions. I believe they believed me, as the sequel tended to show.

Faking the report to get out of that scrape was only a temporary relief, for it ensured that failing some extraordinary improvement in my work there would be another crisis at the end of the next term. I had therefore to do what everybody kept saying I must: pull myself together. In fact, I rose fifteen places in the form, but instead of winning congratulations, I was in the awkward position (the due penalty of lies and de-ceptions) of having to explain why I had fallen from the relative height I was thought to have attained in the previous term. I do not remember, or rather I shall now profess not to remember, how I handled that one. Within a year or so I had put the problem behind me and took a hold on either the first or the second place in the class (at home, of course, only the first was thought wholly acceptable).

These little problems, sorted out sixty years ago, may be of more interest to me than to a reader, but they remain in my mind always and figure in any reasonably truthful account of myself I give myself, and I follow the example of Rousseau in regarding that requirement as in such cases decisive. The success of my primitive lies ensured that for a while I continued to alter the facts to suit myself; fibs and distortions, all begetting further fibs and distortions, were for some time a recurrent feature of my moral life, continuing, I suppose, until there was no further need of them and I could settle for the greater comfort, the relative intellectual ease, of veracity, which, it is pleasant to remember, is the natural preference of middle and old age.

Perhaps it would have paid, even on a hedonistic calculation, to have been truthful at the time and suffer the immediate consequences, instead of living under the threat of discovery in a more despicable offence. But I was incapable of such a calculation, and entirely capable of imagining my mother's distress and anger. What could have been more terrible? My later difficulties in dealing with her were of the same sort, shaped by this early experience. From then on, there would always be aspects of my life of which I couldn't possibly give her an honest account.

When I've observed, in other families, relationships of apparent candour, of acceptance on the part of both parents and children that each has a right to a different sort of life, that each is subject to passions, possessed of secrets, which he or she has no need to justify or reveal, I have been envious, though sometimes wondering whether such open acceptance, such easy abstention from judgement, might not be part of a subtler fiction, a more expert sham, a way of concealing, under an acknowledged right to secrets, secrets darker than those freely licensed. Few are now disposed to underestimate the potential horrors of family life, but I can still feel some envy, and wish that my family had been more skilful at the game of hiding them from others. At least it is a game that calls for collaboration, the shared lie that protects the individual rather than driving him under the cover of noxious private fantasies. I think I now see that the master fantasy of my nonage was the Family Romance, to be discarded only when along with all the other self-deceiving lies it no longer served its purpose. It is a false way of finding out who the child really is and, since he clearly isn't at home with his own people, where he belongs. But he is aware all the time that he can't find this out by lying to himself, by claiming something he's not entitled to, something got by a fraudulent alteration in a ledger or a school report, and always under threat of discovery and punishment. Nothing of the kind happens, no sentence is executed, but that is not important. What matters is that he should not live under the threat, a perpetual northeaster withering joy.

THE PURSUIT OF THAT to which a person is not entitled is likely to be competitive. Unless you had money, as very few people did where I came from, going to a university depended on your winning scholarships, of which, in my territory, only three were awarded annually. They were worth about £100 a year, not by themselves enough to survive on, so one accepted willy-nilly a further obligation, to study an extra year in teacher training, a pledge which provided the necessary £80 per annum extra, enough to get by on at a provincial university, though not at Oxford or Cambridge, which were generally reckoned to require at least £250 a year and were thus accessible only to the children of parents whose income greatly exceeded my father's.

I was by now a slender and rather confident seventeen, interested in girls, of whom I, the virtually only child, knew nothing, and enjoying male friendships. Despite some crises of no discoverable origin, during which I would walk to the end of the pier and remain there for hours in silent tumult, unable to control the movements of my eyes, neck, and arms, I was convinced that the worst miseries were behind me.

So I won a scholarship and, encouraged by parents now relieved and proud, accepted the obligation to be a schoolteacher. To renege on that promise would entail returning four instalments of £80, which was unthinkable, though hardly more so than a future as a schoolteacher. Unlike me, my mother was happily certain that I would in due time come home and be a master at my old school; this seemed to her the height of sane ambition, whereas I had no specific ambition except the negative one of not doing anything of the kind. But I did not say so. And as sometimes happens, the prospect of some apparently unavoidable future crisis was eliminated by a sequence of events, including the war, that could not have been included in the calculations of 1937. To be relieved of the necessity either to teach in a school or to repay that enormous sum was about the only benefit I got out of the war, except of course for the benefit of survival.

IN THE MID-1960s the Franks Report on the University of Oxford caused a certain stir by maintaining that Oxford was to be treated as one of the four super-universities of the Western world, the others being, as far as I remember, Cambridge, Harvard, and California; or perhaps, since it was an Oxford report, Cambridge escaped mention. The claim was made in support of the argument that Oxford needed special favours from the government, if necessary at the expense of non-super-universities, which had probably small claim to be thought of as universities anyway. It was still usual, in my youth, for English people to talk about *both* universities as if there were only two, and in later years it seemed to be generally assumed that I must have attended one or the other of them. Maurice Bowra, a very famous don who naturally liked Oxford as it had been before the war, testified to the Franks committee that the number of applicants for places at Oxford had then been exactly the same as the number of places available in its colleges, which seemed to him a providential arrangement—disturbed, unhappily, by the war and what others professed to regard as the educational reforms that followed it. Two rather small super-universities, then, were all we really needed. As quite a number of novels and memoirs bore witness, scholarship boys who made it to prewar Oxford from grammar schools tended to lead a rather pinched existence, though, conscious of future reward, they rarely wished themselves elsewhere. In any case, my scholarship was tied to one university, so I took my £180 to Liverpool. Life there, as it happened, was quite as exciting, difficult, and metropolitan as I could conveniently handle.

At the end of the century various administrative manoeuvres have resulted in a nominal levelling up or down of the English universities. But of course everybody knows there is still a pecking order, and the old prejudices survive. It remains difficult for southerners to understand the distinction of, say, Manchester University in the sciences, history, and biblical scholarship. And it does not stand alone among the great nineteenth-century northern institutions. I remember arguing, when the Macmillan government was spending heavily on small new universities—conceived as super-liberal-arts colleges in cathedral cities and other such pleasant places—that all this money should be spent on modernising the more grimly

situated Victorian workhorse institutions. I still think it would
have been the wiser course, and it might have done something
to reduce the preeminence of Oxbridge, which is sometimes,
though not in Oxford or Cambridge, condemned as unfair and
even unhealthy.

The main buildings of Liverpool were certainly grimly
situated; the prewar stench and squalor of Brownlow Hill belonged to a different order of civility from, say, Radcliffe
Square. All the same, one sensed a peculiar liveliness in the
place. The old shipping families whose names are remembered
in the university had made the city a close rival to Manchester,
with its great library and its famous orchestra. Liverpool had
very good libraries and a good orchestra, for which it built a
fine new concert hall, opened just before the war began. There
were flourishing theatres and galleries, all striking novelties to
me. I could go for nothing to orchestral rehearsals and watch
Thomas Beecham, Henry Wood, and Albert Coates at work.
Once Coates broke his spectacles and asked bespectacled members of the audience to come forward so that he could try theirs
on and, if he came on a suitable pair, borrow them for an hour.
Anxious to serve, seeking the honour, we trooped up and were
all rejected. Other trivial recollections are oddly detailed: Beecham making the orchestra giggle, then wince; Hans Hotter
swallowing top notes at rehearsal; and the violinist Telmányi
in the Beethoven concerto (a work I knew quite well from an
old 78 made by Jelly d'Arányi, the initial drum taps sounding
like a child hitting a biscuit tin), because of all the players I
have since heard in it none has had such a percussive left hand,
the thudding of his fingers so loud that it almost seemed to
interfere with the music. When the new hall opened, I worked
in it as an usher and so heard two concerts a week, and there
wasn't much of the repertory of the time that I did not come
to know, however superficially. And we had opera, and theatre
I couldn't have dreamed of in my evenings at the local rep in
Douglas.

Liverpool has been unlucky; its occupation has gone. The river, now almost empty, was in my time there crammed with shipping. The gaps and rubble of the war were left untouched for years. It still has the look of a town that has not recovered from a disaster; the docks, derelict or used only for worthy, improvised purposes, suggest a brave sadness. Once handsome early-Victorian streets are now slums. A few years ago I went to accept an honorary degree from the university and was put up at the once grand Adelphi Hotel, where Henry James and many other great folks spent their first night in England amid splendours and comforts now fallen into dereliction. With Michael Tippett, also a graduand, I was taken by car to a reception at the Philharmonic Hall in which long before I'd shown people to their seats. We did not take the obvious and shortest route up the hill, for the riots of a few days before had left smoking ruins, streets blocked by buses full of armoured policemen. It was an affable occasion, but the civilities took place on an island in a waste of strife, racial strife in a city where many ethnic communities had coexisted calmly for a century. There were a lot of poor people in the Liverpool of the 1930s, a lot of slums, but the place was peaceful enough. Even now a kind of camaraderie persisted, being endorsed by habit, by the football team, by the Beatles, and by the self-mocking accent.

Of course even in those prewar days the life of the university was an islanded affair, and the more intense for that. Many of the young men in the halls of residence were plain northern lads from the good grammar schools of Lancashire and Yorkshire, all loyal to their towns, praising or defending Bolton, Batley, Blackburn, or, slightly posher, middle-class Lytham. But not all were poor. The university had a famous school of architecture, full of enviable young men in fashionable clothes, Liberty shirts, and elegant loafers, who would have been at Oxford or Cambridge but for the fame of this school. There were conscientiously dissolute Egyptians, elaborately barbered every morning, pale from their nocturnal carousings. Where these took place I didn't know, but was impressed to note that they often called for full evening dress and shiny top hats. I shared a room with one of the many Northern Irish architects, habitually gentle in manner but with the harsh voice of the province. He irritated me only by his habit, shared by all the architects, of deferring work on his fortnightly "scheme" till the last day or two, and then working through the night under brilliant light. Like almost everybody I met, he was in various ways a revelation to me. Much later, I heard, he fell or threw himself off the roof of one of his own buildings, like the Master Builder.

The warden of our hall of residence was Leonard Barnes, once very well known as the author of *Caliban in Africa*, a Left Book Club publication. Because of a war wound he clanked and limped along on leg irons, always seeming in pain, but courteous and somehow fierce. He was, in person, rather as *The New Statesman* of the time was in print, though less inclined to vacillate. In September 1938 I was in France, but all British tourists were suddenly bundled out of Europe by orders of the Foreign Office. It was a disorderly and wearying retreat, and I arrived exhausted at the hall on the day of the Munich agreement. In the gardens people were still digging trenches. Barnes gave me a drink. I had hardly known what to think about the turn of events, though on the whole I felt glad there was not going to be a war just yet. Barnes was disgusted and devastated by what he regarded as the folly or treason of Munich.

A few months later I watched him limp past me into dinner, his whole bearing reflecting the anger and apprehension he felt at the German annexation of Bohemia and Moravia. He was one of those who influence the young in an unspecifiable way, perhaps by showing so plainly that he knew life was tragic. His heaving gait, his Viyella shirts and corduroys,

somehow suggested that there was a right, sad way of dealing
with existence, at any rate in those days. He wrote a sonnet
about the state of the world and the individual life at the time,
a poem of which I remember the closing lines:

And so will I, like him and Fortinbras,
Make mouths at the invisible event.

Fifty-odd years later I still think of Barnes when I hear or read
that soliloquy of Hamlet's. He believed there was a cause to
be fought for, however black the prospect, and such confidence
is the more telling when the man who holds the view has
himself fought and survived, not unscathed, and with an extremely clear idea of what war was like. I was too shy and
immature to know him well, or dispute with him freely, but
he is in my memory as one of the various kinds of person I'd
rather be.

The students of that time were usually in a ferment about
something it was quite right to be in a ferment about; in my
earlier university years it was the Spanish Civil War. The
Communist Party energetically proselytized, and the more literary students bought and brandished Auden's sixpenny pamphlet, *Spain*. By the time the Republican resistance ended early
in 1939, attention had been more or less wholly transferred to
Germany. Even after the European war began, the Peace
Pledge Union, of which I was still at the time a member,
continued to hold its meetings. It had the bad luck to have
scheduled its annual general meeting on 10 May, the day when
the Germans invaded Belgium and Holland. A pack of Conservative Party members attacked the meeting and were carrying away the passively resisting pacifists when the Boxing
Club arrived, resolved to defend to the death our right to snivel
about our despicable opinions without interruption. There was
a brawl, for which we sanctimoniously blamed not our assail-

ants, the Tories, but our defenders, the boxers. The consequence of this action was the banning throughout the university of all political clubs and societies, a ban which was not
lifted until after the war.

My own pacifist principles were insecure, and might not
even have survived the disgusted disapproval of my father,
who imagined that his friends would cut him if his son became
a conchie; and if they did, he would cut me. I did in fact register
as a conscientious objector, but lacking the moral purity to
hold to that line after the German conquest of France and the
Low Countries, I cancelled my registration. Somehow the Germans didn't sound as if they would be deterred by the methods
advocated by Bertrand Russell or even Gandhi. Russell's confidence in the efficacy of passive resistance depended on his
conviction that at some point humanity would rebel at continued cruelty. The occupying forces couldn't run the country
without cooperation; the Post Office, for instance, would be
at a standstill because everybody would refuse to work. So the
enemy would shoot the Postmaster-General, his deputy, his
regional controllers, and so on and so on down the list, but
they would have to give up before they got far with the mas-
sacre of all the postmen. But we had reason—already—to believe that the enemy was made of sterner stuff. And as the war
went on, such notions came to seem silly, in the old sense of
innocent.

Some of my pacifist friends, in this respect if in no other resembling the enemy, were also made of sterner stuff. They
made a fair estimate of the horrors of occupation, but decided
that any attempt to prevent them would infringe their principles. The agonies of conscientious objection in the quite recent
Great War included a possible sentence of capital punishment;
this was no longer a threat, but nobody supposed that objectors
would have an easy time. If they failed to persuade a tribunal
of the validity of their objection, they would go to prison, a

fate from which most middle-class young men had a reasonable aversion.

There were many complaints, though not, of course, from the general public, about what were called the cat-and-mouse tactics of the authorities; you could serve your sentence, then be rearrested, probably by military police, who would order you to put on a uniform; if you refused, you went back to gaol. I doubt if many men served more than two terms, but some certainly did; a particular friend of mine, of whom I shall say more in a moment, served one sentence in Liverpool and one in Wormwood Scrubs, before giving in and accepting exemption conditional on his undertaking work of approved "national importance." Absolute exemption was rare, and usually given to people certifiably of a religious sect, notably the Friends, though some Quakers also had quite a hard time.

The tribunals were nervous and exciting. The Liverpool body was presided over by a Judge Burgess, held by all to be, within the rules laid down for such courts, a fair and civilised man. One day a disappointed pacifist stabbed the judge in Lime Street Station as he waited for his train, and there was indignation among pacifists, including even those who had failed to convince him of the justice of their cause. He was sent many flowers, and there was genuine rejoicing when he recovered from his wounds.

While all this and much else (including a rather protracted illness) was going on, I was enjoying what I still think of as probably the most exhilarating year of my life: 1939–40 marks the brief epoch of my omnipotence. There seemed to be time for everything: love, play, music, a huge amount of work. I wrote my first book, if that isn't too grand a category to put it in. It was a study of Aaron Hill, an eighteenth-century jack-of-all-trades, theatre manager, dramatist, journalist, poet, and speculator, who introduced Handelian opera into England and wrote the dreadful libretto of *Rinaldo*, which was translated overnight into Italian and played, despite some sneering from Addison and others, with enormous success at the Haymarket. Addison's joking was largely at the expense of the castrato, a voice unknown in England till that time.

The *Dictionary of National Biography* describes Hill as one of the greatest bores in history, but I found him amusing company. His play *The Fatal Extravagance* has a small place in theatrical history, his updating of *Henry V* must be the most ludicrous of all Shakespeare adaptations. His theatrical magazine, *The Prompter*, is a lively source of information about the theatre of the time. Pope put him in *The Dunciad* but took him out again, or anyway obscured the reference, when Hill protested; men would do almost anything to avoid a protracted correspondence with Hill. A man of energy and undeterred by the South Sea Bubble, he devised a large number of absurd projects for making a fortune, and others for saving the nation from the impudent incursions of foreigners. Yet he travelled to Palestine and Greece when he was fifteen, and the Tsar of Russia sent him a medal, which never arrived. I enjoyed the time I spent with him, hours spared from all my other activities, which included a degree course of which Hill formed only a small part. The book, which I have just had a look at, is deplorable, as might be expected. Obviously I was amused by Hill but hadn't the skill to convey my amusement without being prematurely cocky and contemptuous; still, I wasn't yet twenty, and I *was* rather cocky.

It might well be said that there were better things for me to be doing with my time than making easy jokes about Aaron Hill, and I agree in principle, but to write a book can't have been a bad preparation for the sort of life I envisaged, and to do it without anxiety about publication, since that could never have been thought a possibility. Moreover, I seemed to have time for everything, including illness and loss of virginity and sometimes fairly boisterous male bonding.

There is a special intensity in the male friendships formed at this period of life, yet I find I do not recall it—I recall the young men well enough, but not, except in one case, the strength of my feeling for them. We were very straight sexually, but there may have been a suppressed eroticism in some encounters. This was not true, as it happens, of my relationship to the friend who, until his early death, affected me most strongly. This book, for good or ill, is about me, not about him, but I have to say something about him because I admired him as immeasurably my moral as well as my literary superior yet often caught myself thinking him solemnly ridiculous; and that says something that may be important and possibly discreditable about me. Our relationship had two distinct phases, before and after the war; here I speak of the first of them.

I WAS STILL ignorant of English life (though learning fast) and hardly understood the degree to which Peter Ure may have resembled other young English intellectuals of that epoch. If there were others like him, it makes no difference to my story, since he was the only one that came my way; so as far as I was concerned, he was unique. When I first met him, in 1937, he was to me—and to others also—a formidable figure, graceful in movement, with the powerful body of a sprinter (a breaker of school records). His square jaw and grim mouth seemed already to signify resignation in the face of a determined and probably disagreeable destiny: an attitude understandable given the state of the world, but not one that was easily shared by ordinarily exultant youth. Rather surprisingly he liked to play rugby, and played it well, though making it clear that all his pleasure derived from the sport itself and not from the company. He was at the time still a prolific poet, usually heavily Yeatsian in manner but also, in more politically menacing tones, fairly straight 1930s Auden.

His father, once a science teacher, was headmaster of a

grammar school in Birkenhead, his mother a graduate of Liverpool. Both were or had been Fabians. His elder brother was at Oxford and it was held that the family could not afford to send both sons there. Peter, let loose in the world, became a trainee manager at Selfridges, where he ran an information bureau but was too bored to do it well. He was paid £2 a week and rented an attic in Pimlico for 12s.6d., leading a life to which he attributed his excessive carefulness with money thereafter; but it must have had other causes. After a while Selfridges expressed some dissatisfaction with his performance, and he left and came as a student to Liverpool, living at home.

I once had dinner with the family at Meols on the Wirral, the peninsula on the Cheshire side of the Mersey River. I was unused to middle-class houses, and any such occasion would have been a nervous one for me, for I had only rarely entered such places and never eaten in one. For all I knew, everybody in the Wirral who had more than a certain income lived like these people. At dinner I sat listening to a continuous stream of well-formed sentences about important topics. I had never before eaten asparagus, and wouldn't have guessed that in England it is finger food; and when strawberries appeared I refused sugar, not because (at that time) I liked them without, but because after the strain of the asparagus I had simply run out of courage and did not trust myself with the shaker. Peter remarked, in the loud clear tones in which he discoursed on all topics indifferently, that he had always believed sugar to be indispensable to strawberries, since without it they lacked all flavour. His father, in similar tones, explained to him that his remark was unmannerly. A brief, polite altercation followed, and then the conversation returned, as was always probable in those days, to the activities of Middleton Murry and the Peace Pledge Union, subjects on which father and son differed, eloquently but without heat, or to the behaviour of Kingsley Martin and his *New Statesman* since Munich.

The alarming formality of that evening, for so it seemed to me, suggested that in such a house something had intervened to replace not only the ordinary small talk but even those casual yet important expressions of affection, the brief bursts of quarrelling, the random endless chat about acquaintances, that I was myself more accustomed to. And I now reflect that I wasn't entirely off the mark. This man's life had a habit of formality, and related to it was his uncertainty as to when and how strong feelings (including rage) should be expressed. This resulted in a curious instability of temper; it was something repeatedly noticed by the people he later worked with in Greece, and it may have been a legacy from his early life. To cultivate the mind, know the world as it is, seemed in such an environment to require not only decorous speech and manners but a prohibition of the more demotic forms of expressiveness. This version of civilisation allowed no moment of riot, in conduct or in speech. In more than thirty years of acquaintance I never once heard Ure utter a word of slang or an incomplete or ungrammatical sentence. Even his wit belonged to an identifiable literary tradition of nonsense or fantasy. His outbursts of rage were the more formidable, out of all control except for what he could not throw off, this fastidious grammatical constraint. In a note written at the age of twenty-one he records that as a schoolboy, puffed up with the conceit of being, unlike others, a poet, he would be "driven into insane rages" by the other boys. This was a sickness he did not shed.

He was one of the many examples that have been offered to me, and haplessly declined, of an orderly existence. He worked systematically with files and indexes. His poems were copied, in chronological order, into eighteen tall notebooks, the pages numbered consecutively and reaching a total of 1,608. The first poem was written when he was six or seven. He seems to have given up poetry when he became a university teacher after the war. I suppose he made a deliberate choice, or simply felt compelled by the course of events to be a critic rather than a poet. He applied himself to that less exalted trade with the same methods of concentrated labour he had devised for his poetry.

This dedication, hugely admired, was as far out of my reach as his Greek learning and his command of several other literatures, which was so secure that a first-degree course could have added very little to it. The astonishing seriousness of the man appealed to me as much as it alarmed me. It is true that he had a certain lugubrious gaiety, but that was reserved for strictly regulated moments of leisure. Even on holiday there was evidence of refined, all-considering preparation. In the early summer of 1939 I bicycled with him in Wales. The weather was such as North Wales often provides, one fierce downpour after another. I was not properly clad for it, and also suffered a series of punctures. Ure proceeded calmly on his admirable bicycle, securely waterproofed, grimly enjoying the trip.

At one youth hostel our task was what struck me as the entirely unreasonable one of varnishing a floor which, in memory, was as large as a small ballroom; it was Ure, not I, who did it with efficiency and solemn good humour. We stayed at Dolgelley in continuous torrents of rain and mist that obscured the mountain we had ridden so far to see. After two or three days we gave it up and rode on, and when we came to a signpost indicating Snowdonia one way and home the other, he took the first and I the second, decisions conveyed by gestures and accepted as sensible by both riders as they pedalled through the deluge. Going on alone, he would not be lonely, for he had already learned how to be solitary. It was a vocation. I have all these years later barely caught up with him, as usual. What helped him to sustain this choice of life was what I can only too vaguely call a certain religious habit of mind. He professed himself religionless, but his pacifist beliefs brought

him in these years and during his wartime adventures closer
to Quaker friends and colleagues than to anybody else.

He had to think about prison, and while he was doing so
reminded himself in his journal that Goethe had not allowed
a war to interrupt his researches on colour: an example he
recommended to himself and to an unspecified company of
like-minded men: we should "never let anything disturb us in
the pursuit of our intellectual life." He had the little volumes
of the Temple Dante bound into one volume so that they would
count as a single book and be more manageable in prison. Not
long afterwards he was arrested and went to Walton Gaol in
Liverpool. There, and later at Wormwood Scrubs in West
London, he worked on a book about Yeats, which was published after the war. His second sentence was of twelve months,
but after serving two he gave in, to the extent of accepting
conditional exemption. The condition he had accepted was to
do "full-time ambulance or hospital work under civilian control, full-time social relief, or land work."

He felt some guilt at this capitulation but was amazingly
happy. One Saturday morning he was sewing mailbags; the
same afternoon he could walk freely round Shepherd's Bush
Green and be called "Sir" by the bus conductor to whom he
gave his penny. Strolling about London he celebrated "the
extraordinary time-born beauty of the city"—a sentiment
which, considering the filth and decay of London at that time,
could probably be felt only by somebody who had just got out
of a prison, with its "cindery exercise yard" and "intolerable
clothes." He mused on poetry, meditating in his journal on
"those occasional perceptions great lines of poetry bear about
them, at once diffused and close-packed, an aura of meaning
which we cannot lay hold on, knowing only that it acts on our
nerves and the backs of our eyes, yet not a nervous reaction
purely, but something in which the whole being seems to take
part, but without fulfilling itself, but hanging in a kind of

expectant suspension that dies gradually away." This passage struggles to describe a state that privileged readers of poetry will recognise. He goes on to illustrate it from Hamlet's withdrawal of what he says he could tell us at the end: "But let it be": the full disclosure will not be made.

Ure's subsequent career was remarkable, for, having worked in London through the renewed bombing in 1943, he went to Egypt and then Greece, where he quickly learned modern Greek and was soon an officer of UNRRA. In April 1946 he noted in his journal that he "started this war being rudely treated by Walton Gaol warders and end it by drinking gin with generals." He went back to Liverpool for graduate work. The rest of his story I leave for the moment, save for one more word.

He copied into his diary a passage from a novel by Julien Green, a writer he particularly admired: "We are the children of death . . . It calls us from the depths of life. Even before we have learnt language it sometimes halts us in the midst of our games to listen to its voice . . . And all down the years it signals to us." He was to die as he had lived, alone; the notes of his recent reading were on his desk, scrupulous, professional, and there were other notes on himself and his pain.

ON THE WHOLE we were as well taught at Liverpool as students are in other institutions I have known, and the programme of study was more strenuous than any now prescribed. I was not keen to learn Anglo-Saxon, but I did; I went on learning Latin, which I'd been doing since I was ten, but I was now taught it by distinguished scholars, J. F. Mountford and F. W. Walbank, and, rather surprisingly, George Painter, the future biographer of Proust. I took up Italian, under the instruction, also surprisingly, of the future father of Marianne Faithfull. Indeed, I drank wine in celebration of his wedding and continue to take comfort from this connection with true fame.

It is commonplace to say that one was educated by fellow students, but it is probably truer in my case than in most, for I had so much to learn, not just academically but about how to live in a world so different from my own, a world in which I was to be obliged to spend my life. I will mention one such instructor because his whole life was, like its origins, remote from mine. He was not literary, wrote clumsily, was pained to discover the limits of my numeracy. He was a physicist in flight from physics, because his superiors were all at that time dedicated to the production of atomic explosives. He declined to assist them and moved into microbiology and cancer research, so avoiding Los Alamos.

Paul had been at a progressive school, and was devoted to Dr. Helena Wright, a libertarian sex counsellor of considerable contemporary fame. She recommended, among much else, that young men and women should go responsibly to bed together, preferably in their parents' houses. It should be within the scope of the historical imagination to understand how fantastic that preference seemed to me and most of my contemporaries. One of the difficulties of Paul's formation, and that of his circle, as I saw it, was that it was only with other people from the same school or the same milieu that they could really get on. Nevertheless, he sought me out; he had some of that exaggerated respect for literary people that is occasionally found in good scientists, and we were friends for years, his life as rationally ordered as mine was random. Much better off than I, he was conscientiously hedonistic and very generous, giving me money and allowing me the run of his London flat. He taught me something about London and something about life. He liked to talk about his own work and tried to care about mine, but there was little reciprocal understanding. He was one of those men who study their response to a quite casual observation so profoundly that one is about to conclude that they have dismissed it as unworthy of reply when at last some laboured answer emerges.

Later on he changed a good deal, grew to see the virtue of investing and keeping money; he emigrated to the United States, became head of the molecular biology laboratory at Yale, and after that retired to the Pacific coast to carry on his research and his dogged pleasures, one of which was sailing. I have a recollection, shameless and even pleasant, of crewing for him in a Yale Yacht Club race and committing some infringement, so recondite that I did not then and do not now know what it was, which caused his disqualification—not the first time I disgraced myself with him and was easily forgiven. Over the years I provided him with many excuses to drop me, but he was always tolerant of me and my wives; he had fixed notions about the responsibilities of friendship, and anyway, I expect he knew me well enough to have foreseen that disqualification was the most probable outcome of his inviting me into his boat. In the end he equably declined chemotherapy and, working to his last day, equably died. You learn from those whom you do not resemble, and may not wish to resemble, as well as from those who seem more plausibly assigned to you as models.

The end of my undergraduate career coincided with the German incursion into western Europe: it ended, that is, in circumstances of the utmost absurdity. We sat up all night preparing to answer questions on Aristotle and I. A. Richards as the tanks rolled up to the French Channel coast; we sweltered in examination rooms, desperately showing off about Shakespeare, as all hope died. When we were settling ourselves in the examination room to tackle the last paper of all, the invigilator felt obliged to tell us that news had arrived of the fall of Paris.

Since it clearly didn't matter whether one got a good or a bad degree—we had entered an epoch where such things were totally irrelevant—I did well enough. It seemed certain that we should shortly be invaded and eventually occupied by the Germans, prospects which for some reason made us, for the moment, lighthearted and keen not to miss the pleasures we had, in our opinion, earned by our scholarly efforts. In thinking back to the early summer of 1940 I feel something of its careless, nervous, intense pleasures, all the keener because of the probability that they could never be repeated, that a year or so on we might well be dead or, if not, in some situation, at present unimaginable, that we would surely not enjoy. So there was some morbidity in our passages of love and simple junketing, a little more urgency than they might have had at other times, though it is true that the pleasures even of less apocalyptic moments may have something of the same quality, and in them that same voice, sometimes more and sometimes less distant, may often be heard: *Nous nous arrêtons quelquefois au milieux de nos jeux pour écouter sa voix.*

My Mad Captains

No man will be a sailor who has contrivance enough to get himself into a jail; for being in a ship is being in a jail, with the chance of being drowned.

—SAMUEL JOHNSON

Every man thinks meanly of himself for not having been a soldier, or not having been to sea.

—SAMUEL JOHNSON

"I could give you the names of three captains now 'oo ought to be in an asylum, but you don't find me interferin' with the mentally afflicted till they begin to lay about them with rammers and winch-handles."

—RUDYARD KIPLING, *"Mrs. Bathurst"*

ON A CERTAIN DAY, every other Friday perhaps, I can't remember and it doesn't matter now, the troops fell in to claim their pay. When his name was called, the sailor stepped briskly forward, saluted, took off his cap, and placed it on the table. His pay would be placed on the cap. The sum would often be less than he had expected because of various deductions, especially what were called mulcts. This was the archaic word the navy used to mean "fines." Whenever authority was irritated or distressed by something a rating had done, it would award him a mulct. Ignorant recruits sometimes found it hard to understand that somebody who was professing to give them something was actually taking something off them. It might be a day's pay or more, and what with one thing and another, it wasn't difficult for man to be awarded so many mulcts that he got no pay at all. When that happened, an officer, or more likely his writer (the navy word for a clerk: the only writers in the navy were of inferior rank), would cry, "Not Entitled!" and put nothing at all on the cap. The relevant entry in the ledger that lay open before the writer was "N.E.," meaning, of course, "Not Entitled," but decoded by the troops as a North-Easter. The mulcted man would then put on his cap, hand out a parting salute as lively as the one which signalled his approach, about-turn, and impassively withdraw, unwilling to risk any more such awards by a display of chagrin, dissidence, or even surprise. He would then tell his comrades that he'd got a fucking northeaster. The epithet was applied not only to circumstances of disappointment such as this but also to more agreeable awards like liberty or what sailors called "leaf." It was used less frequently in connection with what you might hope to be doing when you got your leaf, and never if the person you were likely to be doing it with was a wife or a steady friend. Worn though it was by overuse, it was especially apposite to northeasters. Sometimes simply to be in the navy was to be in a fucking northeaster that never stopped blowing. Sometimes it seemed that to be alive at all was to have been born in the teeth of such a gale.

CALL TO ME all my mad captains. The first of them was mad in a quite different way from the others. He was unlucky as well as crazy, certainly worthy of a better deal than he got when he found himself consigned, as I was, to service in a sort of parody-navy, though he would have been quite at home in the real one, whereas I would not have found there, any more than in this grotesque doppelgänger, a climate that suited me.

The summer of 1940 might have been a sombre time for a twenty-year-old, for it seemed that the future, unless the war quickly ended in national disaster (as seemed quite probable), consisted of indefinitely prolonged military service. But I say again I remember it as a pleasant though nervous time, offering many satisfactions to which, for imperfectly examined reasons, I felt myself to be entitled. As for the future, let that come when it comes. Meanwhile, there were parties, tennis, bathing, love, and the ordinary terrors, such as the gamble against the disaster of pregnancy, worrying, naturally, but at the same time enlivening.

In September, during the first daylight raids on the docks, I was summoned to London and, trotting naked from booth to booth as the sirens howled, was examined by a team of perfunctory doctors and then interviewed by an amiably rough-tongued civilian who asked me if I had the power of command, was I a leader of men. This was a topic new to me, and I had never had occasion to form an opinion about it, but I assured him that I had this power, and believed I was telling the truth, for like many people at twenty I assumed that my powers were virtually without limit, though I lacked any notion as to how I might have acquired them—hardly from my father, four years a private, liked in his own circle precisely because it would never have occurred to him to lead anybody anywhere; or from my education, in which such leading as had to be done was done by other people, who would never have dreamed of asking me to join them. However, in the omnipotent summer of 1940 I felt sure I must have leadership tucked away with all my other unused capacity.

Taking me at my word, the brisk, overworked interviewer

sent me to Liverpool to be interviewed again, this time by a scholarly captain, a paymaster captain, his sleeves encrusted with bands of gold lace separated by bright white stripes, his breast bemedalled. This was my first encounter with persons of such high rank, though I soon discovered that in the eyes of "executive" officers, paymasters, or pussers, as they were called, even if captains, were not quite the real thing, despite their being regarded with a touch of superstitious awe because of their overdeveloped literacy, their familiarity with an arcane compendium called the King's Regulations, and with the insane naval system of accountancy. But then I was to learn that the real thing was, and perhaps is, not often to be met with.

This captain seemed a rather sympathetic figure, but said nothing, and it took some time for me to realise that this was less because his thoughts were on more important matters, which I would have understood, than because he couldn't think of anything to say. So I said I supposed he would tell me where I should be sent to be trained. He waved this remark aside impatiently, as if there were neither time nor need for such peacetime luxuries. Then, hitting on a subject, he asked me why I wasn't in uniform. "I have no uniform, sir." "Well," he said, "that will hardly do. Very little can be achieved without a uniform. You must get one at once." It seemed certain that there was more to be said, and I sat still while he continued to ponder. Eventually he walked over to his safe, unlocked it, and took from it what looked like quite a lot of money. This he handed to me, saying, "Go to Gieves and order yourself two uniforms, one of doeskin and one of serge. On the serge tell them to sew only half a ring. It is for everyday wear and lace all round would fray the cloth. The doeskin is for number ones. Better buy a greatcoat too." He warmed to the subject and speculated that the tailor was unlikely to be able to execute my order in less than a fortnight. It occurred to me to say in a jocular mode that the troops recently extracted from Dunkirk had not looked particularly well turned out, but his mind was on the future. "So you'll need two weeks' leave," he said. He unlocked the safe again and gave me more money as an advance of pay, which he correctly assumed I should need to see me through this painful interval. I signed receipts and departed, puzzled but reconciled to the fact that in worlds other than mine they did many things differently.

Accustomed as I had been to living on £180 a year, I had never had so much money all at once, about four months' normal supply; and I had no intention of giving most of it to the expensive tailor nominated by the captain. Instead, I went to a meaner establishment in Paradise Street and bought a ready-made uniform—in doeskin, the silly choice—and had the gold lace sewn on all the way round. I added a few other things, including a greatcoat weighing about twenty pounds which I was still wearing fifteen years later when I was much poorer. Then I went off to see my girl, which is what in those days we called young women, and we went to the seaside, where we stayed in a small boardinghouse. Every night the landlady and, as we supposed, her husband made clamorous love on an unstable bed. This struck us as the right way to behave in these difficult times. I don't think we were conscious of any worries at all, unlikely though that must seem.

Returning scrupulously on the due date, I sought out my pale, elegant paymaster captain. He seemed abstracted and hardly knew who I was; perhaps, after all, he had other cares, greater and more martial responsibilities. As before he was stuck for something to say, so he asked me if I'd like some leave; but the money was all spent, and I felt unreasonably sure that if he were once again to unlock the safe, that very action would remind him of our past relationship; so I honourably declined the offer, and instead asked if there was any place I could go to in order to learn my job. After some deliberation he told me to go down to the Huskisson Dock, find a ship called the *Sierra*, and report to a Lieutenant Taylor. "Tell him I sent you to learn the ropes." He sat at his desk and reluctantly wrote a letter of introduction. As I was leaving the room he stopped me and examined my uniform. "Where did you get it?" he asked. "At Gieves, sir." "You did well to go there," he said.

I walked out of the building, haughtily returning the salutes of passing sailors and wondering about H.M.S. *Sierra*. I suspected that it was unlikely to be the educational establishment I'd have chosen myself, but one thing I knew was that as I had never had any choice in such matters, it was absurd to expect to have one now. As a matter of fact, I was to spend the next two and a half years on that ship, and if I did learn anything I wanted to know I can't now remember what it was. I did pick up some things I didn't want to know: to drink far too much, never to speak of women (except of a wife if you had one, or of the wives of colleagues) without innuendo or obscenity, and to deal with the madness of captains.

As things fell out, instruction in this last art began immediately. I found the ship, a bestially ugly thing rearing its bow coarsely above the dockside, held there by cables with rat guards positioned, I noticed, to deny entry rather than to prevent flight from the vessel, which belonged to a company trading in West African cocoa. It had a top speed of about nine knots and in peacetime had carried back and forth as supercargo a dozen or so passengers in reasonably lavish colonial style. The officers, taken over with the ship, were professionals of a different caste from regular naval officers; a closed society or guild, but more amiable than the passed-over naval officers who emerged from early retirement to supplement and advise them—dugouts, they were called, heavy-eyed and gin-glazed, mostly useless but keen on their privileges.

The merchant navy officers nearly all had malaria and from time to time would collapse and lie in their cabins shuddering. Once established, I took to visiting them and offering unwanted conversation. They could offer me a few insights, reduce my ignorance of their world, perhaps even of the world more generally considered. For instance, I hadn't known that in the tropics a man should always put on a jockstrap at sundown and wear a cummerbund at dinner. After a hot day shifting cargo you of course needed a bath, but then you gave yourself the giddy pleasure of the uplift provided by the jockstrap; it was like floating a moment in the cool air of the evening. The tightly wound cummerbund presumably sustained this effect.

These people also shared certain esoteric jokes which came in series, and when intelligible were clearly obscene. One series featured two characters called Mr. Saccone and Mr. Speed, names which happened to be drawn from the name of the firm which at that time was the principal supplier of booze to the fleet. For some reason Saccone and Speed were represented as monkeys in colloquy, with dago accents and an interest in unusual sexual practices. Because I could never join in this game, had never had malaria, never worn a jockstrap, and no doubt for many other reasons, this confederacy of ailing, amiable, and experienced officers found me, despite my willingness to please and to visit the sick, quite uninteresting, odd, and green, which of course I was. I could understand their attitude, which at least was evidence of maturation.

These discoveries lay in the future. As I picked my way across the cluttered dockside and approached the *Sierra*, I entered a world about which, without admitting it even to myself, I knew nothing. All around were inactive workmen, some evidently responsible for fitting a First World War gun on the poop, others sitting among scattered bits of ancient antiaircraft weapons, while others wandered about the deck or the dock, manifestly unproductive.

In those early days the authorities were still unsubtle about air raids. Liverpool had suffered some serious night attacks, but the sirens also sounded at intervals through the day, when there was nothing around except perhaps a plane sent over to have a look at the damage inflicted on the previous night. When these daytime alarms went off, the air-raid wardens rushed about blowing their whistles, and on the docks the noise of riveting and the beat of hammers at once ceased. Since it was by now assumed that no raid was likely to follow, the workmen did not move from their places but got out their cards and played till the all-clear sounded, while the public at large simply went on with their usual business. The workmen apparently had it in writing that they should cease work and take cover during an alert. They scrupulously observed the first part of this order and ignored the second. It wasn't difficult to understand this—every concession, every petty benefit, had been achieved by laborious union action, and to work when ordered not to would have struck them as treacherous or crazy. It would have been useless to explain to them that this was not the right way to behave when the empire was under serious threat and the bastions of democracy crumbling. If the all-clear came just at the moment when an official tea break was due, they ran the one into the other and sat on in the sun, enjoying the dusty, leisured scene.

One of these unalarming alerts was in force as I reached the ship. A large sheet of steel dangled in its slings while its handlers reclined on sacks. The crane driver dozed in his high cab. I had one foot on the gangway when there was a sudden commotion and an officer whom, ill informed as I was, I could already identify as a Royal Naval Reserve commander, hurried down the gangway. I removed my foot. This man had a sharp red face and cornflower eyes. It seems, in memory, that my mad captains all had cornflower eyes. He looked excited but authoritatively angry. Marching up to a group of cardplayers, he ordered them to get up and return to work, pointing out that there was a war on, that ships were desperately needed, and so forth. He said something about Churchill, something about the Hun. The men turned towards him, eyed him curiously, and invited him to fuck off. As if he had foreseen this degree of resistance, the commander now took a pistol from his pocket and pointed it at the group. "Get back to your work," he said. "And for God's sake, try to behave like men." At this the men rose, backed away, and, as soon as they'd opened a certain distance from the commander, ran like hell to the dock gate. A cordon of civilian functionaries now appeared from neighbouring offices, smiling nervously at the officer and hinting that such gestures, however well meant, would not in fact advance the war effort, since their likeliest outcome was a full-scale dock strike. He was calm but disappointed. Later, sharing with me a moment of self-reproach, he said he regretted not having "winged" one of them. "The rest would have pretty quickly toed the line." He had been in similar situations before.

He went back on board and I followed. I explained to the officer of the watch that I had been sent to see Lieutenant Taylor. The gunman, who was still there at the head of the gangway, said, "Why the devil do you want to see *him*?" I sketched a salute and explained my mission. "You'll probably find him in the wardroom," he said. "And don't let me see you again with a button undone." I was hurt by this, because I had spent a lot of time and trouble getting myself up for the part. "That's exactly the sort of thing we have to get right if we're going to win this war," he added. I suddenly realised I was being told off by the captain of the *Sierra*. I surveyed with distaste the unspeakable mess over which he presided, feeling only slightly ashamed to have added to it.

THIS WAS Commander Stonegate, a mad but gallant fellow who as a midshipman had fought with Keyes at Zeebrugge and more recently won a DSO on the Dunkirk beach. His conduct on the dockside was perhaps partly explained by his having taken part in these bloody actions. He was said, falsely no doubt, to have witnessed the killing by a British officer of thirty-eight out of forty men who had tried to surrender to the Germans, presumably to encourage the other two. In any case, he had seen some bad things. He was just the man for the summer of 1940, an expert in lost causes and forlorn hopes, a leader of men, of men often too cowardly or too stupid to follow him; perhaps he needed to be a bit mad, but he was a shade madder than he needed to be. Very likely what pushed him over the top was the extraordinary quantity of pink gin he drank. Of course there may have been other, more private incitements to mania.

Threading my way past the card parties, I eventually found the wardroom, actually a passenger saloon on the upper deck, designated "wardroom" by a freshly painted sign, still unfinished and no doubt waiting, like the rest of the vessel, for the all-clear. Behind the bar was a man who turned out to be Taylor, acting as his own steward. Perhaps the regular barman had taken cover. Taylor was a tall thin man with a very white face, middle or late thirties. He looked quite refined but gloomy. He had been purser of the ship before it was taken over and was now responsible to their lordships for its supply and secretarial requirements.

He gave me a pink gin and offered me a lamb's tongue, which he pulled out of an open tin. He explained that he had some time before decided that what suited his constitution best was an exclusive diet of lamb's tongues. He pointed to several cartons of them stacked against the wall. "They should last me a good while," he said, but added that he was worried about maintaining his supply if the ship was sent to inaccessible foreign parts. He carried an open tin everywhere he went, from time to time popping a pale-pink leathery strip of the meat into his mouth and slowly chewing it. He told me in his quiet, depressed voice that he knew nothing whatever about the navy; he found its methods of accounting and even its manner of conducting correspondence quite unintelligible. He complained that he was the very last person the paymaster captain should have chosen as my instructor. I took to him at once.

In his office he pointed to a great unsorted heap of books and papers, King's Regulations, Admiralty Fleet Orders, Confidential Admiralty Fleet Orders, handbooks explaining how to carve a duck. "You'll find everything in there, I dare say," he told me sadly. For his own part he proposed to account for stores, pay, and so on in an ordinary human way. His accounts would be in order, though not in the order recommended, indeed commanded, by their domineering lordships. Probably he would have liked to feed the ship's company on lamb's tongues washed down with pink gin, for this would have made for simpler accounting procedures than the fussily varied diet demanded. Sighing rather attractively, Taylor now said he must get home to his wife. We walked together to the gangway, he carrying gloves and a tin of lamb's tongues. We saluted and went ashore.

I never saw him again; he got a rather early and blustery northeaster and died two days after our only meeting, presumably of malnutrition and cirrhosis. By another brilliant expedient of the paymaster captain, Taylor's deputy, a Sub-Lieutenant Hewitt, was promoted to the vacant place and I took his. Hewitt was about thirty-five, a grey, clean-linened, brushed sort of man, of most cautious demeanour. He was still deciding whether to marry a woman he had been courting for fifteen years. "You need to be sure with women," he would say. "There's mistakes that can't be corrected." That was also how he ran his office, checking and double-checking far into the night, unwillingly impressed but also alarmed by the careless pace at which I worked. It was he who gave me that advice about the jockstrap, and he also told me that I must always dub new shoes and never entrust their care and cleaning to anybody else.

Our first official duty together was to attend Taylor's funeral and condole with his astonished wife. It was a quiet affair and was just ending with sherry and cake when Stonegate suddenly turned up. He had been in London for a few days, possibly summoned to explain to his superiors why he had threatened civilian dockworkers with a pistol. Drunk to the point beyond which more alcohol can make very little difference, he approached the widow, took her hand, and said in a grave, confident way, "My dear, he can't really be dead, you know. If he were I should have been officially informed." Mrs. Taylor looked slightly more amazed than before, but neither wept nor spoke. "I suppose eating all that tinned lamb upset him a bit," Stonegate continued, as if nothing more was at stake than an unusually prolonged *crise de foie*. He next explained that to his regret he had urgent business requiring him to leave without more delay, thus, for the moment, denying the widow any further consolation, but he turned at the door and promised to have the remaining cartons of lamb's tongues sent round to her house.

Next day I took up my duties as his secretary. My main job was to insert a filling of intelligible prose asking for something, or offering humble compliance with some peremptory demand, into the sandwich of grandiose salutation and valedictory obeisance insisted on by their Lordships. We rubbed along fairly well, Stonegate having what I came to recognise as the usual awe felt by naval officers at what they took to be the superhuman powers of otherwise negligible people who, though presumed incapable of anything else, could write letters easily. The rest of the work was more difficult, since no more than Taylor could Hewitt or I understand the byzantine naval system of accounting. You entered not the true cost of anything but an arbitrary figure selected by authority. The price of beef, for instance, was always the same unless you were told to alter it, and the figure, which memory says was 7d. a pound, bore no relation to what we paid for it. In this way it was possible to feed a sailor on 6d. a day, as their lordships required. Of course the real cost had to show up somewhere, and the relation between the two figures was deeply problematical. Hewitt added everything up, down, and sideways, over and over, in a hopeless attempt to resolve the discrepancies, while I swash-buckled across the ledger, alert to imaginary indications of sense making, seeking occult rational structures. We made a bad pair.

Meanwhile, the ship was somehow patched together and provided with a crew that called for the pen of a Conrad: the sly greaser, the *rusé* steward, and the genuinely naval bosun. There was the dugout lieutenant-commander who recognised in this vessel nothing that reminded him of the navy except the gin at twopence a shot. Officers had a large daily allowance of spirits, which was nevertheless greatly exceeded. Some would spend most of their pay on booze, sitting all day long in the dark wardroom, smoking duty-free cigarettes and speak-ing bitterly of the Geddes Axe, that infamous instrument of government which, after the first war, had, in what seemed to them a frenzy of cost-cutting, prematurely lopped off their jobs.

With such helpers Stonegate, inappropriately on Trafal-gar Day, got his ship to sea, wearing the white ensign for the first time, its weird crew at their stations. He headed north, spending the long night on his bridge, all dressed up with a white collar and a tie, a gold-spangled cap and a greatcoat. At Lamlash, on the Isle of Arran, we stopped awhile and were given too much drink at too many parties involving eightsome reels and the like, by people who mistook us for hardy adven-turers requiring rest and recreation. Then Stonegate was again summoned to London, not, this time, to return. His replacement was signalled. A few days later we heard that, ready as ever with his pistol, he had shot himself. So he got his north-easter. We were never officially informed.

I thought and think of Stonegate as one of those rather grand, in a maritime sense even aristocratic, reserve officers, at best condemned to command vulnerable armed merchant cruisers, at worst to run glorified tramps like *Sierra*, whose careers you need to remember if you catch yourself thinking that Conrad was coming on a bit strong when doing captains at the end—as he so often was himself—of their tethers: the kind, that is, who carry on when almost blind, or carefully check the chronometer before throwing themselves overboard. Conrad must have known captains like Stonegate, quietly excessive men, irrational and brave, who exercised arbitrary power, ordering the lives of men, even issuing brutal sentences without suspecting that in doing so they were behaving otherwise than justly and honourably. Such a sentence, I suppose, was Stonegate's sentence on himself. He knew what it was to command and punish, whether a footlingly armed and ridiculously manned warship or himself. We rather enjoyed speculating that some solemn idiot at the Admiralty had left him alone in a room, mentioning that there was a loaded revolver in the drawer. But no, it was just that he had had enough; and anyway, he carried his own gun.

I am unable, for lack of evidence, to say whether his successor, Henty, was really crazy. He was a round, muscled man with a crew cut, a type I later learned to associate with trawler skippers. His throaty shout and total indifference to naval manners came straight from the fishing fleets of Yorkshire and Lincolnshire. He resembled Stonegate only in his heroic drinking. He took the ship out of the marvellous autumn weather of the Clyde through the miraculous Minches, and round the stormy top of Britain to Sunderland, where we remained, in bleak squalor and without apparent need or purpose, for several weeks. I celebrated my twenty-first birthday there, waiting for a pretty bus conductress who didn't turn up. I wasn't very sorry; she had that charming accent but the conversation tended to flag.

So I went back to the ship, where many of my comrades were prostrate with malaria, which seemed a malady inappropriate to the time and place, late November in Sunderland. Their condition cannot have been helped by prolonged drinking bouts. Some stayed ashore for days, returning with torn uniforms and black eyes, urgently needing bed rest and abstinence. Others remained on board and got drunk more cheaply; of these some wandered about looking vaguely for a fight, while others sat all day in the wardroom, glass at hand, and glowing, you might have thought, with happiness. More temperate officers brought their wives to Sunderland (as they did to all home ports we touched), and these sedate couples would appear in the wardroom, causing a brief burst of courteous attention. This caused me to reflect that one ought never to ignore evidence that women have the power to civilise men, or at least cause them to simulate civility, as well as to drive them out of their minds.

While these matters were in progress, Henty went off on leave and never returned, having, it was rumoured, fallen down a flight of stairs and broken both legs. That was the end of him. He was around so briefly that I had no time to discover in what way he was mad, though I felt sure he was, and that I should eventually find out in what manner. He evaded discovery by taking what, compared with Stonegate's, was a rather proletarian way out.

At this time I saw rather little of my comrades except at meals. They treated me quite kindly, but dismissively, as a sort of handicapped person, a nuisance but at bottom inoffensive, or merely one more disagreeable circumstance one had got used to getting used to. Anyway, I preferred the company of a young "writer" who had been a violinist in some pier orchestra, perhaps at Weymouth. He was the sort of musician I later encountered among Marine bandsmen, technically adept on at least two instruments but largely ignorant of music that was not played on piers or parade grounds. I gave this young man scores of the standard concertos and was amazed that he came close to sight-reading them. He was very excited, feeling as if he'd inherited a fortune nobody had bothered to tell him about while he played his salon pieces.

It struck us both that I should learn to play, so I acquired a violin and a space deep in the *Sierra* where I could not be heard by my comrades, to whom such an enterprise would have seemed terminally bizarre; moreover, such fraternising with the lower deck was, if not forbidden, sharply discouraged. I practised for hours every day, and because my teacher could not conceive of my needing to learn anything elementary, I was soon working on the *Virtuoso Exercises* of Albert Sammons.

This was good fun, and I began blasting my way through Mozart concertos. It was only after the war that I discovered that what I'd been doing was irreversibly destructive, and ensured that I should never learn the instrument even half-decently. All I gained was an increased respect for the technique of people who really could play. Still, it might have gone better if I had not lost my teacher at an early stage in my musical career.

We were always being urged to spot what were called OLQ, Officer-like Qualities, in our subordinates, and it seemed to me possible to argue that being able to play the Mendelssohn Concerto more or less at sight constituted at least one such quality (though I suppose I knew it didn't). Moreover, I may well have had an exaggerated notion of his gifts, learning only later that such ability is much less unusual than I thought. Anyway, I put his name forward, and he was sent away, this quite contented little man from Devon, with his soft voice and liquid eyes. He didn't really want the grand future I thought he deserved, but decided it would be unfair to his wife to turn down the opportunity. I can't remember if he had children. When he got to the place where his OLQ was to be examined, he had also to suffer a medical examination, and they detected a slight hernia, nothing to speak of, but it needed to be put right before he could be trained to be a leader of men, so they operated on him and he died during the operation. Here was another northeaster, this one out of a clear sky. I lost my teacher more definitively than I had intended, and I failed to flourish as a violinist. He had left some things behind—a bow, a mute, some rosin, a chin pad—and I sent them off to his widow. I suppose we have to accept that I was no more entitled to the virtuosity I yearned for than he was to live beyond the age of twenty-six, or than she was to her husband.

SO HENTY FELL, doubtless leaving the carpet soaked in Scotch and penetrated by slivers of crystal. He thus created an interesting vacancy. Up there in Sunderland I reflected that *Sierra* got rid of its captains at a pretty impressive rate. I speculated about the fate of the next one and the possible forms of his mania. Would he be insensitive enough to last longer than his predecessors?

He not only outlasted them but outdid them in many other ways. Commander Archer had not been with us long before he had caused everybody to agree that he exceeded all rational expectation. Up the gangway he came, his face grim and fat, his mouth the shape of a drawer handle. He gleamed from head to foot, skin scrubbed, clothes valeted, boots glittering. He wore many rings and had a great deal of luggage. It was plain that only the best, and a lot of the best, was good enough, and enough, for him. After dinner he descended to the wardroom, which commanding officers enter only by invitation. He responded to the invitation by being loudly cordial, though somehow in a rather dangerous way. His eyes were cornflower blue, but hard to discern, the smallest eyes I have ever seen except possibly those of Peter, my father's assistant. He looked like a fat, well-turned-out pig. He bought drinks grandly and drank himself with apparent abandon, meanwhile weighing everybody up and looking for victims. It soon appeared that he had no use for the simple conversation of friendliness, seeking only to exploit or tease.

He brought with him from Portsmouth a warrant officer who had devoted his life to acquiring the shameless skills of sycophancy. He hung around his boss like the Fool round Lear, but unlike the Fool, he never said anything even obscurely critical. Herbert represented a stage in Archer's own career, during which the way to get on was, as they say nowadays, to kiss ass, which Herbert was willing to do all day long. Archer, long past the stage of doing the kissing himself, needed his ass saluted with just that perfectly servile regularity, and although he treated 'Erbert with amused contempt, he was in a slight degree dependent on him. There was a kind of sympathy between them, obscurely rooted in past service, some of it in the battleship which had carried the Prince of Wales on his then celebrated and lascivious trip round the world. At that time Archer had been a chief petty officer and Herbert a petty officer, or perhaps only a leading seaman.

Their sense of status was quite unlike that of temporary officers; they were mindful that there was a real navy, in which they had served and made their way; they were inexplicitly contemptuous of this wartime travesty, though well aware that they owed their own advancement to its existence. What remained from the good old times was a teasing amiability on Archer's part and Herbert's shameless obsequiousness. But they modified this behaviour to accord with their new ranks, modelling themselves on what they took to be the manners of their former superiors; hence a finicking disdain, and an assumption that one was entitled to the best of everything. What they didn't imitate was the tiny flame, almost invisible by daylight, the spirit of a certain noblesse oblige. They probably believed that sentiment had its origins in an upper-class conviction that ratings were naturally as well as institutionally and socially inferior to officers, a conviction they had long since rejected. They were, however, quite clear about the advantages of rank, and if for some it had entailed notions of honour, they were prepared to dispense with those notions and replace them with guile. So much they shared; but Archer was ruthless and would always get what he wanted, and Herbert, wasting his days giggling, grinning, and capering about, defying odium, would never achieve the transformation of his thin warrant officer's stripe into a solid band of gold.

On the whole, the lower deck disliked having an Old Man who had originated there, because they feared, quite reasonably, that he knew too much, and also that there were some matters of which he knew all too little. Time was to show that he was far from being a good seaman and that he would use his autocratic office for nobody's benefit but his own. But he took his rank very seriously, which was enough to compel everybody else to do the same. It must have been bliss for him to have, at his great age (he was, by my guess, a fat, florid fifty), a command of his own, even if it was the lumbering *Sierra* with its miscellaneous and dispirited ship's company.

Archer ruled from the large and handsome cabin provided by the shipping company for its civilian masters. Somehow, in the interval of retirement between his first and second fits of naval service, he had made some money and boasted of owning boardinghouses in Southsea. Now he set up as a maritime pasha. He would summon me from my distant office not by telephone and not by messenger but by opening his door and bellowing my name. Anybody within earshot would then repeat the cry, and eventually it got to me. "Como!" he would yell. Or "Cosmos!" He never bothered to find out my exact name, or anything else about me, though we necessarily had quite a bit to do with each other, and in some ways I became part of his milieu, always required at his frequent revels and rarely excused from his nightly bridge table.

When the mood was on him he would play cards round the clock, drinking heavily throughout. He never troubled to study the principles of bidding, but was the best player of a hand I have ever known. This discrepancy caused his partners much annoyance, prudently concealed, since he made many overtricks, missed rubbers, and failed to bid slams. It was as if the playing of the cards suited his idea of cunning, his power to divine weakness in an enemy's professions, whereas he was content to leave the sissy business of bidding and making valuable contracts to the uselessly educated middle classes. He would sit there, tiny eyes gleaming, cuffs starched, never tired, never drunk despite the tumbler of whisky constantly refilled, jeering at signs of ineptitude in the other players, berating his partner, and uttering a stream of obscenities in his big cracked voice. Certain sayings were triggered by specific stimuli; if a high soprano voice came over the radio, everybody would turn in his direction and wait for his comment: "She's got an 'air acrorst 'er quim." Having to make this and other such remarks did not affect his concentration on the cards.

Once, in 1941, I travelled with him from the Clyde to Reykjavík in a Polish troopship. At that time shipboard life was still anachronistically luxurious, for officers, that is. We played bridge all the way. One evening when a North Atlantic gale had cleared the saloon of landsmen, he was playing a delicate hand, gleaming with the sure expectation of success, and with only a couple more tricks to make, the ship pitched so violently that he was hurled from his seat and thrown across the saloon. By the time he had picked himself up and got back to the table, the cards were in a muddled heap, but he sorted them out into the original hands, replayed the game, and, slapping down the cards from where he stood over us, won his last tricks and crowed with joy.

The main reason why I qualified for inclusion in his plea-sures was that I wrote his letters. His semi-literacy gave me some authority, for he regarded correspondence with the Ad-miralty as the most daunting part of his job. In the early days he would laboriously draft letters with a blunt pencil on a signal pad. They were usually complaints about the impossi-bility of laying booms—which is what we were supposed to do—with inadequate equipment and too few auxiliary craft, in a location and in weather conditions which would have made the process close to impossible even under the most favourable circumstances. (I think this was true, and the complaints jus-tified.) The drafts would start like this: "Being as the flotations what you promised int come," and continue in the same style. For a while he cavilled at my translations into formal and slightly archaic Admiralty English, but he soon came to de-pend on it and paid me many ironical or obscene compliments. "What the hell are you, Cosmos? A fucking poofter?" It was fortunate that he did not know I wrote poems and songs and tried to play the violin. Before long he just told me what was wanted and left the correspondence entirely to me.

So his dependence on me increased. I ran his social life, tidied up his professional business, and explained the King's Regulations. In return he was, in his way, open-handed, though what he offered was never a gift resulting from an intuition that one would like it. We were once staying in an Edinburgh hotel and had drunk till the bar announced closing time. He had manoevred the rounds so that I, who had bought the first, would also be liable for the last, traditionally a double. It was the sort of tease he enjoyed, and helped by a crony called Commander Drinkwater, always Drinkwhisky to Archer, he made the most of it. On my pay—then, I think, 13 shillings a day—this was quite a serious mulct, and I may have shown that I was a bit upset. So later he made his kind of amends. The party continued in his hotel room, where we were joined by some girls, provenance unknown—he had a knack of surrounding himself with young women, not whores, but willing on terms to go to bed even with this hideous old man (for so he appeared to me). I went off to my room and was just going to bed when he burst in, collarless, fly open, leading a girl who didn't seem the type, being young, and showing signs of shyness. " 'Ere's one for you, Cosmo. I've got 'er sister." This was the first of several occasions when he made or tried to make sexual choices for me. The girl and I chatted uneasily for a while and she slept in a chair. In the morning Archer discovered from her sister that we hadn't done anything; he roared with laughter, dragged the girl into the bathroom, and emerged a few minutes later with his penis on display, the girl following, dishevelled, with an odd shamed gesture. He told the story of this night many times, with variations and embellishments, all emphasising my sexual incapacity. "Cosmo never got it in all night!" he would crow.

His first real act of command was to take the ship to Rosyth, where we were to spend a month getting ready for our great boom-laying mission. My girl came to Scotland and we lived in a workman's house in Dunfermline; it was a good time but arduous. At six, in the dark of a Scottish December morning, I would take a packed, smelly bus to the dockyard. By seven-thirty I'd be aboard and having breakfast, waiting for the relay of yells summoning me to the presence. Archer would go over the pleasant excesses of the previous evening and deride me for bringing a redundant woman to Scotland. Then he would tell me what needed to be written. By four o'clock I'd be on my way home, again in the dark.

This routine was interrupted by seasonal festivities, in-

cluding a grand Hogmanay ball. I watched Archer clumping
round the dance floor with the admiral's wife. The admiral,
Dalrymple-Hamilton, was a member of a well-known navy
family, and was known to Archer, who at some point had
served under him at sea, as Dollyrumple-Amilton. While dancing he seemed quite at home with the great lady, laughing
and speaking, with a courtly bend, into her ear, though he
became formal and submissive during the ceremonies of departure. It struck me that very senior officers, the real thing,
and their women got on more easily with subordinates like
Archer than with reserve officers, even if the latter were apparently more suitable socially or had any number of useful
skills. Regular officers had internalised sketchy but fairly reliable profiles of people like Archer, and would not be inclined
to question his manners or deplore the absurd unctuousness
of the simpering Herbert. At worst they were extreme examples of familiar types. Moreover, it could be assumed that
they would obey any order to the letter, and contrive to do so
without damaging their own interests. They belonged, just as
the admiral belonged, and his wife, too. They were like upper
servants in some grand household, organised as a hierarchy
normally benign, though capable of being severe on any gross
infraction of discipline. Everybody concerned accepted this
arrangement, regarding it as completely natural.

Archer certainly understood such relationships without
needing to think about them. He understood the exact measure
of liberty he could take, indeed ought to take, on a licensed
occasion like the Hogmanay ball. He knew how to look up
and, as it were, by the same instinct, how to look down, how
to treat inferiors with a sort of uncaring kindness, a humorous
indifference that might, in the end, be seen to serve their
interests as well as his own. It was all to do with belonging,
very complete, quite unavailable to the keenest of outsiders,
of whom there were many, pantingly aspiring. Nobody could

possibly have thought I, though certainly an outsider, was keen or thwarted, except in my desire not to be in this *galère* at all.

However, there was no escaping the fact that I was with, though not of, this setup, and small reason to think I should be out of it for a long time to come. The safest assumption about the war, in the winter of 1940–41 and for at least three years after that, was that it would never end, or, at any rate, that a life different from the present—an absurd, quite comfortable servitude—was to be had only in daydreams of which one was ashamed.

Like many another, I would gloomily consider my position. I had been born only a year after the end of the previous war. Around me were men who had actually served in that earlier war, so that military or naval service seemed to them the natural and even the desirable mode of their existence—men to whom the interwar years were a mostly miserable interruption. Their way of life was in principle incompatible with mine. But I already had experience of incompatible ways of living, with quite violent changes from one to the next. I was born at home in a house lit by gas, sharing with many others an outdoor lavatory. Films were still silent. More people had maids than cars. Names were still being carved on the new war memorial, an imposing presence on the seafront. Men removed their hats when they walked past it. There were quarrels about whether somebody who simply happened to have died while in uniform, or even years later, from a sickness contracted during service though probably not arising from it, should have his name inscribed there. Limbless, shell-shocked, and poisoned men were everywhere. November 11 was a day of general mourning, in which even children took part. They attended the bleak memorial services with weeping women and mutilated, bemedalled survivors, singing the hymns which everybody everywhere was at that moment singing, observing the silence solemnly commanded by the firing of maroons, a silence full of the noise of gulls, the last national ritual in which all took part, belonging, because involved in the deaths of many young men. This was a community where people stopped to chat with mourners in the street, and because of complicated family ties and friendships, and acquaintance with the friends of friends, everybody had a pretty good idea of what everybody else was doing and suffering.

Removed from that community to a university where community was based on high spirits and competition among lively strangers, one was settled into another world, very different but in its way congenial. But there were still some old ties: to get onto the boat at Liverpool was to run into somebody with whom one might chat about brothers and sisters, deaths and births. The second war made a bigger difference. It meant an immersion in another culture, and this was true for everybody except possibly for regular soldiers and sailors (though even their lives were changed). It was certainly true for shelter-dwellers and conscripts. For the former there was the forced patience of the queues and the miseries of the blackout; for the latter there was the company of men whose company they would probably in no circumstances have chosen. It was like being sent, in consequence of some awful parental mistake, to the wrong school, of which you could not learn and could never even wish to learn the lingo and the rules and the customs. There was not a resumption of the ways of the old war, nobody any longer used such a word as "comrade," unaffectedly spoken by veterans. It seemed that everybody felt the need to resist everybody else; there was no personal warmth and a good deal of unmotivated hurting. Orders would be carried out impassively, and with a measured compliance that could feel like a silent criticism, as if the will of the person issuing the order could be done so exactly that obedience would seem to demonstrate how pointless it was to have it executed at all, except as one more strand in the wartime rope the navy was tying itself up with. For you always felt that the navy could only have met its own standards of discipline, efficiency, polish, and community in peacetime, the very time when you couldn't possibly have got into it, even if you'd wanted to.

The parties at Rosyth and Edinburgh were the end of pleasure, and by January 1941 it was time for even *Sierra* to do something. We sailed for a secret destination, known only by the Admiralty, the ship's company, and a fair number of wives, girlfriends, and *filles publiques* to be Iceland. Archer got us there, and there we remained, under his curious care, for almost two years.

It had not been foreseen that we should pay so long a visit. The British had occupied Iceland primarily to prevent the Germans from doing so; it would have provided them with an admirable submarine base. The British would also find a positive use for it. Our mission was to lay an anti-submarine boom across the mouth of a great fjord. Hval Fjord offered a huge harbour, big enough to accommodate the Home Fleet and numbers of American warships (they were already involved in the Atlantic though not yet officially combatant), and after the Russians entered the war that summer, the large, and largely doomed, convoys preparing for their fearful trip round the North Cape to Murmansk. All this shipping could rest secure behind the boom, which was covered by an artillery battery on one of the promontories, about two miles apart, that formed the mouth of the fjord.

Or that at any rate was the idea; but we never got the boom laid. It looked simple enough on maps and charts, and mariners weary from the Atlantic liked to think they could rest behind it. But for almost two years we struggled to lay the boom, and when we left, it was still unfinished.

Boom defences are huge, clumsy assemblages of nets and flotations, held in position by great triangular lumps of concrete and having a complicated bit in the middle, a gate you could

open to admit your friends. The materials for the construction
of the boom were lifted out of *Sierra* and put in place by
specialist boom defence vessels, small ships with forked stems
sticking up from the bow like snail's horns. They looked more
like dredgers than anything else but were quite distinctive.
They were commanded by trawler skippers, patient drinkers
hardened by the North Sea but hardly more overjoyed at hard
labour in the cold and dark of the Icelandic winter than our
own malarial officers. In January the daylight lasted no more
than three hours (in cool midsummer this became twenty-two
hours and was almost harder to bear). Now and again there
might be a day or two when conditions allowed something to
be put down exactly where it was meant to go. On the evenings
of these wonderful days Archer, who used sometimes to go
out in a boat himself and work on the boom, would appear to
be quite proud of his skippers.

They were, after all, good seamen; but they weren't equal
to this job, which turned out to be like those torments devised
for malefactors in Tartarus. Gales, rarely forecast, would funnel
savagely down the fjord, gusting to over 130 knots. Ships
dragged their anchors—*Sierra* once even dragged her heavy
moorings and went aground on one of the few sandy beaches
of the fjord. On these occasions the incomplete boom would
be torn to pieces and the flotations blown out into the ocean,
where they provided target practice for passing destroyers. The
heavy gear was lost. These crises occurred, in the nature of
things, when *Sierra* was almost empty. Weeks and months
might pass while we waited for new supplies from Scotland,
and during these times we had almost nothing to do except
occasionally to remind their Lordships of the scale of the problem and the danger to their ships, which continued to sail
confidently into the harbour. Admirals and commodores were
understandably angry, though their anger was unjustly directed at us, when they discovered the true state of affairs and

had to send out destroyers, which ought to have been resting, their companies piped not to watchkeeping but to leisurely making and mending, to patrol the entrance to the fjord.

Archer now suffered undeserved rebuke, and all about him there was much bad temper and embarrassment, but he remained uncannily cheerful. He would send ribald signals to passing ships, draft urgent requests to the Admiralty ("Being as they int no more flotations . . . I ave the honour to request supply most urgent"), and pass the rest of the time fishing. He was delighted by the swarms of dab and codling in the fjord—you simply threw a line over and hauled them in. Sometimes he would pipe a watch to fish, and an hour or two later there would be more fresh fish than the entire ship's company could eat. He would arrange boxing tournaments in the empty hold, with Herbert as a pompous, buffoonish M.C. Once Herbert addressed the spectators as "gentlemen" and was publicly reprimanded by Archer: you don't call ratings gentlemen, only officers.

We were all desperate for something to do. Books ran out, we scoured the ship for old bits of newspaper to read. So the film shows commanded by the Old Man were welcome, though you always felt they had been put on for his personal satisfaction and that he merely found it convenient to let others have a look. Sometimes it seemed the whole war had been put on for the same purpose.

Much of his time was spent in quite passionately doing something that was certainly of no benefit to anybody but himself. He had what seemed an inordinate interest in stores, not just duty-free drink and cigarettes, though these were important, but groceries of every kind. Reykjavík, where our supplies came from, was about thirty miles away by sea—you went round the coast in a little popping drifter. These trips were frequent, for mail had to be collected as well as general provisions, and of course stock for the bar. In Reykjavík you

could also buy some things for yourself in the NAAFI or, with
luck, at the PX, the more generously endowed American
equivalent. Archer spent large sums on goods of all descriptions. Cases of tinned soup and peas, sacks of flour, large con-
signments of whisky and cigarettes arrived frequently and were
the occasion for many jokes and some amazement. As the
months went by, these supplies filled his cabin, first the bedroom, then the outer room. Cases, carefully stowed and se-
cured, were stacked around the handsome double bed. As time
went by, there was hardly room for me on my morning visits;
we would converse over the food mountains, and I would rest
my notebook on packing cases. The place looked like one of
those storerooms you occasionally glimpse through a window
or an open door in a supermarket. Still, he added to the collection, as if intending to have at hand, for his own private
consumption, the food and drink of a thousand ordinary men.

For a while I found something pure, gratuitous, occasionally farcical about this dedicated acquisitiveness. He might
have collected stamps with the same devotion and they would
not have taken up so much space; for there seemed no point
in his hoarding all this stuff except the mere pleasure of collecting it. Perhaps it was because this hobby was so engrossing that he seemed not to share the ennui, the sexual
privation, the hangovers, and the self-disgust that afflicted almost everybody else. The other exceptions were the doctor
and a midshipman, who had been at Winchester together.
These Wykehamists contentedly passed the hours walking the
deck together, rarely speaking to anybody else, and then only
with an evident effort of tolerance. They admitted to one mild
regret, not shared, I think, by Archer, and that was at their
not being involved in the fighting; but Winchester had no
doubt hardened them to such disappointments, and anyway,
they seemed sure this privation, like that of their schooldays,
could only be temporary. So indeed it turned out to be, for

much later on I ran into the doctor in Algiers and he had got a medal for doing something brave in a destroyer. The midshipman, he told me, was dead. In those days the wind blew from all quarters.

It was a time of futility. Some people got very drunk and fought one another. One amiable Geordie drank himself into a stupor and woke many hours later to find that his genitals had been polished with bootblack. A blacksmith—an important man in boom construction—ran mad with a sledgehammer, evaded feeble attempts at capture, and killed himself. In winter months it wasn't even safe to go ashore and play football on the lava shore—you could be cut off by one of those unpredicted savage gales and probably die on the beach. The conditions made inevitable many dreadful moments, especially for anyone with my hopeless fear of heights, when one had to get back on board up a rope ladder from a wildly pitching cutter. In the weak darkless summer weather you could go for a walk on hills that turned out to be no more than huge heaps of sharp stones.

For forty-eight hours every two months you were allowed to take the popping drifter to Reykjavík. In those days it looked like a shantytown, with much corrugated iron, built, no doubt, on an older, less ugly settlement. The cathedral sometimes offered music. There was quite a good bookshop, with English books, and a hotel, justly described by W. H. Auden in the book he and Louis MacNeice wrote about Iceland as not the kind of thing you like if you like that kind of thing. The only drink was sherry, imported from Spain under some mutual trade agreement and exempted from the general prohibition of liquor.

The Icelanders quite reasonably regarded us as having invaded them. They had been pretty sure that somebody would, and when it happened, and they woke at dawn to hear aeroplanes overhead, they turned over and went back to sleep, not caring who was coming, supposing, perhaps mistakenly, that occupation would mean much the same whether it was German or British. In the early days they refused to speak to us, and the troops could only look longingly at the Icelandic girls, or *stulkas*. All that was to change with the arrival of Americans in 1941, but for the time being there wasn't much reason to spend your forty-eight hours in Reykjavík, beyond, that is, the need to escape from the ship and her company.

Contact with the world at large was by letter, though occasionally an acquaintance might happen to visit the fjord in a ship that actually moved. I was asked to lunch aboard the battle cruiser *Hood* by a gunnery sub-lieutenant whose girl-friend happened to be a friend of mine, and was hustled from the table into a launch when it suddenly became known that the German battleship *Bismarck* was at sea. I had enjoyed being shown round this beautiful but aged and imperfectly armoured ship, whose whole purpose at that time was to destroy the German raider, though among her officers there were those who doubted whether she could hope to do it. Three or four days later *Hood* made contact and, hit by a single shell, exploded, all but three of her company of some seventeen hundred being lost. This was as near to great actions as I had come, and I felt my association with the disaster, remembering the ship itself and some of those who had given me lunch and then died in her. Theirs was the sort of experience that, without luck, one might expect to have as a fighting sailor: the real thing, the cold blast.

Considering the state of the boom, there was small prospect of my having any such extreme experiences for some time. We did our fighting for freedom by proxy. Bad news drifted in, terrible things happened to other people. One of our sailors lost his wife and four children in a bombing raid on Hull. For a reason I forget, or perhaps for no good reason, all compassionate leave from Iceland had been stopped, but I thought that in the circumstances I should try to get the rule bent for this man. When I told him I'd see if I could work this, he replied, "Why bother? They were the only reason I had for going home."

Archer was unperturbed by all news, good or bad, and it soon became obvious to me that he was far from sane. To live as he did, like a spider hoarding flies, reducing his handsome accommodations to a warehouse, caring only to measure his self-contentment by the quantity of his acquisitions, was surely crazy. To remain indifferent to the interests or opinions of others, except when to consult them might mean an increase to his store, the encroaching measure of his own greatness: to live thus was surely to be crazy. He was like Sir Epicure Mammon, though for the moment without succubi. The piles of groceries served him as the conversation and re-enacted rituals of Winchester did the midshipman and the doctor.

One cause of wonder was that I couldn't see what, in the end, he hoped to do with all these sacks of sugar, split peas, and the rest of it. How and where would he take it ashore and dispose of it? Of course I could see a use for it in those Southsea boardinghouses, or on the black market, but I was thinking of the impossibility of it ever reaching those destinations. As soon as we touched a British port, the friendly customs men would board us and, as their habit was, head straight for the captain's cabin and the usual propitiatory drink. They would see what I saw every day, only more so; there might not even be space to raise a glass. They could hardly ignore the thousands of pounds worth of contraband piled up before their very eyes. Once I dared to ask him what his plans were. "Don't you worry about that, Cosmos," he said. "I got friends, in I?"

As the months went by and the rest of us grew more and more bad-tempered, more stupid, more hopeless, except of course for the Wykehamists, Archer grew more radiant, always crisply turned out, always derisive, always winning. His com-

mand was of a kind that would irk many seamen, for having
got his ship to the site of the boom, his job, not always ably
done, was simply to keep it there: it served only as a depot,
all the work, admittedly tricky, being done in smaller craft
nominally under his orders. He did not seem to care about
this, and there was reason to doubt whether his professional
skill was anything like equal to his mad self-confidence.

On one occasion a boom defence vessel was for some reason detached and sent to Seydisfjordur on the east coast of the
island. This ungainly little craft had run into a gale even more
severe than the usual North Atlantic winter blows, and broke
radio silence to say she was in trouble. Archer had a fondness
for the skipper concerned—in fact, he probably valued these
boom defence, ex-trawler skippers more highly than anybody
around, and perhaps with reason. So he decided to go to the
rescue.

He already had steam, for fear of dragging his mooring,
as had happened before; and against the urgent advice of his
officers, certainly more experienced big-ship sailors than he
was, he set forth to save his lost lamb. The consternation of
these seamen was increased when he insisted on doing what
they wouldn't have permitted even in far less desperate
weather. Incredulous and terrified, we steamed out through
the shattered boom and took on the storm with the after hatch
open. *Sierra* got a terrible mauling, lacking power to keep
head on to the sea, even if it had always been possible to know
where the sea was coming from. At the worst moment of the
gale I noticed an effect I have since read about, though it would
be impossible to describe it fully—it was as if the entire surface
of the sea had been raised up and suspended like a cloud over
another turbulent surface.

Though still lacking experience of such marine extremities, I don't think I was far out in thinking that the ship could
hardly live in such a sea, and that a man certainly couldn't. As

I sat in the wardroom, feeling more and more gloomily certain of dying very shortly, Archer descended from the bridge, dressed in duffle coat and balaclava. Abandoning navigation to his subordinates, he was evidently not tortured by any consciousness of a mistake on his part. He poured himself Scotch. "Well, Comody," he said, "it seems we've fucking 'ad it." He was quite serene. We watched the battering of the ship and its rapid and dangerous festooning with ice. For hours it seemed quite hopeless, but eventually we staggered into Reykjavík, spectacularly damaged. Of course we never made contact with the distressed boom layer, and I can't remember what became of it. We stayed in Reykjavík for ages and forgot about the boom.

Reykjavík in those years was, I suppose, another part of my education. The arrival of the Americans quickly changed the character of the place—dollars did it, and jeeps full of stuff from the PX, but also the demeanour of these new invaders, a sort of unexamined confidence, an inability to think of foreign parts as unlike America in any way that could not be put right simply by assuming its unimportance. When we had first tried out the nightlife of the town we'd gone to the Hotel Borg Saturday-night dance and induced local girls to take the floor with us. But policemen moved in and quietly took the names of the girls, which, we were told, were printed in the newspaper on Monday as additions to an official list of prostitutes. Perhaps they continued to add to this list until it included the names of almost all the women under forty. But in fact the reserve of the women was not broken down until the Americans inconsiderately changed the culture, after which there were many agreeable temporary ménages and many liaisons of a more casual kind.

The beneficiaries were of course mostly the Americans, since they were far more numerous and had much more money. I had not at this stage of my life encountered many Americans, even singly, and in the mass they seemed remarkably alien. Their army seemed a harsher institution than ours, loudly exacting a discipline that for the time turned the soldiers into foul-mouthed robots. It was on the quay at Reykjavík that I first heard, with astonishment and even shock, the language in which American soldiers habitually expressed, with a kind of mechanised misery, their apparent loathing for the army, for women, for the world they found themselves in. The words they used are now quite commonly heard on the lips of the polite and gently nurtured, but in those simpler times they seemed very startling: cocksucker, motherfucker, cunt, and asshole used as insults. These exiled Americans seemed obsessed with shit, and had developed an idiom that has persisted in colloquial American to this day: it depended on a sort of partitioning or disorganising of the human body, as if to give offence by refusing to treat a person as entire, so that you shouted, "Get your ass over here," or kicked ass, or chased tail. The synecdoche of insult, we rhetoricians might call it. Of course it served merely as everyday linguistic currency and nobody took offence or was entitled to. But it seems I was still not fully hardened to the life and speech of men among men and found it darkened my mood or my mind.

I even wondered what the Icelanders must make of it, knowing English well, as many of them did; but the idioms were strange, for the function of the military patois was of course in part to keep outsiders outside, even other speakers of the language. The Icelanders themselves had a well-preserved ancient language with many deterrent declensions, and they had also a distinctive civilization, with sane marriage laws, no concept of illegitimacy, and no venereal disease. All worth preserving, you'd think, but not immune to the incursions of rival languages and cultures. The British were relatively lacking in imperialist thrust, accepting their unwelcomeness; the Americans seemed incapable of that and came to be thought dollar-wielding tail-chasers. Yet they, not we, were made to feel more at home. Little love was lost between the occupying forces, yet there were those among the British, Archer for instance, who would have taken quite easily to the culture of buck and tail, or whatever might be its English equivalent.

Around Christmas 1941 I met in Reykjavík a British army captain, King's Own Yorkshire Light Infantry, I seem to remember, a man of about forty, who continued my education. His sexual requirements were of a kind I had never even entertained in fantasy; they were indeed so unusual that they probably could not have been satisfied in Iceland even if he'd been made of money. He liked working-class women, preferably barmaids of fairly mature years, and he did not want them for normal sex, from which he had a chilly aversion. He wanted buggery only, and only with partners who also wanted it exclusively. Preliminary enquiries, you'd have thought, must have called for a certain delicacy, but it seems Ashington had at least had temporary successes. What he wanted, though, was a permanent arrangement, marriage indeed. He deplored the vulgarity of all who sought anything less complete, and dispersed his own energies in long and ingenious tirades against most of humanity, but especially against Americans. However, he was a charming man and I valued his company.

That snowy Christmas night we walked, not sober, along the quay, which was lined with American sentries, too many, we decided, for the purpose, and most of them probably angry at having to be under discipline, and cold, instead of enjoying the party indoors. "Look at those poor buggers," said my friend. "They need warming up." From an attic in an officers' club we climbed onto the roof, made snowballs, and lobbed them, soft grenades, at the sentries. Without hesitation two of them opened fire on the roof. We slid down to the eaves on the lee side, got in through another window, and in half a

minute were standing at the bar as if we'd been there all evening. Such were the joys. At twenty-two you naïvely imagine
you're entitled to some joys. I felt none of the shame or regret
that should, on reflection, have followed this absurd and dangerous prank; nor, of course, did Ashington, who had long
ago run out of shame. It was all the odder that I, who feared
heights and of course also bullets, should have enjoyed myself
on the roof. Evidently I was falling under his influence.

Perhaps fortunately I lost touch with him after that evening, but I made friends with another KOYLI called, I think,
Banks, whose self-imposed daily task was to compose a filthy
limerick. I met him when for some forgotten reason I was sent
on an errand to Seydisfjordur. Banks was happily sharing with
a pleasant *stulka* a tiny cabin, decorated on its south-facing
side with dried fish. He had acquired a sparse but useful command of Icelandic, not troubling about those archaic cases and
tenses; his one complaint was that the language of his mistress
was apparently deficient in filthy words, so he had not yet
managed an Icelandic limerick. His life was enviable, his talent
simple and direct, as unlike mine as I could imagine. I can still
remember one of his limericks. It was regular in form, though
coarse in content, fit to be remembered for old times' sake, but
not to be quoted.

Sometimes it seemed to me that I was running out of
brain as well as of civility. If war is generally a stupefying
experience, and it was and is, how much more disabling is the
kind of war I was having, for I had none of the ways of resisting
its lowering effect that I had identified in Archer and the
Wykehamists, in Ashington and Banks. Archer had his suf-
focating stores, his rather nobly mad desire to incorporate the
entire material universe in himself. The Wykehamists, with
their gift of turning things conveniently inside out, took inexhaustible comfort in constituting a superior club in the midst
of outsiders they liked to describe as "mouldy," Ashington had

his absorbing buggery quest, and Banks his pleasant *stulka*. I had none of these advantages. Instead, I had all the prejudices ingrained by small-town life and education, and they forbade me to take any course of action resembling the fantasies that animated my acquaintances and the freedoms they appeared to assume so naturally.

Because of my job I saw more of Archer than the others, and had more occasion to envy his kind of madness. But increasingly I felt myself hopelessly inapt for the kind of life or the choice of lives that seemed to confront me. Observing freedoms, I grew less free. Once I fell asleep on a leather sofa in the wardroom and woke to find that I couldn't breathe, the involuntary system had simply imitated the voluntary and resigned, everything was dark and I felt an appalling panic but could not cry out. Of course I did breathe eventually, but with a convulsion that made others start toward me as if I was ill, which I believe I was, in fact I believe I almost died. They couldn't help and I did not expect it.

In Shakespeare's English "help" often means "cure"— "Love did to her eyes repair/To help him of his blindness"— but one can hardly think of that sense as current, except among people who allow their unhappiness to delude them into supposing that *professional* help can be taken as synonymous with cure, or at any rate the serious hope of it. Cure of what, help with what? I wonder. I am always asking myself why it is that intelligent people are so often willing to seek what they call "help," to go in search of counselling, simply because they are unhappy or cannot make sense of their lives—as if it was an indication of sanity to believe it possible to do this. And anyway, if they cannot manage the affair themselves, what chance has a counsellor who is already in all likelihood convinced that there is no real cause for hope, some overworked therapist whose problems are likely to be worse than the patient's? However much persons of that sort may be supposed to know, in principle, about making sense of life, it's a fair assumption that they have become extremely unhappy in the course of acquiring their information.

Of course I disagree with Sophocles when he advises us to call no man happy, for I have known happy men, all in one way or another mad. The only obviously happy individuals are very small children, and they pay for the enjoyment of that state by being hysterically miserable a lot of the time, so that on any dispassionate assessment they too are in one way or another mad. I am of course aware that I do not believe what I am saying, feeling it right to let it be known that I am capable of such silliness, that it is one of my more important characteristics. I can on occasion remind myself that people in deep and dangerous misery do seek and get help, or that if they do not, or if help is not to be had or arrives too late, they make the incontestably true demonstration of what it is to need help and not get it.

My experience of what I believe is known as apnoea, a condition ordinarily terminal and, I believe, much favoured by doctors writing death certificates, has not yet been repeated. Its effect, though not definitive, was distinctly lowering, and for a time I lived in a no-man's-land between the usual world, where one at least feigned general competence and sociability, and a torpor amounting to an unwilled refusal to do so. I would lie many hours in the bath, watching myself grow fat again, an unhappy eater and drinker. When I heard about the sinking of *Hood* I stayed in the bath all day, getting used to the idea that my friend wasn't to be one of the three survivors. In more active moments I would play the violin with increasingly hideous technical self-indulgence and a face as long as Albert Sammons's.

The temporary relief everybody counted on was the mail delivery. At best every fortnight, at worst with intervals of six or seven weeks, we'd watch the postman climb aboard with his sack, and shortly afterwards cluster round him as he called our names. Sometimes you'd get a whole series of letters from the same person, thoughtfully numbered so that you could read them in the right order. You could follow the course of love from longing to desertion in one batch of letters.

The remedy of love would have been to find a girl. It was actually easier for me than for most others to get to Reykjavík, since there might be papers to collect, or the pretence of them, and failing even that pretence, I could tempt Archer with the promise of a case of condensed milk. But the pastoral happiness of Banks, who had nightly in his bed that nice large girl with flaxen hair (far less common in Iceland than might be thought), was not within my scope, even though the women of the country had softened in their attitudes, persuaded by handsome young soldiers less grim of demeanour than their compatriots, and having miraculous access, in this embattled mid-Atlantic island, to ample stocks of liquor and gramophone records. Iceland had its own hit parade, not corresponding to those of the homelands. An American song called "Yes, My Darling Daughter" was a big hit and so was "Mr. Jones, Are You Coming to Bed?," a chaste triumph for the English singer Annette Mills, but now, I suppose, forgotten. They played their part in many seductions. But success with women called for talents I didn't and never would possess.

My lack contrasted with the abundance of a young Irishman named Harrison. He was a man who by a series of coincidences made several appearances in my later life, even after the war. Harrison was wild in a fairly conventional way, a drinker and sometimes a brawler, but also a seductive charmer. Sheltered persons may make civilized assumptions, for instance that courtship or seduction calls for preliminary conversation or verbal foreplay, some exchange of ideas, the establishment of some common interest as preliminary to sex. But in practice it seems the process can be entirely phatic, talk being merely a means of maintaining personal contact when the real message is an understood undersense, conveyed by oeillades, most speaking looks, privy touchings.

Harrison's intellectual vacuousness could thus be an advantage, especially when there was a language problem, when disinterested discourse was hardly to be expected; but I saw him succeed with intelligent and worldly women. He was thus a master communicator, admired even by Archer. Like a poet, he enjoyed the difficulty overcome. Once he accomplished a rapid seduction when in much pain and for all other purposes incapacitated by piles. Once a drunken impulse led him to invade the surgery of an Icelandic dentist and demand that all his teeth, which as far as I know were sound, should be extracted at once. His appearance after this adventure was as you might expect, and his morale was for the moment destroyed. Rash observers were pleased to see this, supposing that his libertine courses had come to a sudden, self-inflicted, and well-deserved end. But once the bleeding had stopped Harrison made light of the problem he had set himself, and long before the end of the period of toothlessness that has to precede the insertion of artificial teeth, a period when the face is crone-sunken, he had, to the general amazement, completely abandoned chastity.

Later, when *Sierra* was in dry dock in Liverpool, some nurses had been brought on board by the usual expedient of bribing the dock police with whisky. There was among them a plain, hungry girl whom, after an hour or so, Harrison took to his cabin. On his return an hour or so later, he was accosted by a very beautiful nurse who asked him why on earth he'd chosen to go off with her friend, assuring him that she would give him a much better time. And off they went. Desire for Harrison-seemed almost universal.

I met him by accident in Liverpool, Sydney, Seattle, sometimes catching sight of him from a bus or in a bar. Once I ran into him in New York and it turned out that we were both heading for Philadelphia, I to pay a ship's company, he to meet a girl. We made a long stop for lunch and when we got to Penn Station I discovered that I had left my briefcase, full of money, in the restaurant. We rushed back and found the bag where I had left it, untouched. I attributed this mercy entirely to Harrison's luck, for I couldn't imagine that even in the Manhattan of 1943 the bag could have sat there inviolate, waiting for *me* to pick it up.

In Philadelphia we booked into the same hotel, Harrison of course with his girl. Around 2 a.m. he called to say a crisis had developed and he needed a favour: a girl in New York had found out where he was and was on her way from the station. Would I mind if he parked the other one in my room? Well, all right, I said, but won't she mind? But she soon arrived, a little shy but seemingly neither angry nor unhappy. Next morning, a Sunday, both these women disappeared and we walked, along with numerous citizens of Philadelphia, across the bridge to Camden, New Jersey, Philadelphia then dry on Sundays. I had formed a vague plan, of no interest to Harrison, of finding out what Camden had done by way of commemorating its well-known resident, Walt Whitman. We paused at a bar and made friends with some relaxing locals; within the hour Harrison had gone off with a woman. I failed in my Whitman researches, never arduously prosecuted, and walked back across the Delaware alone.

I next saw him later in 1943, when he performed the trick that made him, for a while, famous. We had been sent to join the same carrier in Oregon, where lived a girl who rarely ceased to commend what she described as Harrison's bedroom eyes. Eventually we had to leave what was then the delightful town of Portland and sail down the West Coast, through the Panama Canal, and north to New York. But Harrison wasn't resigned to leaving this girl behind so easily; she took a trip to San

Francisco and he wangled a flight from the carrier to that city, or near it, in an Avenger plane. He spent the afternoon in the city and then had himself flown back, rejoining the ship a hundred or so miles to the south. I have never heard of any similar escapade, though it is unlikely to have been unique in the annals of naval flying.

He was a bastard all right, but it was impossible not to admire him, in the Iceland years anyway, for dealing so competently with a problem that defeated almost everybody else. While they sat around exchanging reminiscences, groaning or giggling over Jane in ancient copies of the *Daily Mirror*, he was, in his chosen way, living. I remember a bald bold-faced officer, who often boasted about his sexual power and endurance, staring at the cover of some magazine bearing a picture of the Princess Elizabeth, then I suppose about sixteen. Suddenly he gave a sort of roaring moan and plunged his face into the breasts of that image, trembling with genuine or simulated lust. Nobody smiled, though Wykehamist eyebrows may have twitched. I could see that men in these circumstances thought of sex almost all the time, but not in any real sense of women. Sex coloured their ordinary language, but women were weird strangers, freaks with unusual genitals and abnormal breasts; they were a territory to be visited or subdued, natives to be propitiated by trinkets, flattery, or booze, before being occupied, in fantasy at any rate, by force.

Our way of life simply intensified an already existing sexual paranoia. No wonder behaviour generally got worse and worse. There were accidents of various kinds. A petty officer is knocked into the fjord by a carelessly hoisted buoy, quite dead when pulled out of the icy water a minute later. A taciturn trawler skipper falls asleep with his foot on the stove while working on his nightly bottle of whisky, and burns off a lot of the foot before the pain penetrates the stupor and wakes him up. There are many defaulters among the troops, and therefore many mulcts—but no deserters. Where would they desert to? The lava desert? Reykjavík, bristling with MPs? And if they could dodge them, what next? There was no way of getting back to England.

Meanwhile, fleets steamed confidently into the unprotected harbour. They included those convoys which were to proceed, all too slowly, round the North Cape to Murmansk. Once we put on proper uniforms we'd long since given up for blue battle dress, except in Reykjavík, and were inspected by a baffled and rather cross admiral. After a year or so our discipline, such as it was, may be said to have faltered; Archer continued to dispense punishments, but less often and less severely. It was hard to devise any that seemed worse than the one we were already enduring. And there were few opportunities to commit great crimes. Homosexual conduct was of course possible, and that was a crime on which their lordships were unrelentingly hard; but no case was ever reported. It is difficult to believe there weren't any, yet it is possible: it simply became the fashion for nothing to happen. We just sat and grew older as lightless winter followed nightless summer and the gales swept down the funnel of the fjord, commonplace emergencies by now, though once made unusually interesting because, to Archer's delight, most of the army camp on the headland was lifted up and blown into the sea.

Very occasionally, in a protracted spell of calm weather, we risked a football match on the lava shore. Since the game was after lunch, and lunch was after a lot of pink gin, exhausted colleagues would soon be vomiting on the imaginary touch-line. Another fine-weather diversion was pony-trekking. The ponies were small and feeble, probably because they couldn't eat lava. Among our more dashing companions at the time was another doctor, Anglo-Irish, who had let it be understood that he was one of those hard-riding gentlemen like Major Robert Gregory, celebrated by Yeats for riding a race without a bit. He no sooner mounted his small beast than it reared and slowly bolted, dumping him onto the desert. Later I was told that this accident was more likely to happen to an experienced rider than to a novice, for Iceland ponies don't behave like horses; they are to be mounted from the offside, and very gently, since they are not accustomed to leg contact and any such pressure makes them bolt. This no doubt explains the equestrian doctor's humiliating fall. He remounted to loud cheers, and the party continued at walking pace, until it stopped at a farm for tea. You knocked at the door, cried "Bless!," and were welcomed with tea, bread, and butter, gravely served.

On one such excursion we had ridden across the dry bed of an inlet, to find, as we returned, that the incoming tide had filled it to a depth of some six feet, something we ought in common sense to have foreseen but hadn't. We had to choose between a detour of some miles, which would be a slow business on these ponies, and simply forcing them to swim across. In fact, there was no real choice, for it was already getting dark; we had to go by water. My pony gave up about forty yards from the farther shore, which I reached independently. The doctor took a photograph of me emerging cold and wet, and because the light was late and strange, my image appeared on the print with a distinct halo. Meanwhile, my spectacles were at the bottom of the sea.

Back on board the doctor sent me to bed, warmly wrapped up but denied alcohol. He thus brought off three coups at once: he had at last found an emergency to deal with, he had a compromisingly absurd photograph, and the prohibition of alcohol gave him his revenge for that unkind laughter. There followed three days of gales, and then, without hope that they would still be there and intact, I took a boat and went at low tide to seek my glasses. I found them at once, unharmed and gleaming, caught between two stones and washed clean by many Atlantic tides. I understood why people made grateful sacrifices to Poseidon.

However, most of our recreations had to take place on board. Archer had ordered a roulette wheel, two zeros, from England and set up a casino, with himself, of course, as banker. On the lower deck gambling games were illegal except for the virtually harmless Crown and Anchor, but we, it seemed, were allowed to lose money more stylishly. And so the time passed. What I felt to be an intolerable existence was, as it must now seem, better than endurable if you think of the conditions under which other people were living—in submarines and corvettes, in the rear turrets of bombers, even in Tube shelters, to say nothing of German and Japanese and Russian prison camps. But I was too young and too self-absorbed to dwell on such comparisons. I persisted in regarding this time as a prison sentence, however comfortable the gaol. If it was a prison at all it was a phony prison, and I was becoming pretty phony myself. Sometimes I was reconciled to the idea that I could go on eating and drinking too much, and losing small sums to Archer at cards and roulette, until, with all the others, I had grown grey, doddering around the dear old hideous ship while somebody in London, who might long ago have seen how hopeless and useless we were, was thinking of something else entirely.

And nothing continued to happen, until, after the best part of two years that somebody in London did tumble to the fact that we were never going to build the boom. Perhaps it couldn't be done; what was by now clear was that we couldn't do it. So once again we sailed away through the wreckage, back to the Clyde.

I was nearing the end of my connection with Archer, still thinking of him as mad, because the now enormous collection of groceries in his cabin couldn't conceivably be got ashore and into the black market or the boardinghouses for which he

must have intended it. Well, I couldn't conceive it, but he
could. He managed the whole thing very deftly with the aid
of his friends, though I still feel I ought not to say how. More
surprisingly, since his was after all surely a record of failure,
he was promoted and joined his cronies in a shore establishment. His new lofty rank took him out of my range, but I did
once run into him again.

Sierra went to refit in Liverpool, a port with which she
obviously had a strong affinity, and her time in dock was
marked by the usual illegal festivities. We left, this time for
Algiers, with a new, sane, but odious captain, and for reasons
I will shortly relate, I returned after a while to Liverpool to
await passage to New York. I now had my last sight of Archer.
I ran into him at the Adelphi, emerging from the dining room
with a blond girl on his arm. It happened that I knew this
woman, for she had turned up at dry-dock parties; indeed, I
had inadvertently seen her naked in the bed of Archer's successor, attended by a half-naked younger sister she was keen
to initiate into pleasures she was still, though only just, reluctant to taste fully. In these circumstances Archer for once
looked weary and rather pathetic, as if the fatigue attendant
on his unremitting quest for women and goods was beginning
at last to tell on him. He was suspicious, as he would not have
been two years earlier, of the jocular endearments I exchanged
with his blonde. When he went out for a few minutes, she and
I arranged to meet later that week. On his return Archer
wanted to know what we had done or talked about in his
absence. This was most unlike him. It seemed he now had
many worries, not the least of which being that he was practically impotent and very restless in his attempts to disprove
it. Or perhaps the girl had her reasons for telling me so, and
I mine for wishing it to be so. Perhaps the impression I had
of an Archer suddenly gone into a decline was born of a wish
to see some justice done, a wish that he should not always be

able to stand menacingly over the company, his face disfigured by the prospect of triumph, on the point of making his decisive trick.

Next morning I got my orders and sailed later that day for New York. I never saw Archer or his girls again. As for him, I suppose he must have died long ago. I still see him, linen perfect, bull head lowered, pig's eyes glinting, voice a West Country din, fly open; his aim always to grab, cheat, outwit, penetrate. Any loss of force, any weakening of his ability to detect weakness in others—of the powers that made him so remarkable a cardplayer—would shortly be followed by total incapacity. He cannot, at close to a hundred years old, be sitting in one of his boardinghouses, breathing heavily over a card table or just staring at the sea or at women passing by on the seafront, his little eyes animated by hopeless calculations of lust or money, with Herbert at ninety simpering beside him. To have lived only for the sake of such designs and desires was to have suffered a kind of madness, possibly too common to have been recognised as such, but in the end certified by time itself. So let us, if only in mercy, consider him dead. As for his blonde, she sent me, a few weeks later, a clipping from her local newspaper announcing the double wedding of herself and her sister to two GIs, one from Kansas, one from New York State. There was no letter, but the mere sending of the clipping supplied the necessary Archerian overtones of triumph, of desire satisfied, of design vindicated, of avarice for the moment quieted. I hope their hedonism survived the test of the future. Here were the female complements of Archer, except that they had youth on their side—but not for ever.

ARCHER'S SUCCESSOR, Mabbott, wasn't crazy, unless it was a sign of madness to adore oneself for achieving command of *Sierra*. He was just as greedy as Archer without being in the least endearing. He installed red and green lights outside his cabin (now more like a boudoir than a warehouse), and when sent for I must wait outside until he turned on the green light. He was vain, unstably authoritarian, most dangerous when his false teeth showed in a smile. He had a habit of slightly convulsing his lower jaw. He took his pleasures with calculation and in small companies—not for him the wanton celebrations of his predecessor. He had found it unwise to trust other people and required them to keep their distance. This attitude, though it was strengthened by the formal isolation of his rank, he could not always comfortably maintain, for he was, I think, lonely, but when he decided to be hospitable, the effect was a general unease. This made my own position awkward, since a degree of intimacy, however false, was forced on us by the nature of my job. Though closer than he liked to think, he was not as close as Archer to illiteracy, and this made my handling of his prose a matter of greater delicacy. Moreover, he assumed that he was capable of interpreting the sort of official document Archer wouldn't even try to read. So my new role was more servile, though at his will I might at moments be recruited as confidant or crony and, in what became almost my most important service, interpreter. It all seemed certain to end in tears, and so it did. I often thought how much better it had been to work with my madmen than with this vain lonely bully.

Meanwhile, and of course, as everybody tirelessly observed, there was a war on. This remark itself exemplified the petrifaction of sensibility war imposes: an observation that may not be fully intelligible to anybody who did not experience the war, even if it could be claimed that peace as we have subsequently known it has its own petrifying power. In wartime people are actively prevented from thinking except in headlines, many of them lies. Simple personal freedoms are sacrificed, and the mind volunteers for, or is conscripted into, banality. In the material world almost everything must be

neglected except munitions, and the memory of London's wartime squalor is not easily effaced, even when the city has found
ways of being almost as disgusting in peacetime. The necessary
acceptance of straitened conditions, the brutalisation of the city
and of the individual spirit, had only one beneficial effect: it
was possible for most people to survive without going mad
with dismay at the prospect of so desperate a world, the piled
corpses at Stalingrad, in the German extermination camps, in
cities suffering thousand-bomber raids. It was acceptable to
have as cause for complaint an enforced dreariness, trivial privations, a general ugliness, especially when they were associated with a common cause, a blackout comradeship or matiness
which, since it could not be avoided, presented itself as chosen,
as admirable.

Before we left the Clyde, Mabbott mustered the ship's
company and actually gave one of those performances modelled
on Henry V at Agincourt. He waved his arm around the an-
chorage, pointing out that the river was full of shipping, a fact
that could hardly have escaped us: there was a great company
of warships, troopships, freighters, as well as anomalies of du-
bious provenance and purpose, like us. He indicated that this
congestion of ships might suggest to us that some big show
was pending. He told us we were about to hit the Hun where
it hurt and that this was the moment we had all been waiting
for. He wished us good luck and leapt lithely off his soapbox.
Uninspired, we fell out.

Now we departed with a vast convoy, and after a few days
heard of the landings in North Africa, which had met with
only slight resistance. It seemed clear that the Germans,
though they had done little to impede the invasion force, would
not allow this completely predictable support convoy to stroll
unmolested through the Straits of Gibraltar, and they didn't.
So after more than two years in the service I had my first
experience of naval action.

When, one beautiful morning, the bells and klaxons sounded, I was sitting in a lavatory, so my encounter with heroic reality was slightly delayed. By the time I reached my action station on the bridge, two merchantmen, both, as it happened, loaded with explosives, were ablaze. Frigates were dropping depth charges. A Catalina, presumably from Gibraltar, was flying slowly round the convoy. The crew of one burning ship pulled away in lifeboats; nobody could stop and pick them up, so they faced a fairly arduous, but not, in the calm conditions, particularly dangerous boat trip to Gibraltar, perhaps a hundred and fifty miles off. Meanwhile, the ship they had abandoned was a roaring furnace. The other casualty, also loaded with explosives, fell astern and was too far off for me to see how it was faring, but it was burning all right, and making large amounts of smoke, something deeply deplored by convoys. A destroyer was shelling it and continued to do so for a long time, but it refused to sink.

After half an hour or so we were astonished to see the lifeboats return to the other ship, their occupants perhaps encouraged by the consideration that it hadn't blown up so far. They could hardly have hoped to put out the vast fires, so we supposed they'd gone back for their belongings. Through my glasses I watched a little chain of men climb a rope ladder and disappear inboard. When they had all done so, the ship exploded. Thousands of tons of such a cargo make a big bang, and after the bang, bits and pieces fell, it seemed quite slowly, back into the sea. Then there was not much to be seen.

The Catalina then did, with great deliberation, something strictly forbidden to friendly aircraft, and flew straight, low and slow, down a rank of the convoy. Since it was possible that the Germans were using captured Catalinas, some merchant captains opened fire on it with light antiaircraft weapons. All such guns were supposed to be fixed in such a way that they could not spray other ships of the convoy with bullets, but someone had blundered, and as the big slow plane approached us, we were sprayed. The Catalina was a good target and we hit it, first with oerlikon fire and then with a twelve-pounder shell, whereupon it fell apart and dropped piecemeal into our wash. A young signalman standing near me was hit in the face by a ricochet; he seemed puzzled, even a little amused, and I took him down to the sick bay. Mabbott was very happy, jeering at people who had obeyed cowardly orders and put on their tin hats. He was delighted to find a bullet hole in one of his cabin ports. There was a big cheer when the Catalina splashed down and somebody at once painted a swastika on the funnel. When we got to Gibraltar Mabbott was told, what had been probable all along, that the Catalina, despite its irregular conduct, was friendly, and that four or five Canadians had died. I forget the exact number.

It may be interesting to note that none of the people who died in this little action need have done so. There was the idiotic boatload who had gone back into the flames to save their money, their photographs, who knows what trivia; and there were the airmen who, for reasons never to be discovered, cruised slowly into point-blank range of friendly guns. Many die as absurdly in all war, though in smaller peacetime wars there would be headlines and indignation, official enquiries, all testifying to the belief that unnecessary deaths ought not to be ignored by the living, that the persons annihilated had some importance in themselves, that a death should if possible make some sense in relation to the life it has ended, that whoever, by his default, prevented it from doing so should be called to account. War changes such assumptions. The word "tragic" is commonly, in peacetime, attached to the word "accident." In wartime this association is severed. After all, the object of the campaign is to multiply by a very large factor the number of accidents suffered by other people. That is, the object of the campaign is to do exactly the opposite of

what we like to think one of our objects in peace, for it is to
expose as many people as we can to the impact of dangerous
metal. Even now, almost a century later, we retain an image
of the Somme, where so much unprotected flesh was exposed
to so much metal purpose-built to mangle it that only parsons
could think of what to say by way of explanation or consolation.
In war the practice of general as opposed to private mourning
is discontinued, and there remains little sense that the fullness
of the world has been even momentarily diminished by the
deaths of thousands, the deaths of friends. My signalman was
all right except for a facial scar, but if he had died which of
us would have thought to mourn? It would have been inappropriate, excessive. There is a time for lamentation and there
is a limit to one's power of apprehending the value and dis-
tinctness of an individual life. The four or five Canadians had
as memorial a swastika on a funnel, and that was at once deleted
when it turned out that they were not Germans. Hugger-
mugger enquiry rapidly established that neither Mabbott nor
anybody else was to blame, except possibly the Canadians
themselves.

I find myself dwelling on this little episode, with a double
sense of shame: that I should be dwelling on it, and that I am
ashamed to be doing so; that I make too much of it, and make
too little. I bring the inappropriate attitudes of peace to a
trifling moment of wartime, and what it really calls for is a
return to the petrified sensibility of that moment. Not having
thought about it for fifty-odd years, all I can safely remember
is the weather, the brilliant November morning, flat calm, the
peace of it interrupted by the thudding of the depth charges
and the rattle of ill-directed fire. It was nothing. It did nothing
to put me on terms with the world into which I had intruded.
The enemy was invisible in submarines, or illusory in the plane;
the dead died for nothing; I learned nothing. Or perhaps I did
learn one thing: that contrary to my expectation not everybody

is scared in action. Mabbott wasn't, and there were others
prepared to be disappointed only because the attack had been
on so modest a scale. To get the full value of combat there has
to be more of a sense that flesh may at any moment be ripped
and scattered while you are doing your best to rip and scatter
back, to sink ships and to drown men; or merely to steer,
signal, notice what is happening all around you, as I, responsible for an action report, was supposed to be doing. In fact,
although there wasn't all that much going on, I found it impossible to make written sense of it, from my point of view it
simply didn't make sense itself. I was baffled by the obvious
delight of Mabbott, qualified only by a touch of regret that it
had not been a much more satisfying action, with more ripping
and scattering; still, that would surely come when we entered
the Mediterranean.

In Algiers *Sierra* resumed the social life. What the *indi-
gènes* thought about it we had no means of knowing, but the
colons soon got over any lingering resentment about the slaugh-
ter at Mers-el-Kebir two years earlier, when the British, uncertain of the intentions of their former allies, prudently
annihilated the French navy. They decided to make the best
of the uninvited arrival of Allied troops in their city. A rich
young vigneron we knew as Charlie became a special friend,
in part no doubt because he found a use for me as an interpreter.
Charlie, who easily got everything else, couldn't lay his hands
on petrol, but he hardly needed it. He would drive along the
quay in a gleaming dogcart drawn by a pretty white pony, his
pretty white *poule*, Maggy, beside him, and present us with a
demijohn of his own wine. He gave parties, sometimes in the
city, sometimes in the mountains, and often we would provide
the food and he the wine he grew and the girls he kept.

In Algiers more generally there was a shortage of food,
even in the black-market restaurants, where the main dish
might be a dish of skinny blackbirds. Sometimes I would go

off in a jeep and bargain with indigenous farmers, who would rush around decapitating chickens. Once we returned with two live sheep, which were made pets by sailors who threatened mutiny if they should be killed. I would go to play bridge with a handsome lawyer and his beautiful doctor wife, but it went without saying that I would bring the food.

The assassination of Admiral Darlan in the Hotel Aletti, centre of local society, was a reminder that Algiers was a dangerous place, where you could not be sure to which party or which general—de Gaulle or Giraud—the French Army and the police felt more loyalty. The immediate consequence of Darlan's death was an irritating curfew, and about the same time the city authorities ordered that there should be each week two *jours sans alcohol*. The second of these prohibitions was tolerable, for it merely meant that spirits could not be sold. You could drink as many aperitifs and as much wine as you wanted, and of course as much coffee, as the chicory and acorn brew was called. The first prohibition proved more difficult, more likely to interfere with Charlie's parties and my quieter but equally elegant evenings at cards. The town was fairly dangerous after dark; there were air raids on the harbour, and I remember standing on the bridge at midnight in the pleasant December air, wearing only a tin hat and pyjamas, feeling for a moment quite at home, quite exhilarated at the din of the antiaircraft batteries, my sleeves flapping in time with the gunfire.

Mabbott grew increasingly vain, rigorous, and demanding; he had no French and was to that degree more dependent on me. He liked to invite hungry young beauties to his cabin for lunch, and take it as a matter of course that they should pay for what they got there in the bedroom next door. I recall an awkward moment when he was engaged in that way and I was in his outer room. The admiral's chaplain called; I assured him that the captain was not at home. He, however, had found

out, from the officer of the watch, that this was not the case.
My embarrassment told the chaplain what was going on. He
seemed to be disgusted with me, unfairly, I think; I could
hardly have come out with the truth. It was with this severe
man that I had gone to the cathedral for the Mozart *Requiem*,
and to the opera, or anyway the opera house, to see a boring
performance of *L'Arlésienne*, a tedious piece despite Bizet's
music, while Fascist youth—Les Chantiers de la Jeunesse, they
called themselves—beat drums and yelled in the square outside. And sometimes we had sat together peacefully construing
Virgil's *Eclogues*—he had been so pleased to find somebody
capable of doing that and wanting to. Now that chaste, re-
warding association came to an immediate end.

Meanwhile, I had various official reasons for often being
ashore, and I came to know something of the city and its white
inhabitants—not the rest of the population, naturally, for the
Casbah was out of bounds, and even if it hadn't been, frater-
nisation with the natives was hardly conceivable. We all made
friends of the *gardiens de la paix* on duty at the dock gates.
Ruthless to their native fellow citizens, they were more than
civil to us. I once went to dinner at a policeman's house and
ate what was probably the best meal I had in the course of the
entire war. When an alert sounded, the policeman grabbed his
gear and ran off, leaving his wife placidly beating the may-
onnaise and explaining how fatal it was to stop doing so even
for a second. The meal continued, rich and slow, and was still
in progress when the husband returned.

In accepting that invitation I was of course breaking the
curfew, and I was challenged on my way back to the ship.
This had happened before, but with Mabbott's connivance I
always had the excuse of some bogus errand; he had, however,
made it clear that if the bluff was ever called he would deny
complicity and leave me on my own. This time I happened to
have fallen in with Harrison, slinking back from some assig-

nation. We were stopped by a commander who somehow detected from our demeanour that whatever business we had
been about was not official. He questioned me in that pene-
tratingly censorious voice in which senior officers of the regular
navy preferred to conduct their conversations with inferiors. I
imagined their wives replying to perfectly simple questions
rasped out in this tone, say about the delivery of laundry, in
educated but timid voices, like Celia Johnson's. I told the man,
with no expectation that he would believe me, that I wasn't
at liberty to discuss my mission, but I couldn't help telling
him the name of my ship. When I told Mabbott about this
encounter, he reminded me, with pleasure, that he had ex-
pressly declined to cover for me in such a case, and he was
evidently looking forward to the sequel. But the complaint was
never made, possibly because my interrogator had his own
reasons for not revealing why he himself was out during the
curfew, probably because when it came to the point he foresaw
boring investigations and enquiries and couldn't be bothered.
It's extraordinary how much, in a lifetime, the lucky can get
away with, or the less lucky when in the shadow of the lucky.

During my months in Algiers I had, as far as I can remember, no intelligent or compassionate reflections on this
interesting and rather sinister city, no real sense of its politics,
its intolerable economic and social divisions—none even of its
military significance, though American and British armies
were pouring through it to take the Afrika Korps in the rear,
while Italian frogmen attacked ships in the harbour and German bombers bombed it more or less nightly. Up the hill
Eisenhower was planning the Sicily landings, in which *Sierra*
was soon to have her first real taste of action. To all concern
with such matters I was immune, but in spite of many super-
ficial distractions I knew myself to be radically unhappy, having no horizon of unhappiness that I could ever hope to cross.
It was a world in which I remained a stranger, which I had

not made; but I had made none for myself that was less alien
or less spurious, though I knew people who had done so and
always felt for them a melancholy envy.

MY ILLICIT NOCTURNAL prowlings could not go on for
ever; indeed, they soon got me into worse trouble and so
brought to an end my stay in North Africa. Charlie was planning an enormous party, with *poules* galore. Shortly before it
was to happen I got to know some people from one of the
U-class submarines, small, unbelievably uncomfortable boats
that had become famous for their exploits of ripping and scattering. I asked Charlie if they could come to the party and he
was delighted. But Mabbott was furious; I hadn't expected
this, wrongly thinking he would be flattered by the company
of heroes. The truth, I think, was that he was jealous of them,
or thought of them as rivals for the favours of Charlie's entou-
rage. The line he took was that the party was his and Charlie's,
that I had nothing to do with it, and had flouted his authority.
He told the submariners that their invitation was invalid, and
forbade me to go ashore until further notice.

This was unreasonable, and also unjust. There have been
a few occasions in my life when, finding somebody's action to
be unreasonable and unjust, I have said to hell with prudence
and responded unreasonably and if possible unjustly to the
affront (anybody can be unreasonable: to be unjust you need
some power). The procedure for complaint was scrupulously
set down in King's Regulations. The subplot of the relevant
passages was that you shouldn't dream of doing it; but if you
insisted, you had to seek a series of interviews, the tenor of
which would once more seek to deter you from continuing.
You went first to your immediate senior; he would be obliged
to advise you to go no further, and you had then to wait for
twenty-four hours before seeing an officer of higher rank; and
so on. Eventually and inevitably this process brought you be-

fore the very person you were complaining of. Mabbott told me to drop the whole business; I declined, and asked his permission to take my complaint to the admiral. Pale with rage, his false teeth in danger of falling from his agitated mouth, he declared a wish to knock me down, but he was not foolish enough to try that, and of course he could not withhold his consent.

I would have been remarkably stupid not to understand that my own position was unsound, for serious enquiry would have discovered that Mabbott's action, however incorrect, arose from incorrect conduct on my part. Why did I persist? Partly because I didn't much care if they threw me out, though conscious that whatever I was made to do after that disgrace certainly wouldn't be more agreeable than my present job; partly because of a trait I have on a few occasions in my life been surprised to find I possess, a sort of unconsidering recklessness, of pleasure in self-destructiveness. There was even, in this mixture of motives, a small but I think genuine, even altruistic, desire to see justice done against a petty tyranny.

I was summoned to the hilltop and interviewed not by the admiral himself but by a rather genial flag officer on his staff. I supposed this was just about all right, I could hardly insist on the actual presence of the great man, and anyway, I was running out of fervour. So I accepted this substitute; moreover, I was actually rather impressed that with so much on their hands (the invasion of Sicily for a start, though of course I didn't at the time know that that was what the fuss was about, only that something serious was afoot). He told me to go back to my ship; he would see that everything was straightened out. As I started out down the hill, the admiral's car stopped and he offered me a ride to the harbour. This was not at all what I had expected—nothing at all seemed to have happened, nobody cared about my case or, for that matter, Mabbott's. There was, it seemed, a war on. Mabbott now became suspiciously friendly, and may have known more than I did about the next move; for almost immediately I was relieved of my job and told to make my way with all convenient speed to New York. Somebody was exercising prudence. I was simply removed from the scene. I knew very well that nobody in New York needed me, any more than anybody did in Algiers.

GETTING TO New York was a slow business. First I went back to England in an almost empty troopship, accompanied by one of the heroic submariners and an army major who carried two submachine guns wherever he went. These men drilled fanatically for hours, swooping and charging round the deck. I declined all invitations to join them. There was also a reserve lieutenant who had got into some trouble and was being moved out of the way. He had consulted a witch in Algiers who told him that on a certain day, which was to occur during our passage, he would lose both his legs in an explosion. Another witch had—independently, he thought—confirmed this prophecy. After a while, since we seemed insufficiently impressed, he remembered a further prediction, that anybody in his vicinity at the time of the explosion would lose more than his legs. It was interesting to note that on the stated day we all grew quietly nervous about this and stayed up till midnight, jeering with relief when the day had passed.

Another passenger, technically a prisoner, was a captured Luftwaffe pilot we were supposed to be guarding. He was a tease, threatening to jump overboard at Gibraltar and swim to Spain. He didn't try that and remained throughout confident and amused at our follies and delusions. When we sailed up the Clyde with dozens of aircraft over our heads, he could not understand why they were British; he had been told, or pretended he'd been told, that his lot had achieved total mastery in the skies over Britain.

Weeks passed without my finding a passage to New York.
I went on a course on how to run the galleys of a capital ship
(quite useless, of course), wandered about for a while as one
does on these occasions, and then left, in another empty troopship, a French liner, for New York. All the traffic was of course
in the other direction. As I foretold, nobody in New York
knew or cared why I had come. I ran errands and enjoyed
myself. On my first night in the city I was taken by one of the
beautiful young women provided for our entertainment by the
English-Speaking Union, to Carnegie Hall, where I was astonished that the concert opened with the wrong national an-
them, and also by the conducting of Dimitri Mitropoulos, who
used no baton and twitched remarkably. Then I left my partner
and went to supper with Alicia Markova, to whom I bore
greetings and some kind of present from the dancer Claude
Newman, a charming fellow I'd recently run into. He had done
me the honour (which he did almost every young man) of
trying to seduce me, and, unwounded by my refusal of that
honour, entrusted me with this task. Mme Markova was gra-
cious, patient, and paid the bill.

In New York we had, in addition to pay, an allowance of
$6.50 a day, enough, at that time, to do a good deal more than
just live. Although I knew vaguely what to expect, nothing
could have been more surprising than the New York of 1943;
the most amazing discovery was that it was sparklingly clean,
or anyway seemed so after London. Its gaiety was also different,
the bustle and brilliance of it very unlike the dark satisfactions
that were all London could offer.

After a while I had to go to Asbury Park in New Jersey;
there were many British there, not liked by the residents, who
found much to complain of. The hot-weather rig of the Royal
Navy was particularly resented on the ground that for men to
wear shorts was obscene. We obediently adopted American
trousers. A British flag was discovered, by a busy old fellow

with a theodolite, to be an inch or two higher than the Stars and Stripes beside it. Our commandant suggested switching flagstaffs. All this was understandable—back at home the natives were beginning to complain about the American "occupation." It did little to cool the ardour of the affair with America that I had begun in New York. But now it will be thought that like all love affairs it was begun in illusion. Nobody will believe that New York was not only overwhelming but clean; and nobody who remembers the 1960s but not the 1940s will believe that Asbury Park was petty, priggish, on the lookout for anything that could be construed as sexual misconduct.

Next I was despatched to Portland, Oregon, a pleasing destination, though getting there was hell. I took a detachment of rather mutinous men and was not much good at leading them, partly because I sympathized with their plight, though it was exactly my own. We were crushed into a slow train in July heat, with nowhere to sleep and, for the first day, nowhere to sit down. So we arrived in Chicago weary and filthy from the smuts that came in from the open windows. There was a wait of eight hours, and I didn't see how I could keep them together for that length of time, so I dismissed them and told them to reassemble at the station an hour before we were to continue the trip. I then took a long and beautiful shower in the station, wandered around, ate, and was punctually at the place of assembly. Two men had gone missing.

On the next leg we did have seats, but at Minneapolis another man, this time a CPO, disappeared. After that the trip was not so bad. We had bunks. It took six days for our diminished band to get to Portland, where I was almost immediately summoned before authority and informed that the CPO had lodged an official complaint, somehow making out that I was responsible for his having, as the navy puts it, "run." How he made his case was never explained to me, but in that

respect this little crisis differed little from many other episodes
in my naval career. Nobody seemed to take my misdemeanour,
if it was one, at all seriously, and I felt unreasonably miffed at
this, sensing that if I'd been regarded as a serious person I
would have been given more serious treatment, if only a serious
scolding. Insofar as they thought about me at all, they were
too busy trying fretfully to find out why I was in Oregon
anyway, and thinking of something to keep me occupied.

In time all became clear: the Americans were putting
together an escort carrier for the British, and I was a prematurely arrived member of the new ship's company. I was able
to visit the hull and to infer that as it was still at a fairly
rudimentary stage—no sign, for instance, of a flight deck—I
should be in Portland for a long time, as indeed I was, learning
the different ways of enjoying and conducting oneself that were
enjoined in that distant, lost America of 1943, with its strange
dating rituals, its easy gaiety. Portland was then a charming
town, full of birds and roses; I saw it again thirty years on and
it was not the same, my pleasant hotel grown into a skyscraper
and everybody less happy, but still a town one could live in.

THIS NAVAL section was meant to be a brief *scherzando*
passage, linking the inevitable importance of youth with the
dread insignificance of age, but as time went by, it appeared
that the interim cannot have been as pointlessly amusing as I
had believed. But enough: I omit details of the happiness of
Portland. The lid was fitted onto the Liberty-ship hull, and
we left with farewell parties and unrealisable promises to return. Then we sailed down the coast, through the canal, up
to New York, and across to Scotland with a fast convoy.

Now this was almost the real thing. We had a proper
active service captain, shortly to be an admiral, and he had a
proper active service secretary, who knew a lot of technicalities
I hadn't picked up, though I did not believe he was by any

measure as good a letter writer as I. I was reluctantly trying to learn another trade, having been put in charge of aircraft stores. I had suffered a course in this subject but never came near to mastering it. Aeroplanes need thousands of bits and pieces, and crafty persons who know about these will cheat an incompetent storekeeper and make off with valuable items like silver solder. I dispensed a lot of dope—dope in those days was not marijuana but smelly stuff required to keep healthy the fabric of planes. I was close to useless but had shrewd cover from my petty officer.

Carrier life suited me better than *Sierra* had done. There was plenty of space and the whole business of launching and retrieving quite large planes from a quite small deck I found interesting. The first plane to land on our deck broke the arrestor wire, Harrison's charge, and tumbled into the sea. The pilot was fished out and given a cabin next to mine, where he lay moaning in terror and crying out in his sleep. Later we had Seafires, the naval adaptation of the Spitfire, which despite the adaptation had a very high landing speed, and the sight of Seafires toppling into the sea was almost commonplace. More pilots were fished out. I never tired of watching the man who led them in to land, standing rather dangerously on a sponson and waving two yellow lollipops to guide the pilot. Later on I wrote what struck me as an ambitious poem on the subject of the relationship between this man and the pilot, or even between this man and life in general, but the poem, though not lost, is not repeatable here, since poetry resembles violin playing in belonging to the list of the many crafts I have attempted and abandoned, in some cases more than once.

In February 1944, we sailed with a new ship's company from Sheerness, bound for the Clyde, where (it was understood) we were to "work up" with a view to attacking the battleship *Tirpitz*, sulking in a Norwegian fjord. This would have been a desperate adventure, but we never even got to the

Clyde, for somewhere off Lowestoft we were mined. This was
not supposed to happen: we were preceded up the swept channel by minesweepers whose equipment could deal with mines
of all sorts; but this acoustic mine eluded them. The mine
exploded under the engine room with alarming and impressive
results. We did not sink; there had been much attention to
techniques of damage control, and many of us had just been
on a course at St. Paul's School, where we had jolly times
pretending to blow holes in large models in large tanks and
studying how best to prevent them from sinking. What happened was that everything was smashed, the main engines
lifted and moved from their beds, and there was not even
auxiliary power to be had, even for a cup of tea. The explosion
happened at lunchtime; I had a glass of something on the way
to my lips; and I remember best the frightful destruction of
glasses and crockery, and the barely disciplined haste with
which we made our way from the depths onto the tilting flight
deck. Some people were lying about looking dead, but they
were only stunned, and as I ran towards the bridge they rose,
like figures in a resurrection painting by Stanley Spencer.

There was a long struggle to get a towline to a destroyer,
but it proved impossible in the sea that was running. Finally
a specialist tug took us over, and we made the slow, cold, and
dangerous voyage back to the Medway. I suppose it was quite
an achievement to get this wreck into port. Later we went into
dry dock at East Ham, where a skeleton crew, including me,
spent most of 1944. I borrowed Paul's flat in Shepherd's Bush
and every morning at six-something made the impossible journey by tube to Plaistow. There was little to do—really useful
people, gunners and fighter direction officers, were sent off to
help with the Normandy bombardments, while we, in due
time, watched the khaki hordes depart for the coast, studied
the course of the V-1 buzz bombs, at which, after the first few
days, we were no longer allowed to shoot, and took such plea-

sure as there was to be had in the hideous London of 1944.

All this while men were at work repairing what came to be known as the hole in the elephant's bottom. By the time they had finished it was late in the year and there was no further need for us in the German war: the *Tirpitz* had been sunk by the RAF, the sea war was virtually over, and the convoys were safe. But our war was not over; we acquired a new ship's company and a new captain—sane, though deeply fond of the novels of Dornford Yates—and were sent off, along with many more important ships, to the East.

We found ourselves beginning the next year in Sydney, and were often to return there. Of the pleasures of that city I shall not write here, but they were not negligible. I have a clear recollection of the genial officer who never wanted to go ashore, and was loved by all because he was always willing to be duty officer and let everybody else enjoy themselves in Sydney. On their return to the ship he would greet each of them solicitously: "I trust you had a successful evening, Lieutenant. I very much hope you achieved an insertion."

I was now more contented; I had grown into the life I had had to lead these four years and more. I even had friends aboard, a clever fighter-direction officer, a refined dentist, a philosophical and libertine major—I cannot remember what he was doing in a warship, only that after the war he grew very calm and ran a good restaurant in the Lake District. There were some abstractedly pleasant, mostly doomed air crews, who preferred their own silent company. Ashore, in the artistic colonies of Sydney, there were poets, patrons of poets, and parties. They did something, less than I now feel was necessary, to restore and reshape my imagination. Perhaps I was now too old, and too far gone into the navy, already wondering what on earth I should find to do when I had to leave it. But that was some time off, and there was still the Pacific war. We could not guess how close that was to its end.

For the first time I was employed in a genuine warship and about to take part in a real war, huge forces confronting one another on the vast battlefield of the Pacific Ocean. Bristling with warplanes, equipped with American cipher machines and heavy axes to smash them up if threatened with capture, we went off with elation to join our allies, who were on the point of invading Okinawa. The large and by former standards very powerful British squadron was very small by comparison with the enormous American fleet, presumably the largest ever assembled. It was the time of the kamikaze attacks, at first devastating to all ships but especially to carriers, especially if they were, like ours, unarmoured and virtually a huge floating tank of high octane fuel.

Like Stendhal's hero at Waterloo, I had very little idea of what was happening, or even of where the battle was; I think we were involved in a diversionary attack on Sakishima-gunto. Refuelling was done at sea, and we had stores for ninety days. It was easy to forget what land looked like, as if that ocean had no shores, like the one my memory dragged out of Ovid, in his account of the Creation. But all this activity was without apparent purpose, for we saw nothing, and the enemy must have perceived without much difficulty that there were more important matters to attend to than our manoeuvres. We despatched aircraft, catapulting them into the bright air, and later welcomed some of them back; we scanned the shoreless world for Japanese planes, not knowing that by this time they had very few, and none to waste on us. Okinawa fell, and we went back to Sydney.

For a while after that, we were nothing but a tramp, ferrying aircraft between Brisbane and Sydney, but soon we became one of the thousands of ships massing for the assault on Japan. We got as far as the Manus Islands, on the equator, a colossal American naval base, where we idled and swam, and lamented that in view of the estimated million casualties in the

Japanese landings (notwithstanding the much lower figures now being offered, that was the estimate we were given at the time) we had probably survived five years of war to no purpose except to be eliminated in its last days. We were at Manus when the atomic bomb was dropped on Hiroshima. The general opinion was that it saved our lives, and we were unethically pleased about this.

The rest of the tale is vaguely humanitarian, for the ship was sent to Hong Kong to carry concentration-camp survivors to Sydney. Hong Kong was horrible: dirty, empty, hot, diseased, and starving. We were inoculated against everything imaginable before being allowed ashore and were very sick from the inoculations. Put in charge of the emaciated passengers, I was given a working party of Japanese prisoners of war who tore around, under a bullying Japanese NCO, as if slaving for the Emperor himself, so that I had to persuade him to order the men to slow down, they were making me tired.

The Hong Kong camp whose inhabitants we took on was a mixed one, so there were women and children in the group, I forget how many, but certainly too many to add to the complement of an already crowded warship, which in any case had no accommodation suitable for couples or families. Another problem was the supply of water, always, on long voyages in hot climates, rationed. However, we were full of good will and determined to make our guests comfortable, even if we'd have to limit further our own already restricted comforts. A shower was an absolute daily necessity, but we allowed ourselves thirty seconds of water apiece, a man standing by with a stopwatch to make sure there was no cheating. Our guests were not so limited. They were all undernourished and some had beri-beri—the sick bay was busy, and so was I. Yet as they grew stronger, everything began to go awry. I remember that last voyage from Hong Kong to Sydney as one of the more irritatingly instructive of my naval career.

First the women complained that even the Japanese had not parted them from their men, as I had done. I explained— what might have been obvious—that warships were unfeelingly designed without thought of marital cohabitation. Then they were indignant that they had sometimes to pass by half-naked sailors in order to reach the heads, or toilets. I explained why this could not be helped, and stressed that these men had willingly ceded some of their own space and comfort to their suffering betters. Finally they complained that they were required to share their unsatisfactory accommodation with a half-caste Filipino woman.

Now, it happened to be the case that the Japanese, by allowing married internees to live together, were indirectly responsible for the birth in captivity of a fair number of children. All were still very young, and their presence was a major part of our problem in keeping everybody happy, or at least quiet. All these babies had been delivered by the Filipino woman, who was a midwife, and it was recognized that in the absence of a doctor she had done very well and perhaps even saved lives. The other women respected her professional abilities but thought them quite irrelevant to the present situation; they weren't used to sharing quarters with a person of inferior race, and the humiliation was the greater because, as they tediously and unnecessarily kept telling me, a ship of His Majesty's was British territory. The woman herself was more amused than upset, amused by the resurgence after years of humility (it had been expedient or necessary in one way or another to defer to the captors) of attitudes she had long since learned to live with. She was also amused by my youthful indignation, my unrealisable wish to teach these appalling women a lesson. If I could have rehoused her, she would have complied quite happily, having no special desire to stay where her presence was causing so much distress. She laughed at them, and at me for supposing I could do anything to change them.

Meanwhile, their menfolk also began to recover their health; they got up committees and made demands, some of which I could meet, even when they were of doubtful legality, like the demand for a bar. They got one, but its opening hours had to be restricted, which caused these mostly petty officials to rail against petty officialdom. They seemed to think that during their four years of captivity the world, and especially British colonial arrangements, must have remained exactly as they were in December 1941. They had imagined that on boarding my ship they were stepping back into that world, but they soon found out how much standards of civilized behaviour had slipped. They were business people and policemen with automatic contempt for Chinese and other non-whites, and they were astonished at the treachery of the English lower classes who, while still in khaki, had ousted Churchill and installed a Labour government with a large majority. (We in the East had no vote in that election, but the general view among my comrades was that it didn't matter, since a Labour victory was unthinkable; I still treasure the memory of their dismay when they read the result. This was not what they had been fighting for.)

I spent much time with these boors and their women, downmarket versions of E. M. Forster's Turtons and Burtons; what made the experience even more horrible was that as they grew healthier under our care they became more odious. They came to despise me almost as much as the Chinese, but saw a need to be careful about the way they showed it, since I remained, as the result of what they saw as a collapse of naval morale, their provider and, unlike the coolies, capable of kicking back. Of course I took no reprisals. I remember the relief I felt as I escorted them ashore at Sydney, all the greater because, in fulfilment of my expectations, none except the Filipino nurse bothered to say thanks for what in my view, though not in theirs, were the remarkable civilities and kindnesses they had received during their long voyage.

After another spell in amiable Sydney it fell to me to go home. I managed this by hitching rides on aeroplanes, with long stops en route, at Colombo, Karachi. Cairo, and Malta. At the time people got used to staggering around the globe in this manner, but this journey now feels like a dream, so I establish its reality by consulting my copy of Joyce Carey's novel *The Horse's Mouth*, which is inscribed *Colombo, December 1945*. And I was much taken with the beauty of the shopgirls of that city. What else? The long stay in Malta, where north-easters blew into your eyes clouds of dust from the bombed buildings; where I went to see a movie called *The Man Who Came to Dinner* in a cinema with a hole in the roof through which showers of rain occasionally poured, obscuring the screen and interfering with the pleasure of the sole patron, me.

Finally I hitched a ride from Malta to some airfield in the west of England, where it was snowing. I didn't much like the look of winter or, to be truthful, of England and my future in it. Still, I had some right, not much but some, to a temporary happiness; like Ulysses, who also had mishaps along the way, I could say without too gross exaggeration that I had *fait un beau voyage*. One of my few literary triumphs in the war years was a translation of that sonnet of Du Bellay's, which won the prize in a *New Statesman* competition. But I was now twenty-six, and I had no idea what I was going to do, except for the negative certainty that it wouldn't be seafaring. A little more positively, I was fairly sure that it would involve writing of some sort, and reading, if I could buy the leisure to do it.

III

The Rest

. . . et tout le reste est littérature.

—PAUL VERLAINE

Some mornings, fresh from dreams in which I take part not as an old man or indeed as a young man, but merely as well-known me, I look into the shaving glass and see hardly anybody I recognise, only an allegorical representation of Eld. Where now is that person to whom such considerations of age need not apply? He belongs to a mythical realm, not some Cockaigne, not a happy land far far away, just some place in which he is miserable or jolly, confident or embarrassed, in familiar ways, but in which he is his unquestioned self, and always so, without variation through time.

This arch-self becomes inaccessible, obscured by the broken face or mask in the looking glass, which, less broken yesterday, will be more broken tomorrow; hardly a relation of the self as dreamed. How, then, to get in touch with more fugitive selves, those others who bore my name and were also in their turn to be severed from the dream archetype? Eld has lost them along with almost everything else, certainly everything that has to do with the awful keenness of bodily pleasures which, I recall, once shook me, or perhaps, since they persisted from one self to another, I should have said once shook them, now to be recovered only in rare moments of drowsing in sunlight. What I, what all need is a madeleine or a *phrase de Vinteuil*, even stumbling on an uneven but memory-packed paving stone might do it, cause the boulder to roll back a moment from the entrance, exposing the real and not the shadow.

T. S. Eliot said that we can discern patterns in our lives "only at rare moments of inattention and detachment, drowsing in sunlight." But you can't write a book while drowsing in sunlight. Of course there are ways of faking the pattern, as Nabokov does when he claims in his autobiography, *Speak, Memory*, that the thing to do is to hold the narrative together by means of what he calls "thematic designs." It is a way of patterning many disparate events and selves and of offering an illusion of wholeness, a life, or part of a life, rendered as a tribute to some aesthetic force that controls or eliminates fact in some higher interest: a box of matches recurs, it has nothing to do with vice or virtue, it is a cohesive device more interesting than death or revolution, promoting a magical integrity irrelevant to human hopes or pains. I call that faking, though with admiration; it is a species of the good writing that cannot help eliminating truth from autobiography. It tempers the prevailing northeaster of time. It is a means of giving life the calm coherence of myth.

Still, the time of life so far described in this book was itself or has become a time of myth, its world a region of fantasy. Even if it is not an illusion that I and the other people I've spoken of ever existed, they now exist no longer, whether or not they are dead. But henceforth I have to confront what seems a real world, real because it has not had time to sink into fantasy, it is still peopled by historical personages, however distorted by memory their identities may be, however indifferent I may be (as Nabokov was) to their fates. From here on there seems to be less chance of feeling good while lying and faking.

Moreover, at this stage it's a bit late to start asking deep questions about the possibility of telling the honest truth about a self, and far too late to worry about the nature of the self, how it came into existence, how it accommodates what appear to be in important respects different selves. If the honest truth is demanded, let it be remembered that few, and of them not many very honest, have been willing to claim that they told it; moreover, it is undeniable that its principal enemy, in autobiography, is, as I have suggested, not mendacity but good writing.

"I'm writing well today"—a silent claim occasionally made by most writers, even autobiographers—is a way of saying, "Today I've been *beautifully* economical with the truth." Rousseau boasted that he had an irresistible impulse to set down everything about himself without bothering about style. He would do it so completely that the reader could from then on claim to know two people, himself and Rousseau, and to achieve this knowledge would have to put up with the whole truth, unvarnished and uncut, even if he complained that he didn't need to be told all this. "Maybe you don't," says Rousseau, "but I need to tell it." Ah yes, the need to tell. But there is that other need, to try to write well. In spite of these protestations Rousseau couldn't help writing well; he needed also to do that, even if his readers didn't care, though if they really didn't care, why does Jean-Jacques continue to find readers? And, as he was willing to admit, he cheated quite a bit in order to keep up the pretence of not doing so, thereby frustrating his stated intention of telling the truth at any necessary length.

It is true that he had a passion, not shared by all autobiographers, for showing himself in disgraceful situations, sometimes even exaggerating their disgracefulness, and in his

later pages went on tiresomely about the wickedness of his
false friends and persecutors, so that we read on more and
more dispiritedly, like Browning's moon glad to finish. It is
true, too, that he liked to read his stuff aloud to audiences in
order to enjoy more keenly their reactions of shock or disgust
or boredom, while at the same time relentlessly offering them
assurances that he was not merely a fellow who inevitably
shared many characteristics, amiable or otherwise, with them
and with the great majority of mankind but in spite of these
similarities remained, you'd have to allow, a pretty rare kind
of person.

No doubt everybody who voluntarily writes autobiography—and circumstances in which one could be compelled
to do so are quite difficult to imagine—feels a bit like that;
and it might even be claimed that almost everybody who has
heard about the possibility of constructing even the most private, the most silent narrative account of his or her own life is
some sort of autobiographer. And all are aware of an implicit
promise to tell the truth, if only to themselves. Perhaps the
silent autobiographers manage to be more truthful, who can
say, but in the course of writing it down, the others will discover, if they didn't know already, that the action of memory
depends on the cooperation of fantasy. This is the truth.

Writing truthfully of one's life therefore requires what may
seem to be a scandalous breach of the promise to be truthful.
And it can be further argued, even more disconcertingly, that
in the ordinary course of his written narrative, as of the inter-
minable day-to-day account he gives himself of himself, the
autobiographer will remember only in order to forget what he
cannot bear to remember. He may be aware, at a quite conscious level, of certain specific suppressions: as Philip Roth
put it in *The Facts*: "Even if it's no more than one percent
you've edited out, that's the one percent that counts." But there
remain to be considered omissions of another kind, when the

editing is done unconsciously in the service of lifelong resis-
tances to a ghastlier truth that allow it to be expressed, if at
all, only in repetitive neurotic symptoms; this is the editorial
effort that sends you running to the psychoanalysts with their
tragic conviction that memory is, in truth, merely an instrument for concealing the truth, the hundred percent that really
counts; the story they will induce you to tell, by only half-
attending to your rambling narrative (so unlike anything that
could be described as good writing, just as their form of attention is just about as unlike good reading as possible)—that
story will be very different from anything that could be published outside a professional journal, and even there the analysts
are on their best literary behaviour, seduced by the notion that
there needs to be what pre-programmed readers will recognise
as a coherent tale to be told. Hence Freud's fascinating case
histories. Hence also the way we tell our dreams, describing
a façade, giving them pseudo-classical forms, unable not to
write them well.

IN SPITE OF all that, in spite of its uselessness, people
will go on asking the question whether there is such a thing
as a self; how, if it exists, it is constituted; what it has to do
with those clownish, distressed, cheating, honourable, sober,
drunken selves that gesticulate at the roadside as one drives
smoothly down the highway of memory. According to David
Hume, "There is properly no simplicity in [the mind] at one
time, nor identity in different [times], whatever natural propensity we may have to imagine that simplicity and identity,"
and he certainly wasn't the last to question our natural propensity to imagine that we each have a self, a self that might
speak for all those discontinuous states. "A single string speaks
for a crowd of voices," as Wallace Stevens raptly if obscurely
remarked.

Indeed, it is now commonplace that the self is a recent

invention or illusion, that external ideological pressures compel each of us to make one because, as subjects, we are easier to keep in order. But I think it was good of Hume to allow us a *natural* propensity, so that we can at least think we have a certain primordial right to choose to have selves, or possibly only to imagine that we are doing so, rather than simply suffer them to be imposed on us. I have difficulty with the idea that I, or for that matter you, can be understood as merely the site of conflicting discourses, merely the product of practices we have no control over and no direct knowledge of. Frankly, if I could not continue to assume, unphilosophically, that I have a self, I shouldn't be bothering with all this. I do see that my self is not immune, in its formation, to social and ethical prejudice and control, but I cannot feel that these are powerful enough to eliminate a certain continuity. Or anyway, a *natural propensity* to assume it, a modicum of identity in different epochs (to be sought, naturally, under differing appearances); and a natural propensity also to take responsibility for all the selves subsumed under this hypothetical self. Or anyway, to assume a right to speak for them, even in a manner that by trying to make them seem interesting falsifies them, insofar as what does not exist can be falsified.

So: it is the moment of the liminal rite, the passage from myth to fact, the start of all the rest of it. The return to real life after more than five years of ersatz took place at a large and dismal demobilisation unit at Oldham, near Manchester. I suffered a perfunctory medical examination by a doctor smelling of gin, and was then offered a choice of civilian clothes, blue pinstripe suit or grey pinstripe suit—off the peg, like my first uniform, but far less pretty. Then out into the dark, for that December day light had not broken, indeed was never to break, over Oldham; and down the intolerable streets, all frost, smoke, and despair, to a station from which I could go anywhere I wanted if there was anywhere I wanted to go, being now a man set free but suffering a serious attack of self-disgust, and contemplating a world and a future with which he could discern no possible connection.

As a way of marking time I visited the Isle of Man, and communicated my depression to my family. Then, learning that my old ship, labouring along in my needlessly rapid wake, had finally reached Devonport, I took slow trains to Plymouth and collected my belongings, including the violin which, since I last saw it, had been fatally damaged, possibly in a storm, possibly in some end-of-term romp.

My old comrades were charged with taking the ship back to America. It appeared that the Americans were celebrating the end of the war by ordering the destruction of military moveables like aircraft, jeeps, and trucks (anxious, it was said, to sustain demand rather than create a slump in the automobile factories). Vast numbers of planes and trucks and other vehicles were dumped into the Pacific. Drivers would take their vehicles down wooden piers and jump out just as the trucks or jeeps toppled over into deep water. But the owners wanted their carrier back, presumably to have the pleasure of breaking it up themselves. Of course there might have been difficulties about scuttling it, and then again they may have been thinking of its scrap value. It could be converted into new cars and tractors, but in that case why didn't they load it with planes and trucks and jeeps, which could also have been recycled?

Such speculations were possible only to one whose life was still to a considerable extent stuck in the past, like Milton's lion at the creation, pawing to get free its hinder parts. I found myself wishing to go back with the old ship (actually she lived altogether for only a little over three years, and spent one of those grievously wounded in dry dock, a huge hole in her bottom) and see her solemnly into the breaker's yard. There might be a touching little ceremony, and that I would have enjoyed. But I was no longer qualified, once again had no uniform, and couldn't very well attend the obsequies in my pinstripe suit; so after a rather sombre drunken weekend, I took my leave of her, pausing for a last look at her crest, which I had designed and for which I provided the motto: *Debellare superbos*, it read, to the great satisfaction of its original, perfectly sane captain. He had assumed, when I offered a translation, that he had been chanced upon a young man both warlike and classically trained. He had of course been unable to foresee that his ship, as well as the arrogant enemy, would get debelled.

THE REST OF LIFE did turn out to be literature, though it also consisted of seeking work, getting it, and eventually giving it up. But at this stage I had no idea whatever of how to go about finding work, and was indeed quite good at ensuring that I did not get it. I applied for a job at the Royal Naval College and even went to be interviewed at splendid Greenwich, but was very properly turned down. The navy was where I'd spent my years between twenty and twenty-six, without at all wanting to, and instead of being glad to be out of it, I was hankering after it, afraid to try anything else. I had also recognised and was ready haplessly to indulge my habit of getting into milieux where I couldn't expect to find myself at ease, possibly because in those peace-shocked days I couldn't imagine being at ease anywhere. It was quite out of the question that I should ever be easy at Greenwich. It was already obvious that wartime personnel wouldn't really do in peacetime, and it is plain enough that I could not have worked there without getting into trouble with the navy and also with myself. I knew this well enough at the time, but also felt that whatever I found myself doing would be pretty disagreeable and that I should do it badly, so why not this? Australian jobs were being advertised and I applied, seeking the relative comfort of a known and recent past, but I wasn't wanted and was quite glad of it. My fighter-direction officer friend, unable to resume his medical studies because he had allowed himself to get too old, devised a scheme for importing canned Australian asparagus into starving England, but we had no capital, and anyway, he soon found his enterprise ruled out by the impenetrable government import restrictions of those exhausted days.

So the only way to sustain life was to take up a postgraduate scholarship I'd acquired at Liverpool in 1940. It was an unhappy expedient. I was by now too grand to enjoy being *in statu pupillari* and the money was barely enough to survive on. The immediate future was certain to be, like those deprived days in Algiers, *sans alcool*, but this time truly so, and without very much of anything else I had learned to regard as agreeable. I took on a dreary piece of research and sadly idled away the dark days, sometimes by playing bridge from morning to night. Obsessed, I'd wake in the morning already calculating the chances of finding a four after breakfast. I am bad at giving things up, so I take a special pride in having decided, in 1947, to give up bridge completely. I have never played it since.

In those times, however, it was a way of getting placidly and warmly through some hours of one's life. It was a comfort. The rest of the population—but it would just have to look after itself—was also having to exist on rations that had become meaner since the end of the war; even bread was rationed now, and in the atrocious winter of 1946–47 there was a fuel shortage, so that we were without electric light all day and were allowed no heat till nightfall, and very little then. Again, this was the general condition, but I took it personally, sitting in my small room in my dyed battledress and duffle coat, staring at the cold radiator, preoccupied with my own discontents, or calling on my tutor in my pinstripe suit. Even if you had a pocketful of money and a full clothes ration book, there was nothing in the shops to be bought.

Sure that I would die before long—such a pity to have

survived the war and then succumbed to a mortal boredom—
I paid little attention to most of the people around me, let alone
to any evidence that many of them were actually enjoying life.
Those were the days when, in the perhaps fallacious memories
of some authors, good folk took their pleasure in contented
poverty, like the girls of slender means in Muriel Spark's novel.
But even for them it could not last, for avarice and other sins
for which they had a natural propensity, not to speak of such
northeasters as a leftover German bomb, appropriately ended
their peace, to which they were in any case not really entitled.
The sadness of all this is compensated, in Mrs. Spark's story,
by an impressive religious allegory. I did not know the pleasure
or the peace, and hardly bothered to accuse myself of the sins;
nothing of higher-level significance could possibly have been
inferred from my dull days over dull books, my dull thoughts,
my sadness at the very idea of myself.

One conviction survived in the gloom and in the teeth of
the evidence: that I was to be some sort of a writer. Already
in my later twenties, I might have given some thought, and
possibly did, to the consideration that I was leaving it a bit
late, that I had nothing to support this admittedly lukewarm
ambition except a couple of plays, some poems, and a long
story. I suppose I deluded myself with some excuse for my
infertility, those barren years at sea, but of course I was en-
viously aware that others had written well in barracks, hospitals, places even less friendly to the business of writing than
mine had usually been; and there they were in *Penguin New
Writing* and in other journals, and even publishing books, like
Roy Fuller, or dying and leaving behind accomplished poems,
like Sydney Keyes and Keith Douglas, when the best I could
manage was *New Statesman* weekend competitions. I rather
admired, or perhaps just felt I should rather admire, though
incapable of emulating, the apocalyptic verses so profusely published in *Poetry London*, which was edited by the handsome

and unreliable Tambimuttu, its covers brilliantly adorned by Henry Moore's lyrebirds. I subscribed but received not a single copy. Even in that I failed.

As to my plays—I am still amazed that, having had them beautifully typed up, I had the nerve to send them to the Birmingham Rep, and even more amazed that Barry Jackson, an important, busy man, should have taken the trouble to write me quite a long letter pointing out what was wrong with them—roughly that since they were palpably the work of somebody who evidently knew nothing about the theatre, they would be impossible to stage; and further, that even if they had not been so hopeless in that respect, they were irritatingly hazy about what they were meant to be doing and saying. So much for the theatre.

My long story went to Olaf Stapledon, the godfather of science fiction. He wasn't my choice, and I was aware, without disrespect, that he could hardly have been a worse one. There was a rather enlightened scheme whereby ex-servicemen who aspired to be writers could be put in touch with some established figure who would criticise their work and hint whether it was worth going on with it. Stapledon was kind, but he loathed my story, which was as unlike his sort of thing, which I rather loathed in return, as might be imagined. He did his best for me, inviting me to lunch at his club and patiently discussing my work. Suddenly he asked me to show him my hands. I spread them out. "Aha!" he said. "It's obvious you do nothing with your hands—no digging, no carpentry, nothing manual at all!" This was clearly what he had expected. He disapproved of, or could not believe in, writers who could not use their hands.

Perhaps he was right. I have always envied people who know how to do practical things, but have never brought myself to try. I have often been mocked for my assumption that the way to find out how to do things is to find the relevant book on the subject, as if unaware that not all knowledge can be had from books. That you can learn how to do things by doing them has somehow always seemed mysterious to me. Many years later, in a review of William Golding's novel *The Spire*, I wondered where he had gone and what he had read to find out so much detail about medieval cathedral building. I even looked up some of the possible books myself. Golding wrote to me as follows:

You said in your article that you'd like to know where I got all that stuff on medieval building methods. The answer—only for God's sake keep it to yourself—is that I didn't get it anywhere. I invented it by thinking what it must have been like. For all I know to the contrary they had bulldozers and forklifts: but if they *didn't*, then they must have used the most elementary methods which are as easy (because limited) to imagine as a neanderthal foodgathering existence. The only research I did was one hour in Salisbury library with the foundation charter of the cathedral. The rest is sheer sleight of mind . . .

What Golding failed to mention was that he was always at home with the idea of making things, and of making things work (boats, for instance), and that was why he could do the sort of thinking required. If the question is, How did they build cathedrals? some will rush off to a library, others will go to Salisbury or somewhere like that, stand in the crossing, and look up, or remain outside and ask themselves how the spire came to be bent. Then they go to work. I should stand in those places and, absolutely none the wiser, head for the nearest library. You have to have the sort of mind that understands the principles.

Another thing comes to mind as typical of Golding: he once asked me whether I was keeping up my Greek. When I admitted I wasn't, he asked, "But what will you do when you retire if you can't read Homer?" Greek was basic know-how. Having it, you could see how Homer worked, and also Achilles. That's where I fall down.

It is probably a consequence of this incapacity that my attempts at novel writing have been so pathetic. I don't really know how things are done. Iris Murdoch enjoys, or used to enjoy, getting huge bells out of lakes and cars out of ditches, and to be able to do that in persuasive detail must be a great source of confidence when it comes to making characters work. It used to be said that to write, epic poets should have encyclopaedic knowledge, so it must be good also for their descendants, the novelists, at least to be able to surmise how very complicated things are done. Or even simple ones. I recall that in the days when some of us were wild about the newly published *Doctor Zhivago*, that accomplished novelist P. H. Newby, who does know how things work, refused to share my enthusiasm, describing Pasternak with genial contempt as the kind of novelist who didn't know how to get a character through a door. This criticism may be unfair to Pasternak, but after all, he had, as Aufidius says of Coriolanus, "a merit/To choke it in the utterance"—virtues enough to allow most of us to stifle our criticisms of such technical limitations. I had no such merit; my fiction, my theatre were marked by a failure to persuade the characters to do anything, but also to say anything of much interest. It was also emerging that my poetry wasn't up to much, so there was nothing left for me except to become a critic, preferably with a paying job in a university.

THAT WAS HOW I belatedly entered adult life at around twenty-six. As a liminal performance it was pretty poor, since in a sense I at once stepped back from the threshold and became a student again. That wasn't all, for before long I got married. It occurs to me that this is the point where, if I were Rousseau, or perhaps even some quite ordinary autobiographer, I should say something about that. But I don't intend to. I will say here only that I was twice married. I cannot say much more on this point about the forty years in which I shared my bed with one woman or the other, because I am in absolutely no sense doing so as I write. They were in their entirely different ways close friends, and the first of them, the correct beauty, the censor, the terrified, gave me the great gift of children. I believe that the second, the wild one, and I were, in our good times, *copains*, but for reasons that no longer exist we later weren't. It is quite useless for me to speak of the woe that is in marriage, or the delight either, since they are not here, I cannot summon them. This is not the place to come for information on marriage. I am an old man and sleep diagonally, as I continually remind myself, sleep comfortably, in my large bed, in which I cannot even imagine and probably could not easily bear the protracted presence of another. I salute my wives, but now only as occasional visitants to my dreams, they who by some accident of fortune entered, and remained for four decades, in what is and, as I now clearly see, always should have been, a solitary or at any rate a non-conjugal existence.

Of course it did not always seem so. But enough of that: I return alone to this page, anxious about very little, sad to extremity, aimlessly dissolute. I recognise a version of myself in that character who lived so uselessly, stupidly, self-destructively, through the war years. That is to say, he has for some reason held on to his ticket, he is around now, he can be certified as me. Certainly a quite different version of him could be offered, at least as true, at least as false, but equally capable of presence. Memory, as I remarked, cannot operate without the support of fantasy. Without its maieutic attentions nothing can be delivered, not even convincing lies. When in working order it can give to the moments it selects arbitrary and baffling contours a little resembling those of a dream, in which the details prove on analysis to have mutual relevance, though they have only a strained relation to any facts.

This very morning I woke out of a dream of disgrace: I had been giving a series of readings of something I'd written, aware that it was not good, though the audience, seated round at a long table, seemed patient. Then the late Graham Hough, a friend but an unsparing critic, began to chatter rudely to his neighbour. He grew louder and more offensive, and I had to ask him to be quiet, whereupon he petulantly denounced me and all my works and walked out. When I looked up, most of my audience had silently followed him, and only two of the twenty or so were left. I went to my office and found a black cat on my chair.

Now, I could assemble some "day's residues": I had been reading in a Sunday paper of Graham's rude response, long ago, to a lecture of George Steiner's, and this had reminded me (if that's the word) that despite our wholly amiable relationship, he had always enjoyed making disparaging remarks about books of mine. And it seemed that he had two good reasons for being rude to me. The first was that he had spent more than three years in a Japanese prison camp and I hadn't. The second was that I stayed away from his funeral. The audience, friendly but reserved, had no such telling grievances, but it was a version of a graduate class I had recently taught at Yale, always feeling that I couldn't quite make out what they would have liked to have from me, that I was performing inadequately and letting them down, though they were far too polite to give any sign that they thought so too. And behind that memory was another, of my inveterate conviction that I was far from being a good teacher, not an easy thought to have constantly in your mind when what you have principally done to earn a living has been to teach, or profess to. When I mention this particular shame to close friends, they say how absurd, what about So-and-so, and remind me of the quite long list of my successful pupils, professors all over the place from California to Jerusalem, even some real writers, one or two quite famous. But this is not consoling; all these people would very likely have still "done well" if they had never set eyes on me.

Back in my office there is the cat. On the previous night a television programme about superstition had reminded me that encounters with black cats are considered unlucky in Italy but lucky in England. I think they were lucky in the Isle of Man but can't be quite sure. Hence my retreat to the office, where in good time I should think of some cause to be brave or even cheerful, at least to shrug off my recent disgrace; but even that refuge contained a symbol of ambiguous fortune.

This summer I stayed in southern Tuscany with an Italian friend, a candid, affectionate woman, catlike only in curling up, purring, and falling gracefully asleep. We were out very late one night, having driven a long way to attend an opera about a bird, by a composer called Dove—but she did not menace author or work—and got back at three in the morning. That day she had guests at lunch, and after the meal fell asleep, took a catnap, slumping forward on, as it were, her paws. I continued to engage her guests in polite talk, until it was obvious that she wasn't going to stir, and then, with some embarrassment, they left. Later they telephoned to say they had left behind a camera and a pair of sunglasses and hadn't time to come back and get them. I offered to bring them to London. The reason why they had been forgotten was that they were lying under my sleeping hostess. She had deprived these aliens of protection from the fierce Tuscan light, and of the power to use that light to record her territory. Other details, remembered and invented or both, could be added to any account of this incident, so that the entire episode, when adorned with material that might in the ordinary way seem tedious, with portraits of the persons concerned in the tiny drama, not least with associations developed even as one wrote it all down, would look more like a dream, and have the kinds of potential meanings we seek in dreams.

So, in a limited way, it is with autobiography. The percentage of truth we leave out may after all show through somewhere, even if we fake the record. The amount of faking we are allowed is debatable: not as much as Nabokov, perhaps—he who without apology preferred good writing to fact—but faking all the same, though in our faking there must be something it would only be slightly absurd to call the truth. But it is really a question of the weather, the private weather, unpredictable as dreams yet recognisable as a climate, that the autobiographer must describe.

IV

Incomplete

that inward eye
Which is the bliss of solitude . . .

—WILLIAM WORDSWORTH

To be alone is not necessarily a blissful condition. The inward eye can be overworked, though except occasionally at weekends solitude now suits me well enough. Unfortunately I hadn't discovered that in 1946. Living in devastated Liverpool, in one cold room, with no money to buy a drink, nothing to wear but my pinstripe suit, applying myself dispiritedly to a task in which I took no pleasure, I got such comfort as he could provide from Peter Ure, the sombre friend of whom I have spoken and in that bleak time virtually my whole acquaintance.

I feel ungrateful as I say it, but I would have settled for companions more irresponsible, more empty-headed, more like the ones I had just said goodbye to. Though habitually disconsolate, Ure returned to normal life with a better past and a more promising future than mine. He should have been, on any dispassionate view, in much better shape than I was. He, and not I, had known what it meant to be truly useful. And —a matter for awed envy—he had a book in the press. But he was unhappy all the same, homesick for the Greek landscape and language, as well as for his own usefulness in both. Ready as always to call on a poet to do his thinking and feeling for him, he described his condition with a quotation from Rilke: "So badly does one live because one always comes incomplete into the present, inept and scatterbrained." As a characterisation of the speaker rather than of me this was badly chosen; none of the epithets Rilke used could reasonably be applied to him. All the same, it would be plausible if unsubtle to call him depressed.

He risked dramatising his low spirits by providing them with almost too apt a setting. He found himself a rundown flat in which we would sit drinking coffee, the only beverage he felt he could afford, and conducting conversations of low tone among its remarkable furnishings—crazy leather armchairs with the springs sticking up from the seats at prohibitive angles, unbearable brown wallpaper and skirtings. One freezing night he came to dinner at the hall where I lived, and was struck down, as were all the other diners, by the diarrhoea which in those days quite often followed a communal meal. His bitter account of his sufferings in the night somehow made them seem more distinguished than one's own, as no doubt Rilke's would.

There was something dauntingly impressive about his large gloomy voice and his complicated sentences, though occasionally they seemed suddenly quite hilarious and reminded me of the faint and almost improper possibility that there remained in the world things to giggle at. He had saved some money from his UNRRA days but lived even more frugally than I had to; he found excuses for his meannesses, well knowing them to be implausible. I remember meeting his train when he arrived, bearing everything he owned, at Newcastle in 1947. A porter struggled over the long bridge across the lines with an overloaded handcart and hailed him a taxi, for which service the man was tipped with a threepenny bit, worth a fraction more than the modern decimal penny, though it's fair to say that in those days it might buy you a cup of tea at an all-night coffee stall.

He lived below his income in other ways, too. Already a well-equipped scholar and soon to be recognised as such, he was always aware that somehow he was putting forth less power than he knew he had. So he had already failed. "Time's eunuch," he would call himself. Why, suffering a melancholy that needed the relief, the animation of a kind of society I could not provide, he shrank as he did from the pleasant, untaxing, affectionate, even admiring company that was available I couldn't understand. Once, he invited me and some other people to dinner but found when the company was assembled that he couldn't face the duties of host and, asking me to take them over, withdrew. I admit that he provided me with some solace in the desperate days, but not as much as I needed.

Eventually his life settled, as mine never really could, into what seemed habitual and to him tolerable patterns, from which he would only occasionally break free. He formed a taste for driving long distances in fast cars. In 1966 he visited me and my family when we were living in Gloucestershire. He accepted lunch but refused an invitation to stay over, because he wished, he said, to push on into the southwest. It was a soaked West Country day. What would he do when he got to Dorchester? Go to the cinema, he supposed. He liked the company and the children, but not for long. He was often ill, so that his not being quite well seemed almost a matter of course, an understandable hypochondria, another way of being different and alone; but as usual he was saying less than he meant when he said he wasn't well, and so he died.

Having earlier hinted that this man almost inadvertently educated me as an undergraduate, I have now had to reintroduce him into my story as a principal postwar memory—

as a means of suggesting the atmosphere of those heavy times. Another phase of our relationship was very different, began when we were simultaneously appointed to lectureships at Newcastle. University life, at any rate in the redbricks, was more strenuous then than it would ever be again; the students were mostly ex-servicemen, veterans in their late twenties, eager to get their lives restarted, some with wives and children to think about. Their demands were fierce. Ure worked without haste and without rest. I stumbled emulously after him. But our closest association was about to end. He remained in Newcastle, somewhat out of the range (he mildly complained) of metropolitan editors and publishers and the BBC, whose acquaintance I was making, though he did some reviewing and some broadcasting as well as writing several books, all respectfully though not ecstatically received.

It is natural enough but also slightly indecent to wish he had known not only more fame (as he deserved) but more ordinary happiness, a few lovers, a few holidays from a conscience and a consciousness much too exacting. Fame he did want, but only the kind that comes from the approval of the just, those he would refer to without embarrassment, thinking of Spender's poem, as the truly great. He might later have wondered whether there were any such judges around. He became a serious student of Stoicism, a discipline prophylactic against vulgar disappointments. He has been dead twenty-five years and I continue to admire him and even, in some privileged moments, feel his presence half admiring, half deploring whatever I am trying to do at the time. I still have difficulty in imagining anybody so different from myself who might nevertheless find something in me to like, even to envy.

IN THE DARKNESS of 1946 I came to know a far less admirable yet still prodigiously endowed figure who, in his way, played an equally decisive part in my life. That he should

have done so was at the outset very improbable, but existential
.catastrophes must always be sudden. This man, D. J. Gordon,
was vain and ambitious; he had his deserved successes, but his
hopes of more general fame burned out years before his death
at sixty-two. In the selfish way of autobiographers I speak of
him here only in order to say something relevant about myself.

Sometime in 1946 I found myself sitting in Gordon's
Liverpool study correcting the proofs of his long and extremely
learned article on Ben Jonson's masque *Hymenaei*. My original
research supervisor had noticed that my interests, such as they
were, differed from his own, in their direction and also, possibly, in their seriousness. I was supposed to be editing Abra-
ham Cowley, whom I regarded as on the whole tedious, though
I was curious about the very learned notes he wrote for his
unfinished epic the *Davideis*. This sort of thing also amused
Gordon, and he correctly believed that one of the most effective
ways to learn the trade—it had the additional advantage of
saving him a lot of bother—was to be involved in one's teacher's
own work. So I was handed these proofs and asked to check
all the references.

Gordon was of all the men I have known the one most
excited by scholarly problems; you could see this excitement
in the movements of his body and hear it in his strange, com-
bative, self-assertive voice; and when the moment came to
reveal the solutions in public, he did so in an appropriately
dramatic way. The *Hymenaei* piece happened to be one of his
best and most characteristic achievements and was later,
though hardly at the time, regarded as a work of real importance, almost a new start on the subject of Renaissance my-
thography and courtly entertainment. Jonson was learned, but
like other learned authors of the time felt no shame about
copying erudite information from obscure compilations, man-
uals, a whole library of forgotten sixteenth-century reference
books. (Cowley, I discovered, though a lesser figure, was another such; perhaps all learned men, especially learned poets,

were and possibly still are such.) Gordon accumulated a large collection of these works, tracing the original information they provided in the text and notes of Jonson's masque, and setting the whole thing in the context of the Stuart court, where masques, with elaborate costumes and machinery by Inigo Jones, reached an extraordinary level of magnificence. Performed once only, they were, so to speak, antiquarian and magical potlatches; but they were also of considerable political significance, not only because they were impressively expensive but because they fostered and flattered the dangerously absolutist tendencies of the dynasty.

It was not Gordon's usual way to behave like most other scholars and simply write up his results for publication. Rather, he would prepare a lecture on the chosen topic and ensure that its preparation, and especially the occasion of its delivery, should be appropriately spectacular. He looked forward to these occasions as opportunities to give an unforgettable performance in an impossible blaze of academic light. He was practically unique in thinking the academic profession as, in some ideal manifestation, akin to the theatrical. "I am by nature a *régisseur*," he would claim. From his gait on entry to his last word, all was theatre. I borrow his friend Ian Fletcher's description of the performance:

The audience was stunned: the idiosyncrasies were in full flower— that provocative swing of the body first to the left, then to the right; the uncanny cadences. At one point the audience heard: "I am still waiting for someone to tell me about" [a favourite locution] whatever or whomever it was, followed by a pause while his eye flicked over the room as much as to say, "and I am most unlikely to find that person here."

He would begin by describing the occasion of the masque or entertainment, or the startling character, unaccountably neglected by all previous commentators, of some work of art—

for example, the Rubens ceiling in Inigo Jones's Banqueting House at Whitehall, where many of the great masques were performed. He was fascinated by the complexity of the Rubens allegory and laboured long to explain its programme. The ceiling panels had been taken down during the war, and he had been able to examine them, in company with his mentor Fritz Saxl, director of the Warburg Institute—dedicated to the study of the classical tradition, the *nachleben* of antiquity— before they were restored to the ceiling. Later he always maintained, correctly or not I don't know, that one of the panels had been put back wrongly.

The opening passage of the lecture would contain some thrilling disclosure that opened up a new vista on history, some moment in the narrative that would turn out to be critical: Rubens leaves London! The Earl of Arundel commissions a curious portrait of his wife! As a Scot with ambitions in the south, Gordon had a special interest in the Scottish king James VI of Scotland and I of England, and he liked to recall that at the time when that king, to the annoyance of his new subjects, was flooding England with Scotsmen, he had rewarded a scholar named Gordon for writing a French panegyric on his accession by making him Dean of Salisbury; unfortunately this was a *John* Gordon.

The lecture would require many slides, always projected on two screens, which was the usual Warburg Institute way of establishing, by a sort of historical stereoscopy, startling new perspectives on art history. The mannerisms, the strange, hootingly genteel voice, had the power, if not to astound the audience, as Fletcher put it, certainly to induce in them a rather wild mood, a mood of mingled excitement, admiration, hilarity, and derision such as I have never encountered elsewhere. The gesticulations, the rehearsed pauses, the refined sneer or downward glance of contempt that accompanied allusions to other workers in the field, the little *moues* of self-satisfaction, all these combined to make his lecture as good as a play; not a mere farce, because he was usually saying something new and interesting and, after all, saying it memorably.

Preparations for such performances, or even for the subsequent publication of the paper, would be long, slow, and intense, requiring the collaboration of many minions. After he became professor at Reading (where he summoned me in 1950), he had more of these to call on. I remember how, in 1952, the entire resources of the small department (except perhaps those of John Wain, whose habit it was to watch sardonically from the touchline) were mobilised to assist his writing of a paper on Chapman's continuation of Marlowe's *Hero and Leander*. It had been child's play to solve the allegorical meaning of the nymph Teras and explain the metamorphosis of Hero and Leander into thistlewarps, but the iconography of Ceremony was proving much more difficult to elucidate. It occupied us all for weeks.

I had long before—I won't say fallen under the spell, for I was always fully conscious of a certain absurdity in such proceedings—I had been delighted to learn that scholarship of the kind the world at large might well think dull and without importance could be carried on with such panache. It did something to reconcile me to the manner of life I had somehow dropped into. I didn't deceive myself into supposing I could ever do the same sort of work with the same sort of dedication, but those early days, the *Hymenaei* days, showed me that there could be virtuosity and passion in scholarship, and whatever he chose to talk about, whether Jonson, Beardsley, or Henry James, Gordon's work had those qualities. These gifts, rather rare in the erudite, even rarer in run-of-the-mill scholars, I didn't seriously aspire to, but there were also methods to be learned, and demands on imaginative resources, and these, I liked to think, might be more attainable and more capable of satisfaction.

When I first met him, Gordon was still not much over
thirty, but his persona as *scozzese italianato*—the expression is
Luigi Meneghello's and is adapted from the saying *Inglese
italianato, diavolo incarnato*—was well established. Less the
dandy than he later became (there were few dandies in 1946,
and at this time he had very little money), he was still dis-
tinctively dressed. Even in the battered tweed overcoat, protection against that dreadful winter, he seemed very exotic
amid the dirt and undisturbed bomb craters of Liverpool. His
black hair, worn very long for those days, his extraordinary
laugh, always tinged with scorn, above all that odd hooting
way of speaking, his habit of pronouncing words on the intake
of the breath, which I have never met with elsewhere—all this
marked him off. Neither the laugh nor the manner of speaking
was suitable for ordinary social usage. Such habits are, I think,
signs of deep solitariness. For all its trace of Edinburgh re-
finement (like that of the ladies Muriel Spark remembers from
her youth as always saying "Niverthe*lace*") that accent was
private and deeply unsociable. Students hearing him for the
first time couldn't understand what he was saying. For all the
magnificence of his public performances he was alone and
lonely. Ian Fletcher remarked that he was never *in place*, always
restive, strange, "with his bird face, nose perhaps predatory,
the trapped brown eyes and the eerie tune of the voice." That
tune partly derived from his fluent but frequently surprising
Italian, according to Meneghello blemished by astonishing ar-
chaisms: *Questo lurido paese,* he would hoot, ignoring the fact
that *lurido* in modern Italian means filthy or squalid, not pale
and wan.

He spent a year in Florence before the war and came to
know the poet Eugenio Montale, author of the great late poems
addressed to his wife "Mosca." When Gordon first called on
the poet, bearing an armful of flowers, Montale opened the
door and called out to his wife, "*Mosca, c'é un giovanetto con*

dei fiori!, Here's a young fellow with flowers!"—a glimpse of
Gordon for once at least not out of place.

It is said by people closer to him than I that the year in
Florence was sad, dark, and disastrous; yet Italy remained
almost the chief interest of his life. His single most passionate
concern was with Palladio's Teatro Olimpico at Vicenza, on
which he planned to write an exhaustive study. He also
dreamed of mounting in that astonishing theatre a performance
of *Coriolanus*, for the sake of the *frisson* to be got from this
contamination of two violently discrepant Renaissance con-
ceptions of the antique. Like most of his plans, and largely for
the same reason, this one never came close to fulfilment. But
he was elected to the academy at Vicenza, and his death was
more thoroughly lamented in the local newspaper and in the
proceedings of the local academy there than anywhere at home.
That academy meant more to him than Cambridge, where he
did his early research; his true bases were in fact not modern
universities but such autonomous and specialised institutions
as an Italian Renaissance academy and a German centre of
research, the Warburg Institute.

He had the manners as well as the dress and vocal affec-
tations that appear to be characteristic of British art historians,
so it is almost impossible to imagine him in the army, but he
did serve about eighteen months before he was discharged as
unfit; whatever the matter was, it left him with some minor
cardiac infirmity. He slept every afternoon and read detective
stories in the night. From the army he went to his lectureship
at Liverpool, where he remained till 1946, the year in which
our paths crossed.

The purity and scope of his scholarly ambition, his arrogant and explicit contempt for hacks, second-raters, and rivals were such that he was not greatly loved; sometimes his
bizarre manners deserved a necessarily secret compassion, for
his circumstances were not those in which a repressed homo-

sexual could easily be happy. Later in life he preferred to work
with a collaborator, and his pupil John Stokes says there was
in this choice "an element of desperation, an excuse to get in
touch with people; but the idea of the shared enterprise probably stemmed from the personal legend of Saxl and the Warburg." Certainly his grief at the deaths of Fritz Saxl and his
successor, Gertrud Bing, was extraordinarily intense. He was
so lonely that he was glad to have somebody like me, who was
always willing to hear him talk, to use his remarkable library,
and now and again to go with him to the movies. He was keen
on doing this at least once a week, though contemptuous of
most films—I remember his sneering at the pretentiousness of
The Third Man.

At Reading in 1946 he at once and as usual incurred
grudging admiration and amused hostility. Before long he succeeded to the chair of English. At the beginning of 1950 I
joined his small department, where the sceptical John Wain
was something of a nuisance to him, though a source of continuous amusement to me. After a hiatus of three years I was
able to resume the practice of learning from Gordon. As far
as I ever became a serious scholar, it was his doing. He taught
not by precept but by example; that was why I had found
myself sitting there with the *Hymenaei* proofs and a vast pile
of Latin and Italian books.

He had a passion for distinguished visitors and would
prepare for them at great personal expense, both financial and
emotional. When Mario Praz came, I drank too much at dinner
and on the way home fell heavily off my bike; although Praz
had shown me nothing but kindness, this accident was attributed to his famous *malòcchio.* The most absurd of these occasions was the visit of E. M. Forster somewhere around 1953.
It was February and a day of heavy snow. The car bringing
Forster from Cambridge was hours late, Gordon was in an
agonising fuss, and an audience of undergraduates had its pa-

tience further tried by John Wain, who singled out the most
slovenly of them and asked whether they thought it right to
dress like tramps when about to meet a great writer. Forster
was in his seventies and after such a winter journey could be
presumed to be weary, but it did not occur to Gordon, at last
on his favourite spot, gesticulating before a large and attentive
audience, to curtail his elaborate introduction. Finally Forster
spoke in his easy ambling style about his visits to India, but
he had just got to the point of saying, "A great deal has been
written about my book *A Passage to India*, and I don't think
I understand it all, so I'll take this opportunity to tell you what
I think about it," when Gordon rose, edged the great man
aside, and announced that we should have to stop there, since
the vice-chancellor was expecting the speaker to tea. Though
often outrageous, he wasn't often as silly as that, and I thought
of the Indian magistrate Mr. Das, who presides over the trial
of Aziz in *A Passage to India* and brings the proceedings to
an end, though "nearly dead with the strain." I felt sorry for
Forster that day. After dinner he was told to sit at one end of
a sofa while admirers, one by one, were led up to him and
allowed to share the sofa for five minutes or so apiece, absorbing
his wisdom. This was apparently an old English custom, re-
pellent and now, I think, obsolete. Gordon appeared to be
under the impression that the day had been a great success.

His choice of Jonson's masques, and the aristocratic ba-
roque theatre more generally, as his principal interests, was,
very likely, motivated not only by his taste for recondite and
difficult scholarship but by the unusually intimate connection
between these topics and arbitrary and supreme political authority, something he would have liked to have had himself.
The Stuart courts combined sumptuary display with learned
texts in support of absolute monarchy. Here, as in the festivals
of the emperor Charles V, employer of Titian and Ariosto,
were poet-scholars, musicians, painters, and architects in the

service of a sort of sublime propaganda. As Gordon said of the Banqueting House, it was not only a place for banquets and masques but the principal room of state: "The decoration of such a room was a public and political act . . . This was a world where the 'real' and the 'historical' could cohabit with the feigned, where the hard political programme could, without distortion, undergo translation into symbol." Such symbols, such mythologies of royal power could not survive the moment in 1649 when Charles stepped out of that very Banqueting House onto the scaffold in Whitehall. After that, the ceiling became, "as an act of state, irrelevant." Even his later passion for the 1890s couldn't alter the fact that after January 1649 the world became altogether less satisfactory to Gordon.

There was here a genuine nostalgia for a lost world. The masques themselves, each destroyed after a single performance, were emblems of lost magnificence; so was the image of Charles I sitting in his cabinet with seven Titians on its walls, pictures soon to be sold by Cromwell. The world outside encroached crudely, disastrously, on this magical realm, the spirit of which might be restored, if only rather dimly, by great scholarship. To provide that was to join in some sense the greatness of which he, at that time almost alone, had learned to speak with assurance. This achievement justified what others might regard as vanity or pretension. He conducted himself always according to his own estimate of his importance, without regard for the world's opinion.

I think of my own time in his department, roughly the 1950s, and especially the earlier years of the decade, as, in a slightly crazy way, the most valuable I have spent in any job. The university, in the days before the expansion of the 1960s, which took it into its present park setting, was still very small, and housed, mostly, in pleasant but decaying buildings. Surveyors had limited classes in some of the rooms to a maximum of five persons; they recommended that one should head for the chimney if the floor showed signs of collapse. A pleasant common room looked out onto a lawn dominated by a great tulip tree, and it was possible to know many colleagues in other faculties, a benefit that has almost disappeared from the modern university. The formidable Warburgians were frequent visitors, including Ernst Gombrich and even, on occasion, representatives of the American branch of the firm, Rudolf Wittkower and Erwin Panofsky. And there were distinguished local scholars ready for conversation. Perhaps it wouldn't be impossible to point to equally impressive groups in some modern common or combination rooms, but it might be harder to represent them as normally in easy, serious talk.

However, it was in the tiny English Department, managed with a strange blend of caprice and contempt, that my education continued most vigorously to flourish. All concerned are now dead; the latest to go was John Wain, the only other lecturer in literature. Wain was in his mid-twenties, four years my junior, and had recently arrived from Oxford, where his career had contained every conceivable recognition except, for mysterious reasons, a fellowship. He was abnormally quick-witted and far from mealy-mouthed; he used his wits to needle Gordon, who early sensed in him a difficult rival. Wain cultivated a manner of life antithetical to his boss's, covering his naturally beautiful manners with a veneer of proletarian, beer-drinking coarseness. He was harsh, irreverent, and rode a motor scooter, which he called, inaccurately I think, his hot rod. He had friends who would have thought Gordon a figure of fun; one of them was Kingsley Amis, whose celebrated powers of mimicry he almost matched, not least when he used them to emphasise Gordon's peculiarities of voice and manner. The dashing, iconoclastic Al Alvarez, still an Oxford undergraduate and founder of the Oxford Critical Society, kept in close touch; he would arrive at high speed in his green sports car to consult Wain about the current state and prospects of poetry. The one person Wain almost naïvely and wholeheartedly admired was Philip Larkin, whom he had known as an undergraduate at Oxford. Forty years on, it may seem strange that Wain had to dash around bullying people to subscribe to *The Less Deceived*.

More remarkably, he had close friends much older than he: C. S. Lewis; Dan Davin, story writer and publisher of the Oxford University Press; and others who shared his intimate knowledge of Oxford pubs. They liked him because he was funny, but also because he understood scholarship. His challenge to Gordon consisted in his being in his own totally different way a man of learning and imagination. Gordon didn't know how to meet it, because it wasn't according to the conventions as he interpreted them. It was hard to accommodate Wain's candour and intelligence to the quite different rules of the game imposed by Gordon's own fantasies. You might say it was as if some turbulent and articulate Leveller had broken into the Banqueting House. There was no way of keeping Wain down; for one thing, he was a teacher of exceptional powers, which justified almost any disruptive behaviour. So he raged like the hectic in the departmental blood, a fever and an enchantment. Gordon's response was a reluctant mixture of admiration and resignation, with only an occasional bout of irritation and resentment.

Wain, rapidly gaining ground in a larger world, didn't stay long. In 1950 there appeared, as the last item in the last issue of John Lehmann's *Penguin New Writing*, his celebrated essay on the poetry of William Empson, a founding document of what was later called "the Movement." He had also written a book about Arnold Bennett, his predecessor as a Potteries author, and was entangled in hopeless negotiations with a ghostly South American publisher; parts of the book turned up in his collection *Preliminary Essays*. Shady publishers recur in the careers of Larkin and Amis, and perhaps in those of other young persons dying to get into print. The first poetry

collections of Wain and Amis were published by the Fine Arts
Department of Reading University, printed, along with a number of less celebrated debuts, by the typographer William
McCance on a handpress, in editions of a hundred or so. But
soon publication was no longer a problem. Wain took over
from John Lehmann the Third Programme magazine, *New
Soundings*, at a time when that programme was very influential. Soon he wrote and published *Hurry On Down*, and
advised us all to write novels, it was so easy and so profitable.
The success of that book took him out of the academy, and he
did not return until, twenty or so years later, he was elected
Professor of Poetry at Oxford.

Gordon cannot have been sorry to see him go, though the
rest of us were. One source of civilized hilarity remained to
us—Ian Calder, a dazzlingly odd, encyclopaedic young man,
a scholar of the kind both Wain and Gordon could admire. He
was only loosely attached to us, his home being the Warburg
Institute. He was probably the greatest living authority on the
Elizabethan mage John Dee, whose library he was studying.
Calder and his family were thought to have provided the in-
spiration for some of the most shocking of the early stories of
his friend Angus Wilson, who would occasionally come to
Reading and observe, aghast, some of Ian's more outlandish
schemes and activities. Calder was endlessly bright, amiable,
unpredictable, and informative. Having him around was a
great help, though it was disconcerting to discover so often
that you didn't really know something you thought you knew.

He was held in much esteem by the Warburg sages,
though they were worried by his freakish adventures. His life
began to go awry when he took a very small part in an amateur
production of *Two Gentlemen of Verona*. Deeply stagestruck,
he now conceived a desire to direct and play the title role in
Marlowe's *Jew of Malta*. He sold all he had, including his
grand piano, and hired Toynbee Hall, a small London theatre,

for his production, which was by no means a success. Gordon, who liked Calder, looked on impassively as this absurd self-sacrifice was played out. Now lost to scholarship, the theatrical Calder went off, it seems, to Teheran and directed Shakespeare's plays on Iranian television: another flamboyant young man lost to academia, taking his ambitions into the great world. I saw him again at the memorial meeting for Gordon in 1978, now plump, flushed with drink, but still smiling sweetly above his bow tie and as full of recondite information as ever. Quite soon afterwards he died.

Gordon himself, though he would of course have liked to do his thing in a larger world, was wise enough to see that he could dominate more successfully in a small university. There he got his way less by winning the consent of colleagues than by exploiting the wary respect felt for him by the vice-chancellor, John Wolfenden. He grew richer, the result, I gathered, of an unexpected revival in the value of some Cornish tin-mine shares, and his entertainments thereafter grew more magnificent. Grand dinner parties were given, groups of shabby colleagues presided over by the dandy in the brilliant waistcoat. He hankered for lost or imagined happinesses at Cambridge or Henley: warm summer nights, the flash of fine young half-naked bodies; some Forsterian inner circle of the plucky, the sensitive, and the proud he thought to have existed once, and might exist still, though he could never find it, or at any rate find an entrance to it. Those parties, for all the splendour of wine and dessert, didn't do the trick; my memory is of coldness, coldness getting to the party by bus, social, formal coldness when there. They merely varied the consolations of a life short of solace, made tolerable by scholarship, by performance, by friendships that were by his own insistence not with equals, not total.

These were his best years. Soon he, and his associates, had to deal with his first serious bout of alcoholism. All his

major work in the Renaissance was done by 1957; even articles
appearing later were written earlier. He was, at the time of his
first breakdown, about forty and had published no book. He
now applied the research methods he had developed to later
literature, partly influenced by a book of mine, partly by the
arrival, made possible by my lobbying, of Ian Fletcher as a
replacement for Wain.

This momentous recruitment couldn't possibly happen in
a modern university. I had got to know Fletcher through Donald Carne-Ross, a polymathic Third Programme producer in
the great days when listening figures were regarded as vulgar;
in any case, listener research couldn't deal with numbers under
about fifty thousand, so there was happily no way of knowing
how few people listened to the sort of things we did. Fletcher
was a librarian somewhere in South London, a man totally
lacking paper evidence as to his education, but already a notable collector, haunting the Farringdon Road (now, after so
long, bereft of its book barrows). He was already an authority
on the poetry and minority journalism of the 1890s, and a
scented poet with a taste for highly scented poets, not only of
the 1890s but wherever they could be found. We collaborated
in a programme about Marino, a seventeenth-century Italian
poet whose fame, once immense, had vanished. We would meet
at the cathedral-like Henekey's pub in Chancery Lane, reputed
haunt of Decadent poets; you drank your bottle, brought by
a waiter in a white apron still looking like something out of a
fin-de-siècle poster. There was even a private postbox said to
have been devoted, in the 1890s, to the making of homosexual
assignations.

Fletcher's talk was of use to me, for I was working on a
book which had to do with Arthur Symons and also with
dancers and music-hall personalities. He was unknown except
to an amused, admiring small circle; but the recherché learning
for which he was later to become rather famous was already

impressive, and it seemed absurd that he should spend his days, as he said he did, examining the hands of schoolchildren who proposed to borrow library books. So I arranged a lunch and introduced him to Gordon. They hit it off wonderfully, and after a discreet interval, I suggested that Fletcher was the sort of man we wanted in the department. Gordon hesitated only briefly, and Fletcher was summoned to an interview.

When this event took place, I was giving a lecture in a remote classroom. To my great surprise I was interrupted by the entry of the head porter in full fig, an unprecedented occurrence. He had been sent by the vice-chancellor, who was chairing the interview committee. When I arrived, Wolfenden told me to sit down in the candidate's chair, cheerfully informing me that as my candidate had proved incapable of speech, he had no choice but to ask me to be interviewed on his behalf. I had always been bad at interviews, where a certain degree of self-belief is quite urgently needed; my tendency, in youth, had always been to say I was incapable of doing whatever I was being asked whether I could do. ("Could you undertake a course of lectures on late-eighteenth-century poetry?" "No, I'm afraid not.") But the surrogate interview proved to be much easier, so tongue-tied Fletcher got the job. Soon he was roaring and booming around the place as if he had never for a single moment been short of words. I regard this as probably my finest academic achievement.

Fletcher was a great success, not least with Gordon, who now developed his interest in Beardsley and his contemporaries. By one of those odd historical flukes that are more common than some historians seem to believe, he had, as an Edinburgh undergraduate, met John Gray, quintessential 1890s author of that prettiest of 1890s books, *Silverpoints*, a work said to have been paid for by Oscar Wilde. (Gray, as Gordon remarked in characteristic tones, "was not—the Law Courts said—the original of Dorian Gray.") The poet became a priest and set up house in Edinburgh with his companion, André Raffalovich, author of *Uranisme et Unisexualité*. They ran some sort of salon, and there entertained, along with the cream of Edinburgh intellectual society, the youthful Gordon.

So a seed of interest had been lying dormant and could now be induced to sprout. Fletcher could tell him as much as he could possibly want to know about the Rhymers' Club and the whole "tragic generation" of Yeats. Before long Gordon was able to mount a fine Yeats exhibition, which travelled to Manchester and Dublin; the catalogue was several times reprinted. He loved the long labours involved in setting up exhibitions, and he loved making the acquaintance of Mrs. Yeats and the occultist Gerald Yorke; above all, of the photographer Alvin Langdon Coburn, who early in the century supplied, under the direct instructions of the author, the photographs that illustrated the New York Edition of Henry James. Coburn was old but lively; he had known everybody and recognized Gordon as an accomplished Jamesian as well as a learned eccentric, and in his case deferential historian and littérateur. When he died he left Gordon a Cézanne lithograph of *The Bathers*, which, like much else that he valued but lost the will to protect, was stolen in the chaotic last days of his life.

Gordon's first alcoholic episode ended well enough. It had become impossible to ignore the signs: he would be drunk before nine in the morning, and was increasingly liable to commit outrages of all sorts, some comical, some embarrassing, at meetings, lectures, examinations. He was dried out and, accepting the humane advice of Wolfenden, took sick leave and spent it in Beirut, then known as a place to go for many varieties of pleasures, and not only the licit ones. He came back temporarily transformed, lively and confident. But back in Britain the Scotch-Calvinist superego reasserted itself; it would not let him live the life he needed, and he soon began to drink again, never forgetting that in doing so he was killing himself.

I saw rather less of him in these later years, partly because in 1958 I left Reading for Manchester and then, in 1965, Bristol. Unfortunately there was another reason for coolness. I became co-editor of *Encounter*, a monthly which, at that time, enjoyed much esteem on both sides of the Atlantic. In the spring of 1966, Melvin Lasky, who though technically co-editor was really editor-in-chief, departed on a long trip to South America, leaving me to do more or less as I pleased with the paper, and I saw a chance to give the arts a more prominent place in it than they had normally had. The Victoria and Albert was putting on a large Beardsley exhibition; Gordon was at least as well qualified as anybody else to review the exhibition, and I commissioned a long article from him. Almost for the first time *Encounter* would have a lead article on the arts and an unpolitical cover dominated for once by the head of an artist, Aubrey Beardsley. That same anomalous issue carried a long review of an edition of Foxe's *Book of Martyrs* by Frances Yates and a selection of Wallace Stevens's letters with a commentary by me; anybody could see that Lasky was away.

It happened that at this time *Encounter* was beginning to be plagued with difficulties caused by rumours about the sources of its funding; more of that later. They were becoming critical just at the time Gordon was writing his article. I must have forgotten that for him to have done so without the usual desperate fuss of consultation and correction was inconceivable. Fletcher told me about the earlier stages of composition, comparing the author to Moriarty at the centre of his web: "Graduate students were despatched like heralds in all directions, secretaries were usurped, so that life in the department faltered; taxis were continually summoned, phone calls booked to all parts of the continent." This was of course quite normal.

Later, however, events took a nastier turn, for Gordon became involved in the approaching *Encounter* crisis. A draft of the Beardsley piece arrived on my desk, and I thought it excellent. It contained a characteristic excursus on the philosophy of exhibitions, but its substance was a newly "historicised" Beardsley, treated as "the epiphenomenon of a communications system." This system is described as deriving from late-nineteenth-century periodical advertising techniques and other manifestations of a new kind of art intended, in the words of Arthur Symons, "for the street, for people walking fast." The photograph and the poster made the reputations of such performers as Yvette Guilbert and Lillie Langtry; modernity became a saleable commodity, and the publishers John Lane and Elkin Mathews sold it. Gordon discussed individual works of Beardsley with acute originality, and along with Brian Reade's catalogue of the Victoria and Albert exhibition it certainly raised understanding of the period and the artist to a new level. Though he lived for more than a decade longer, this was Gordon's last work of any extent, though he did organise another good Beardsley exhibition; this was a form of display at which he, not surprisingly, excelled.

At the time I was living in Gloucestershire. I should have known better than not to expect a visit, and Gordon arrived at my house with another draft and a mass of notes. We spent a weekend walking and working on the essay. During his stay I had many telephone calls from New York, for Robert Silvers, the editor of *The New York Review of Books* and a friend of both Dr. Conor Cruise O'Brien and myself, was keen to arrange a peaceful settlement of an action for libel O'Brien had brought against *Encounter*. Naturally Gordon overheard some of these long conversations; naturally he was interested. Since he was almost unnaturally devoted to gossip, he went home and talked knowingly to a friend about the case, a complicated affair which, having heard only one side of the conversations, he hadn't completely understood. This friend carried his talk abroad, and Gordon was in danger of being sued for slander, a prospect which threw him into a state of fantastic alarm.

I found it odd and irritating that in the many desperate

telephone calls in which he agonised over his predicament he showed not the least sign of bearing his betrayer any ill will, so at one point I asked whether it wasn't rather absurd of him to continue to speak of this person as a friend. I was forty-six years old and long out of Gordon's sphere of influence, but he found this comment unacceptable, perhaps insubordinate; anyway, he was silent for a few seconds, and then hung up.

For my part I was in no hurry to renew our relationship. He had caused me a lot of trouble at a time when I already had plenty, and it was a year or so before anything happened to break the ice. This occurred when, in 1967, I sent him a copy of my book *The Sense of an Ending* and he telephoned: "I was afraid to open it; but now I see what you were about. It is autobiography . . . very *moving*." I recall this remark not only because it broke a silence but because I didn't understand it, and still don't, though retaining enough respect for him to hope that someday I may find out.

In his turn he sent me *The Renaissance Imagination*, a collection of his essays edited by Stephen Orgel, which went back as far as the *Hymenaei* article. I had earlier protested against his resigning the job of collecting and editing these essays to Orgel (who was, however, a very good choice if one had to be made). I had argued that he was still in his fifties and ought not to behave as if he were already dead. I had not seen, as John Stokes did, that his permanent passion for collaboration was a sign of deep insecurity and that this was one more, admittedly odd, manifestation of it; but I might have known he would resent my remark. He got over it, and it was a friendly act to send me the book. I wrote at length to say I thought it a monumental achievement, adding that I had myself long ago been blown off the course he had tried to set for me, or, though I couldn't have matched it, I might have done something less impressive in the same line. He telephoned again to say he found my letter very *moving*. He spoke this word as if it had a special sense and not its usual meaning. I suppose that was in 1975; it was the last time we ever spoke together.

I had seen something of the increasing squalor of his last years, lent him a book which, when I retrieved it, was also squalid, *lurido*, beyond further use. Young men he picked up in London would go with him to his house and, when he collapsed, remove his pictures from the walls: the Cézanne and a lovely Gwen John drawing of Arthur Symons among them, probably sold for a song in London.

I could see little here but petty tragedy, but the reports of those who watched his decline at closer quarters modify my impression of unremitting decline. People who had known him as long as I remembered him as a slender, domineering, foppish young man, later a dreadfully disappointed, dissolute old man. But he made younger friends, who had not known him in his prime but were still enchanted by his strange oracular manner, his immense reading, his slightly contemptuous generosity. He was admired by young people at Studio Vista and *The New Left Review*; I have no clear idea how he made their acquaintance. And older friends, closer to him and more loyal than I, took care of him in his worst moments.

There was between us a barrier, perhaps of envy, perhaps of something more obscure, compounded of differences in sexual orientation, disappointment on his part that a pupil less gifted should become better known, though falling so short in so many respects—insufficiently dramatic, impossible to contemplate as a potentially gorgeous performer. Above all, I think, there was a failure on my part, a certain obtuseness to his character and his motives, the product perhaps of a native clumsiness in understanding persons of fine organisation and aggressive individuality; or a failure to intuit the whole pattern of a life so intensely devoted to scholarship and to such power, whether real or illusory, as scholarship may bring with it.

Still, I like to think I can say of myself what Cleopatra said of the messenger: "The man has seen some majesty and should know." There *was* grandeur, obvious to all who daily dealt with him, though not always easily descried by others. He was denied what he would have valued much too highly: the conventional honours of the British scholar, the Fellowship of the British Academy, the honorary doctorates—and would suspect, in my view rightly, that he was denied them by some who were his malignant inferiors. The breakdown in health and the belated appearance of the book are parts of the explanation; the remoteness of his interests from the conventional academic run of things is another. Finally, there was that strange, scornful manner, to which it was thought he had no right in terms of achievement. He was disappointed but in the end didn't care much. I hope he knew, in the ruin of his age, that there were those who would keep in memory or imagination a vision of him, swarthy and slender, in yet another exquisite new suit, arriving on the platform to do what he most delighted in, to give the performance so painfully prepared: to exhibit before an amused and admiring audience that scholarship which was to him a true instrument of understanding, beauty, and power.

Errors

Many errors,
a little rightness . . .

—Ezra Pound

A GREAT INTIMACY, never directly expressed but very secure; the nod or glance is enough to signify the happy solemnity, the shared acceptance of a poem, even of a line of verse. For a moment all's right with that world. A possible world?

The academic study of vernacular literatures, especially of the literature of one's own language, has rarely dealt with such rightnesses. Historically it has always been a substitute or an ancillary. In England it came into existence to serve serious persons lacking privilege, as a substitute for Greek and Latin, more suited to the needs of women, nonconformists, and others denied access to the great schools and universities. If their courses were to have even a semblance of rigour, they must be, like a training in the Classics, heavily philological. The old universities weren't impressed, and joked about "the godless institution in Gower Street," meaning the University of London, which you could enter even if a Greekless female atheist, and study this ersatz philology; but the other nineteenth-century universities also opted for it.

Their courses might not tell you much about poetry, certainly not about modern poetry. A reasonable command of Old and Middle English was necessary to the study of English up to the time of Chaucer; after that there seemed to be nothing much to learn except the history of literature, which usually turns out to be the history of lots of other things. In the United States the study of literature was a byproduct of language-learning and an aspect of what is still called rhetoric rather than philology, but the more advanced study of literature took much the same line.

To talk about literature is to give a rhetorical performance about rhetorical performances. This secondary rhetorical phenomenon develops its own independent laws and interests. Modern rhetorics, as taught for example by Paul de Man, are extremely sophisticated and tend to be self-reflexive, to be performances about themselves. One way and another, the direct experience of literature is largely neglected; on both sides thus, to borrow from a sad sonnet of Shakespeare's, is simple truth suppressed.

The experience of poetry is normally assumed to be something that cannot be directly discussed. Yet it does of course exist, and at least some students of literature take up the subject because they know the experience and would like to know its meaning. What they get is philology, linguistics, history, including history of ideas, and it is on their memories of these disciplines that their success is judged. Great success can be achieved by candidates who care very little about poetry. It is not unusual for able students to admit or even to boast that the part of their studies that directly confronts literary texts is the part that interests them least. Many of their teachers share and encourage this attitude.

If we could begin all over again, it would be useful to recall that poetry was once assumed to be a teachable subject. The demise of that notion is in part a consequence of devel-

opments internal to the poetic tradition, especially the decay
of confidence in the accessibility and value of learnable techniques. There is no point in deploring that historical development, but it can still be argued that people who have actually
written Petrarchan sonnets, villanelles, sestinas, ballades, and
so forth, whatever the merit of their performances, actually
understand more about poetry than people who haven't, and
may have a better understanding of more modern, less com-
municable, technical achievements. They will know better why
poetry is important, if it still is.

There are in the United States senior poets of high technical virtuosity—it is almost enough to name Richard Wilbur—
and some who love to explain and exemplify the luxurious
virtuoso possibilities of traditional forms, the skills that may
help to train original voices; and here I need only mention
John Hollander. At least until recently, the current of American poetry has flowed away from such poetry. Teachers of
literature, though they probably like the idea that a few of their
students actually write poems on the side, have generally been
suspicious of "creative writing courses," regarding the actual
composition of poems as a leisure activity that has nothing
much to do with the real work. Recently, however, I have
encountered, in a graduate literature class, students who have
been taught to write poems as a major part of their studies.
Belatedly, I am almost convinced that this is where the study
of literature ought to begin.

I read a poem by George Herbert and come to one of
those lines that might be used as tests of a genuine understanding of poetry: "to sever the good fellowship of dust," or
"Then shall the fall further the flight in me," or, more difficult,
the remarkable ninth line of the sonnet "Prayer" (you need
the whole poem to see why that line is perfect). I look up and
see faces, on cue, gleaming with the experience of poetry: "The
land of spices; something understood." Books are written about

such topics as Herbert's understanding of Calvinism and so forth; and that's fine, these are real subjects. But the owners of those faces probably understand Herbert better than the learned authors who shuffle, cough in ink, and read Calvin.

But we cannot begin again. In this respect things are as they are, and will almost certainly get worse.

I KNOW I ought to know a bit more than I do, and ought to be readier to speak, about these and other aspects of my profession, if only because it occupied me, with diversions, for almost half a century, in England, the United States, Canada, Australia, even in Italy, Switzerland, South Africa, Japan, and China. There is a family resemblance in the practices of all the universities I've visited in these countries, but there are also local variations that would call for exposition and are best left to someone who finds them more interesting. And the great changes in the last half-century, especially in the last twenty-five years, though interestingly catastrophic within the profession, are more likely to bore or bewilder than to enchant most people outside it.

It is true that I've had a ringside seat at all this, and perhaps I should compel myself to say something subtly explanatory about it. I try to do so with little assurance, and with the reservation that I am the victim of a disabling conviction, somewhat at odds with the evidence, that none of it really has anything to do with me, not now, anyway. Perhaps it never really did. The new literary theory was another country in which I went to live without feeling truly at home, even when it still seemed exciting, even before it became drugged with self-regard, even when it seemed necessary to receive and question it, to criticise its arrangements with what must have seemed a forced severity.

Once more the *métèque*. No doubt there have been times in my life when I have felt easy, enjoyed the peace that must come from an assurance that one is in the right place—a peace so natural that it is not remarked at the time of its holding, when the question of belonging simply doesn't come up. But I've not known that benign ignorance since 1940 at least. Perhaps I never knew it. Even in the society of the friendly tenement we were but secondary citizens; even at school I was among seniors, perpetually young and negligible; and in the years at college in a strange country still, for all the thrills and all the fun, still a *métèque*. I have been too ready to abandon what is never more than a temporary environment, quick to move jobs, quick to resign, glad to abandon one exile for another. It seems always to have been so; I willingly sacrificed the certitudes, such as they were, of the small society, the familiar streets, tasks, pleasures, friends of Douglas, keen to move into a world of learning of which I knew nothing, for which I had no preparation.

Searching for a clue as to what place books and learning held in my life during that prehistorical epoch, what I remember is the newsagent, his chaotic shop with its dingy heaps of atheistical pamphlets and all the small wicked volumes of the Thinkers' Library; the arrival at our house, every Friday night, as regular as the farmer with his eggs, of the newsagent's bald son, always, as memory dictates, in streaming oilskins, his spectacles awash, bringing not only the weekly local paper but the latest indignant, sneering issue of the *Freethinker*; or that Scottish shipyard worker who, on his holidays in Douglas, gave me my first instruction in Marxism and presented me with the two Pelican volumes of *The Intelligent Woman's Guide to Socialism, Capitalism, Sovietism and Fascism*, a work which, on reflection, I should have to list, in the improbable event of somebody requiring me to do so, among the forces that have shaped me, insofar as I can claim shape. And yet I have more frequent and easier access to reading that bored or baffled me—certain odes of Horace, for instance—than to Shaw's admirable prose. Why? Because *nunc est bibendum* and *diffugere nives* had to be taken slowly? or because one's still under the illusion, if it is an illusion, that Horace is a better introduction to the mystery of complex language, of syntax conducting its tense, pacific struggle against metre? Or is it merely that Horace can still seem, academically and socially, a greater asset?

Meanwhile, across the water (one of the ways in which we would refer to England), other young people were being educated more systematically and successfully. These were the people with whom I should have to live, however inimitable their splendour. The thought that I would need to do more than live with them, that I would also have to compete with them, was almost too daunting to be entertained. Competitiveness was not something that came naturally, but I had some practice, since the problem of matching, competing against, parental expectations continued urgent; there was still a requirement that I should be well placed in the class list. But these pressures were domestic and hardly at all related to my own image of a future in which success would come from doing something better than my contemporaries, except insofar as that was necessary to avoid tearful maternal disappointment. But perhaps the superego, resistant to all the forces the id has thrown against it, has perpetuated that necessity, so that even as an old man I grow uneasy if I am not at my desk by nine, and am attacked by guilt after a couple of idle weeks in the heat of Tuscany, when no man can work. *Traa dy lioaur.* Remember, time wasted is time lost—time that is needed if one isn't to fall behind in the endless struggle to belong somewhere, if only with oneself.

There may have remained to me, at twenty, some ability to assimilate, not easy and natural, and tinged by a certain conscious pride at being able to do it. What finally established me as a hopeless outsider, or non-belonger, was the navy, and I sensed that I was lucky to have been drafted into a sort of poorish photocopy of the real thing, just as I was lucky to have

stayed alive when more correct fellows, who responded as
bravely as their elders expected, were getting killed. It's said
that it was quite usual for young men in the 1920s to feel bad
at having missed a war in which the probability of dying was
a good deal higher—we knew this from Christopher Isher-
wood's guilt about never having faced what he called the Test,
and from similar confessions. It may be that National Service
exempted the children of the 1930s, too young for the real
war, from this slightly mad guiltiness, but I think survivors
of the war, even if never exposed to imminently lethal action,
often have somewhere in their heads the notion that they have
remained alive by some slightly underhand trick or evasion,
that they have joined the club of the peacetime living without
disclosing what would have had them instantly blackballed.
They can be fairly sure of never being found out, except by
themselves. A bolder spirit might want to argue that it is the
ordinary members of the Life Club who are the real offenders,
that although they might well, if called upon, be extremely
brave, they seem in the absence of any such challenge to have
no idea of what it feels like to confront people ruthlessly dedicated to the idea of ripping you apart or drowning you.

It makes a difference, and it may be thought that persons
lacking such experience should be required to sue to those who
have for admission into *their* society. But it doesn't work like
that, it never did; for example, those who gave up most of their
twenties though contriving to hang on to their lives were afterwards given no quarter and asked to compete on equal terms
with those who hadn't. It is therefore possible for survivors to
be at odds with, to feel unqualified to associate freely with, the
living as well as the dead, each of these classes manifesting, if
only by body language, signs of incipient distress and rejection.

NEVER SURE that I wanted them, or was properly qualified to take them if offered, I began in late 1946 to apply for
lectureships. Sometimes I was called for interview, and as I

have already remarked, I found interviews impossible to manage. I remember one at Bedford College, where the poet George Fraser and I competed for a post that paid £350 a year. The committee was large, learned, and terrifying, and neither of us survived its probings. Informed of our failures, George and I walked around the lake in Regent's Park, telling each other how hopeless were our prospects. Fraser had been at the centre of a group of army poets in Cairo, and had already established a reputation as a literary journalist in London, so if he couldn't find a job, what chance had I? He survived, employed by the *TLS*, and he most patiently organised, with his wife, Paddy, a salon in Beaufort Street, Chelsea, where once a week poets shyly congregated to read their new works. He was thus a figure of some importance in the London literary world, but in the end he too wound up, after certain painful vicissitudes, in the academy, and spent his last years as a venerated teacher.

Leeds University had two vacancies, which seemed promising. I applied but was turned down without hesitation, and the electors sensibly gave the jobs to Arnold Kettle and Harold Fisch. I tried but failed to persuade myself that I'd been turned down for the sake of an ephemeral joke. Kettle became the most influential of English Marxist critics; Fisch later emigrated to Israel, where his learning still flourishes in the austerely orthodox atmosphere of Bar Ilan. There was no room for my name in that joke.

Much the oddest of my interviews was at Reading. Gordon had gone there, as I have said, and was immediately keen to fit me into the small department, then run by a Scot, a Burns scholar called Dewar. The weather in the early weeks of 1947 was uniquely awful; the entire railway system was disrupted and no train ran according to timetable. I was supposed to be in Reading in time for dinner, and spent ages prowling anxiously about Paddington, looking for somebody who could direct me to a suitable train. I chose the wrong counsellor, for the train I boarded rushed through Reading and did not stop till it reached Leamington Spa. Getting from there back to Reading meant long waits on frozen platforms, and when I reached Reading it was midnight. No taxis, naturally, so I walked through the snowdrifts to the hall of residence where Gordon lived. He had sensibly written me off hours before, and the hall was of course locked up.

I was once again in what friends throughout my life have thought of as a typical muddle. So far, obviously, I have always got out of them when they were life-threatening, and I got out of this one. To be out all night in such weather being unthinkable, I approached the building across the road, which was a Dr. Barnardo's Home, and knocked many times on the door. After a long while I was grudgingly admitted. I described my plight as piteously as was compatible with masculine reserve. They heard me out, then threw me out. No doubt they decided I was a menace to the children, though I was still so innocent that the idea of my being a potential child abuser never occurred to me. I wrote down those who so cruelly denied me as professionally inhuman, and I take my revenge on them annually: of all the begging envelopes that come through my door only Dr. Barnardo's fails to win my pound.

Crossing the road again, and now desperate, I got into the grounds of the hall and began without hope to look for a window I could open. I found one and climbed noisily through it, whereupon a light was switched on and a naked youth rose shrieking from his bed. He turned out to be a lad who worked in the kitchen, and I'm proud to say that, summoning a desperate resourcefulness, I not only succeeded in calming him down but got from him directions to Gordon's rooms. They were open (as they wouldn't be now) and there was a gas fire extravagantly burning while its owner was in bed in another room. I found whisky and settled down beside the fire. A mouse walked slowly across the carpet and sat beside me. The warmth filled us both with creaturely charity. After a while Gordon, never a good sleeper, came out of his bedroom and nonchalantly greeted me. He produced a tin of biscuits and went back to bed.

Next morning, exhausted, I was interviewed by Dewar and Sir Frank Stenton, the great Anglo-Saxon historian, who rejected me without hesitation. They sensibly preferred the youthful John Wain. When, three years later, I did get a job at Reading, it was only because Gordon had by then succeeded Dewar as the boss and could dispense with formal interviews.

I should probably never have got a university job at all but for what I like to think of as the superior perceptiveness of Lord Eustace Percy, then in charge of what was still King's College, Newcastle, in the University of Durham. It had far outgrown its parent and was, very appropriately—for the factories and shipyards of the Tyne were in those days still at work—an institution strong in engineering and quite lacking the cloistral atmosphere of the cathedral city; but it did not neglect the humanities. Two jobs were on offer; it seemed obvious that Peter Ure would get one of them, and there were such hungry and overqualified candidates for the other that I still wonder what strain of aristocratic perversity, what atavistic passion for gambling, or simply what unimaginable acumen prompted Lord Eustace to pick me. And so I got my first job. I was almost twenty-eight.

I didn't stay long in Newcastle, but took off for the softer south and the Reading experiences I've already mentioned. Reading suited me so well—better, in some respects, than any other place I've taught in—that when the university moved to a park outside town I, who had never owned a house, bought one opposite the park gates and prepared to live there for ever. The pay was bad and I had young children, but I was in the first stages of a *deuxième carrière* in broadcasting and literary journalism and was managing well enough. Thinking of future expenses, and uncertain of the favours of producers and editors, I halfheartedly applied for professorships here and there— Belfast, Southampton, one of the smaller London colleges, I forget which, and finally Manchester, where, in defiance of precedent, I failed to make a fool of myself at the interview and got the job. This remarkable event occurred on the day in 1957 when the Manchester United football team was destroyed in the Munich air crash, so for that reason if no other there was no dancing in the streets. From 1958 to 1965 I stayed in Manchester.

The university had a kind of grim friendliness and a justified assurance of its own value, at a time when the metropolitan claims of Manchester were weakening but still pretty strong. (*The Manchester Guardian*, still so called, had only just begun its gradual move to London, the Halle Orchestra flourished, the Rylands Library was, and of course remains, one of the greatest in the country.) The mood of the place was always to oppose the south, and the university had, or professed, no inferiority feelings about the ancient universities; if bright people came to Manchester, sharpened their talents, and left for Oxbridge, that was their business, and they might well come to repent their foolishness in leaving a serious place for institutions that devoted themselves to feasts and gaudies.

It was at Manchester, when I was nearing forty, that I belatedly learned a little about how to conduct myself as a professional academic. Only a little, of course, for I was still haunted by the sense that I had no business to be in this business; and I also retained that habit of deference that has been a curse largely because the only way to break it seems to be by intemperate action. I wish I could believe that these defects were imaginary, or perceptible only to myself, but there can be no doubt I was at the outset quite unfitted for the job; I'd known this, and tried to get out of it by telling Gordon that if he'd get me a Readership (the rank below full professor) I'd withdraw from the Manchester appointment while there was still time. He affected to consider the proposition, then informed me that I might be worthy of a Manchester chair but hadn't yet quite reached the standard required of a Reader at Reading. Of course it had been a mistake to give him this perfect opening; after twelve years of his society I ought to have learned that one of the defining characteristics of bitchiness is that it cannot afford to miss such chances. And I was aware, at the back of my head, that he actually wanted me to leave; I had moved on enough to be in some slight degree envied. He wondered, or pretended to wonder, how I'd got the job before my book *Romantic Image* broke upon the world, but soon conjectured that I'd been lucky. *"Omne ignotum pro magnifico,"* he intoned. So off I went, wife, babies, and all, to the chill and smoke-infested north.

In those days, as perhaps in these, the person arriving from a distance to take command of a strange department could rarely expect an unqualified welcome from colleagues who believed themselves, and not without reason, to be at least equally well qualified for the job, and he needed plenty of tact and self-assurance, neither of which I had much of. Moreover, I didn't understand that malice, which I have experienced in myself but always on a temporary basis, can be for others a perfectly usual way of responding to the challenges of private and professional life. Anyway, it was some time before the older hands consented to treat me as something better than an impudent interloper, owing his new job (they conjectured) to certain domestic enmities that had cancelled their chances and made it necessary to appoint an outsider. But they were, it finally appeared, essentially civil, well-brought-up, and well-educated men who were not implacable, and, as the more acute memories of their disappointment faded, they perhaps came to see me as harmless, if never acceptable with enthusiasm, so they made their peace. Now they are all dead, and I think of them as friends and even, in generous moments, as generous souls who did what they could to make me tolerable.

My colleagues included an alcoholic and one or two slackers, which is about the normal proportion. All the others successfully conspired to protect them from me, wrongly presuming, until the contrary became obvious, that I was capable of decisive action. The professor of English Language, joint head with me, was pale, fat, and asthmatic, but good at protecting his turf. He spent a lot of time lying on his office sofa to ease his back, and it is in that posture that, long dead, he recurs to my memory. He owned so many books that in order to accommodate them he had bought the house next door to the one he lived in. He despised Oxford, Cambridge, indeed all parts south of Sheffield, but was a real old-style scholar, and correctly guessed that I wasn't, but he bore with me until, after seven years, I announced that in a few months I intended to leave Manchester and go to Bristol, after which betrayal he never again spoke a word to me.

I found out by experience that running a department is a laborious business, requiring you to fight, as they say, your corner, to distinguish true from false amiability, and so forth. In my first year I found myself competing with other departmental heads for newly authorized appointments. I had a good paper case for another assistant and I made it as convincingly as I could, but at the decisive meeting I was challenged by a famous astronomer, who wanted another helot to man his telescopes, and when in the course of his impressive oration he passionately asked whether Professor Kermode was really ruthless enough to strengthen his own department at the expense of closing down Jodrell Bank, much in the news at the time because it was tracking sputniks, I was so amazed by this brilliantly shameless tactic, and so abashed, that I abandoned the competition at once.

As we left the meeting, Eugène Vinaver, who was the professor of French, a very wise, courtly, distinguished man and a subtle combatant, asked me back to his room, where, he suggested, we might share a cigarette. He meant this literally, for he took a cigarette out of his case, produced a small pair of scissors, and cut it in half. As we smoked the fragrant fragments, he explained to me the hopelessness of going into meetings of the kind we'd just left without preparation, without, that is, hours of persistent and crafty lobbying. I couldn't imagine anything I might have said in the way of pre-emptive strikes that would have made any difference to the outcome of a struggle between me and Jodrell Bank; but in future I went to a lot of trouble to solicit support, which was sometimes given as promised, and sometimes not.

Manchester was still, in the late 1950s, an intolerably smoky city, so we lived out on the Cheshire fringe, which the prevailing winds were supposed to protect from city smoke. This meant a tedious daily drive into the centre but it was what responsible parents did, in an attempt, often vain, to save their children from chronic bronchitis. So I suppose I missed a lot of whatever fun was going as relief from the high seriousness that characterised the working life of the university. But there clearly was fun of a superior sort; the presence of *The Guardian* guaranteed that. I began reviewing for it and went on doing so until quite recently, when a *nouvelle vague* broke over it, somewhat to the disappointment of old stagers like me.

The old *Guardian* families, the Scotts and Wadsworths, had a special place in the life of the city. Manchester, archetypally civic, was of all the universities I've known the one that had the most binding relations with the non-academic life of its district. London, which in any case has many other centres of learning, is too large and its university too scattered for any comparable bond, and Oxford and Cambridge simply are the intellectual life of their cities, so that there is really nothing to bond with.

The peculiar virtues and advantages of the great city universities, among which Manchester still has a certain preeminence, are not easily understood in the south of England. I've always thought it significant that of the six British copyright libraries (to which all publishers are obliged to send free copies of their books) one is in Wales, one in Scotland, one, anachronistically, in Dublin, and the other three in London, Oxford, and Cambridge, the last of these apparently marking the northern limit of high-powered scholarship. Long ago A. P. Herbert proposed a great extension of the copyright privilege to as many as forty libraries—a notion very disagreeable to publishers, who dislike being compelled to surrender even six copies of each book and would rather see the privilege abolished than enlarged. Herbert got the divorce laws changed, but he failed in this attempt to defeat southern prejudice.

In the 1960s, when the Macmillan government was proposing to spend a great deal of money on new universities, there was a good case, which I argued in print at the time, for spending it instead on the existing civic universities, which would at least have been more economical than starting a lot of new ones from scratch. The change would have deprived a few cathedral cities of what promised to be welcome new amenities, and possibly prevented some useful innovation, but it takes a long time to build a major university, and if you could weigh those disadvantages against the benefits that might have accrued from improving the sites and the endowments of the Victorian creations, it might just turn out that the money would have been better spent on them.

Although I arrived with prejudices formed in London and the south, it soon became obvious to me that it was unnecessary to think of being at Manchester as any kind of scholarly deprivation. For the work that interested me at the time, the

Rylands was a more than adequate library. I had imagined that I should need to be continually in the train, heading for the British Museum; but I hardly ever needed to go there. Like the Halle Orchestra, the Rylands was the product of Victorian cotton riches. Its original endowment was wonderfully lavish, and I've heard that in the early days it had so much to spend that it could buy everything it wanted and still have funds it didn't know quite what to do with—hence, for example, the magnificence of some of the bindings. Even the great American libraries are no longer quite as well provided as that; and by the time I read and lectured there, the Rylands had much less to spend on acquisitions. It has been taken over by the university library, but it is still there in gloomy Deansgate, all the old riches hidden behind its black walls.

So much for Manchester. Though never deeply attached, I didn't particularly want to leave; but my children kept catching bronchitis and we were advised to move to a less testing climate. Bristol is a pleasant place, and I worked there with admirable people; but I rather quickly established—as I might have foretold, since this seems to be true of more or less everywhere—that it wasn't exactly my place. I found different explanations for this new attack of alienation. I reflected that I was in my middle forties and might well be in Bristol for the rest of my time, wearing good tweeds and walking my dogs on the downs—I who had never owned tweeds or a dog. I missed my first term there, giving a lecture series at Bryn Mawr which became a quite successful book called *The Sense of an Ending*; so my stay was for only five terms.

We settled in Gloucestershire, fifteen or so miles north of Bristol, in an old farmhouse on which somebody had rather absurdly imposed a pseudo-classical front. It had a vast garden, a paddock, and the largest greenhouse outside Kew, very decayed. The house remains in the memory of my children as the happiest they have known, and I am now sad and even

shocked to reflect that in 1967, when Noel Annan beckoned
me to University College, I inconsiderately dragged the family
off to Hampstead. My children had been about to go to Bristol
schools—the boy (a good musician) to the Cathedral School,
the girl to Badminton. But off they went to London, into an
uncertain educational future. In the short term it turned out
rather badly for them. There was, I now see, a sort of des-
perateness or wildness in my behaviour at this and other times,
for at moments of decision I am by temperament likely to make
the wrong choice, even if others have to suffer for it. What is
this insatiable wish to have no road not taken? Why does a
timid man, regardless of his own and others' comfort, habitually make the bold, disconcerting, wrong choice?

ALL THE SAME, in some respects the move to London
turned out well. As I'd been warned to expect, I encountered
much fiercer and nastier opposition than in my earlier jobs.
At that time there was, at University College, no escaping the
fact that one was head of department; your contract made you
responsible to the university for the conduct of the subject,
and everybody else's made them responsible to you. The arrangement had certain advantages, including a splendidly com-
petent and beautiful administrative assistant, whose talents for
unobtrusive organisation in my business affairs, whether of the
college or beyond it, I didn't fully understand until I had her
no longer. There were also obvious disadvantages. James
Sutherland, my predecessor in the Northcliffe Chair of Modern
English Literature (as F. W. Bateson famously remarked, it
was like being Mammon Professor of God), bought me lunch,
handed over some keys, and gave it as his general opinion that
there was a stormy passage ahead and he was getting out just
in time. It is pleasant to think that at ninety-five or so he is
still enjoying his retirement, having missed twenty-eight years
of worsening academic weather.

The other established chair, until recently dedicated to medieval and linguistic studies, was occupied by a boisterous bully who held lunchtime court, surrounded by sycophants, at the Marlborough Arms in Torrington Place. When in London he spent much of his time in the pub or on the telephone to his brokers; three days a week he retired to his house in the West Country. He had been known to send a young colleague all the way there to bring him something he'd forgotten. He'd had his own internal candidate for the job, a drinking companion, Bardolph to his Falstaff, and I was to expect malice from both of them. But a month or so before my first term started, this man suddenly died. It was easy to imagine how horrible my life would have been if he'd lived the normal span. Even in his absence his henchmen, especially Bardolph, did all they could to make my life difficult and often wretched. But by a piece of luck his successor was Randolph Quirk, not yet, in those days, a lord, not even, indeed, a sir. Randolph was another Manxman, and we had known one another since we were schoolfellows of about eleven. He was miraculously efficient, and easily combined with his prodigious output as a grammarian the power, patience, and energy to manipulate committees. With me holding the ladder, as it were, he contrived some radical renovations in the department, the most important of which was its severance, for examination and indeed for all practical purposes, from the rest of the far-flung, awkwardly governed university. The department still had a core of rather resistant old hands to whom the declaration of independence was a more serious matter than it seemed to me; but by 1970 we were at peace with one another.

University College was certainly large enough and distinguished enough to be independent, and this virtual autonomy gave us a freer hand. Except in the sciences hardly any institution now grants permanent and more or less absolute control to a single person; it is an arrangement thought of as

German, and old-style German at that. And it must have
seemed a very bad plan to those labouring under the whip of
some capricious autocrat; but I couldn't have been that if I
tried. With appointments I had a more or less free hand, though
as a rule I consulted at least the senior colleagues, but for good
in some cases and ill in others I brought about certain appointments that might have been more difficult to achieve on
a more democratic system. There was a feeling that we were
slightly different from other English departments in having
more immediate contact with a wider world of letters, and
could introduce suitable persons from that world; hence the
appointments of A. S. Byatt, a scholar and already a good
novelist though not yet famous, and of Grey Ruthven (recommended to us by Robert Lowell, snatched away from us by
Edward Heath, and thereafter known to all the world as Lord
Gowrie). Stephen Spender spent some years with us, and then
Dan Jacobson, though that happened in the reign of my successful successor, Karl Miller.

Throughout these years my private life was in a great
muddle. It was even hard to say where I lived; it might be in
Hampstead or Dulwich, Regent's Park or Golders Green or
Battersea. Or, for that matter, Connecticut or Massachusetts,
New York or New Hampshire. Yet it was the only period of
my life when I felt, perhaps only imagined I felt, in charge of
it, in the way drunken drivers feel in charge of their vehicles.
It had long been clear to me that I was a far better chairman
of a committee than a member of it; that I felt easy when
lecturing to large audiences though I was timid in seminars
and hardly ever dared to ask a question from the floor. So the
enforced autocracy of University College suited me well, and
so did the sense of playing a part in a large enterprise.

A seminar of mine which achieved some celebrity could
probably have developed as it did only in London, for although
it began conventionally enough as a weekly meeting for grad-

uate students (some of them unusually gifted), it soon broke out of these bounds, partly because, the topic being fiction, we brought in writers interested in the theory of what they were doing, for instance Christine Brooke-Rose and the late B. S. Johnson. American scholars took to dropping by. One of them constructed elaborate paper models of poems—one of which he took to Vincennes, where, to his great sorrow, it was seized and destroyed by insurgent students. Others laboured to extend Chomskyan or transformational-generative grammar above the level of the sentence, a quest that came to resemble that of squaring the circle. Visiting speakers tended to come back to discuss the contributions of others; we had inadvertently formed a club, and the proceedings increasingly assumed a festive and unacademic yet still serious air; there was no time limit to the sessions, and when they formally ended, everybody went off to a pub and carried on the talk.

The other reason why this at first perfectly ordinary enterprise acquired some wider significance was the date, the late 1960s and early 1970s. For now began the new approaches to literary theory that a quarter-century later have so altered almost every aspect of the subject. In the early days there was no sense of revolution, only of an extension of existing interests. When, in the nineteenth century, English departments got going in Britain and America, there was a strong tendency to present the subject in the most scientific light available, partly to justify its usurpation of Classics, partly to compete with hard science for prestige and money. The consequence was a lot of compulsory philology, Anglo-Saxon, Middle English dialects, in the hardest cases Old High German and Icelandic. The trade journals, with names like *The Journal of English and Germanic Philology, Modern Philology, Studies in Philology*, and so on published studies in literary history but nothing that could easily be called criticism, and there were similar constraints on Ph.D. topics. But we had already gone a long way to changing that emphasis. The different notions of criticism exemplified notably by I. A. Richards, Leavis, and Empson were by now familiar, and the Cambridge English school had from its foundation soon after the Great War excluded the old-style philology from its programme. In America the New Criticism, having penetrated the academy against stiff philological resistance, was by now almost an orthodoxy. So although we were interested, we were not astonished when, in 1966, Roland Barthes attacked Raymond Picard in his essay *Critique et vérité*.

Picard, a philologist of the traditional French kind, had violently attacked Barthes's *Sur Racine*, a work which took a psychoanalytical and anthropological line on its topic, in a pamphlet called *Nouvelle Critique ou nouvelle imposture*; whereupon Barthes, on behalf of the French new critics, issued his polemic against what he called *lansonisme*, Gustave Lanson having provided, in his *History of French Literature* (1895) and his five-volume *Bibliographical Manual of Modern French Literature* (1909–14) the groundwork of orthodox university study.

We applauded Barthes sympathetically, though confident that he was fighting in France a battle we'd won long ago in the anglophone world. And we looked forward, naïvely as it turned out, to a future in which the French might catch up with us. Meanwhile, Barthes pleased us because he wrote so well about fiction, especially the *nouveau roman*, and we regarded that as being very much in our line.

In short, we did not bargain for the changes that were to follow so quickly. There had been a revival of interest in the linguistics of Saussure, and Claude Lévi-Strauss had shown that Saussure's ideas of language as but the preeminent instance of structured sign-systems, and of a possible general science of signs, could be applied to anthropology and, of course, more generally. Then the French, belated but less belated than the rest of us, discovered the Russian Formalists, whose origins were different but who had affinities with Saussure. It now appeared that delicate structuralist methods could be devised for the description of texts as well as of sentences. These descriptive systems were in principle value-free, which is why it became fashionable to write complex descriptions of the James Bond narratives. Barthes was good at this kind of thing, and in a 1966 issue of the journal *Communications* he published an influential "Introduction to the Structural Analysis of Stories." Other contributors to that memorable number were A. J. Greimas, Claude Bremond, Umberto Eco, Christian Metz, and Gérard Genette, all very soon to be familiar names.

The French invasion had begun; but although we enjoyed trying our hand with these new tricks (and some were trying to reconcile them to Chomskyan theory, which was not in the same way derived from or related to Saussure), more difficult, more revolutionary developments were closing in on us. Barthes's *S/Z*, a remarkable book-length analysis of a Balzac short story, occupied the seminar for many weeks. Barthes was now the great name. In those days French sages, including Lévi-Strauss and Lacan, regularly spoke to large audiences at the Institut Français in London, and I myself took part there in what was intended to be a dialogue with Barthes, though he spoke for so long that by the time I'd said my little piece there was no time left for discussion, which was all right with me.

Barthes was a gentle man, a literary man, a lover of Stendhal and Flaubert, not at all the iconoclast, the fire-eating revolutionary he was sometimes taken to be. He kindly attended my seminar, assuring me that its members might, if they chose, speak English, but that he would respond in French. We began on this basis, but it soon appeared that he did not understand what was being said quite well enough to make an adequate reply in any language, whereupon to my great satisfaction everybody now buckled to and spoke nothing but French. Somebody asked a question about *Tristram Shandy*, a novel of inexhaustible interest to theorists of fiction, and Barthes at once confessed that he did not know the book, or for that matter many books not written in French.

When somebody else associated him with the avant-garde, he demurred: at best, he said, the *arrière-garde* of the avant-garde. But already *S/Z* had moved on from the simpler structural analyses, and in 1973 *Le Plaisir du texte*, with its bold, elegantly erotic approach, was received with delight. Barthes was in these years as prolific as he was famous, and he was producing other books that also interested us, but less directly. He gave us quite enough to think about as it was. I believe his fame has waned a little, but he seemed to us then to be the prince of modern critics, and I think he deserved and still deserves that title.

As the seminar developed, news of it reached outlying parts, and its intellectual resources were considerably increased by visitors from Cambridge. They included Jonathan Culler and Stephen Heath, young converts to structuralism. Culler was working on a thesis which became a celebrated book, *Structuralist Poetics*, and he would later be the clearest and probably the most celebrated exponent of post-structuralist and deconstructionist thinking in America. Heath had recently returned from Paris and Barthes's seminar; he was a friend of Philippe Sollers and Julia Kristeva, and a contributor to *Tel Quel*, a flamboyantly avant-garde structuralist or post-structuralist journal which, after many theoretical and political convulsions, including a fit of Maoism, expired as late as 1982. Heath, modest but adventurous, became the virtual leader of the English group. A vilely printed book called *Signs of the Times*, which he had written in collaboration with two disciples, was passed from hand to hand; later he wrote, in English, an excellent book on the *nouveau roman* and, in French, an authoritative study of Barthes.

We were advancing far beyond our initial state of amateurish curiosity concerning formalist analysis and the techniques of the *nouveau roman* into the darker jungle of what is now simply called Theory. In these very early days it was regarded by many respected elders as at best a joke, a hobby, or a stunt; the old guard was not yet troubled, and its bitter and mostly ineffective counter-attacks were quite far in the future. At the time there seemed no need to bother.

This was so even in Paris. I recall a conversation at a Christmas dinner, in the fantastic Ile St. Louis apartment of the novelist James Jones, with a man from the publishing house that issued *Tel Quel*. He clearly regarded the journal as window dressing, tongue-in-cheek, a form of promotion, and otherwise of no significance. He found it very amusing that this oddball journal was so solemnly studied across the Channel. And certainly what was sometimes called the French fever was taking hold; these innocent early symptoms gave way to the more desperate and delirious indications of its later stages, and the names of Foucault and Lacan, Derrida and Kristeva almost eclipsed that of Barthes. As it turned out, the British rather held back, still regarding the Channel as a moat against infection, and the major epidemic occurred a little later in the United States, hindered only a little by the fact that among those likely to be interested, relatively few read French easily. But the appearance of translations, and the authority of Paul de Man, who soon discovered an affinity between his own work and that of Jacques Derrida, very soon made Theory a dominant interest of the academic literary establishment. It still is. It has shown a remarkable ability to accommodate various political positions and interests, not least an indigenous feminism that has fairly comfortable relations with the French version.

The academy has long preferred ways of studying literature which actually permit or enjoin the study of something
else in its place, and the success of the new French approaches
has in many quarters come close to eliminating the study of
literature altogether; indeed, there are many who regard the
word as denoting a false category, a term used to dignify, in
one's own interest, one set of texts by arbitrarily attributing
to them a value arbitrarily denied to others. This position many
find grateful, either because it saves trouble or because they
have ideological objections to the notion that certain sorts of
application can detect value here and dispute it there; or because they are, as it were, tone-deaf, and are as happy with
the new state of affairs as a professor deaf from birth might be
if relieved of the nightmare necessity of "teaching" the Beethoven quartets.

The door that was opened in the late 1960s let in many
unexpected visitors. Perhaps the extraordinary *événements* of
May 1968—which shook American as well as European universities, though nowhere except in Paris did it threaten instant
political revolution—gave these intellectual movements their
energy, and the sense that vast alterations in the method and
presuppositions of what the French call the human sciences
were inevitable and irreversible. Certainly the innovations have
showed great staying power; the work of the founders has been
assimilated, not only by people who've learned the patter but
by serious, committed teachers who have serious, committed
pupils. Those elders who have repeatedly predicted that the
whole business will simply fade away, like other such movements before it, must now feel that they were wrong. Some
kind of better-informed reaction may be in train, and may be
desirable, but there will be no return to the pre-revolutionary
positions. Back in Bloomsbury, at the end of the 1960s, we
may have been amused and excited, but we hardly understood
the seriousness of our novelties, which have by now changed

in various ways the manner in which we think and talk about the arts in relation to other interests and to the new, aggressive politics of feminism.

The seminar is still remembered with gratitude, even by participants whose work has taken them a long way from any position I could myself occupy—beyond what, in some cases, I can easily understand. As Jonathan Culler is the best-known American, so Christopher Norris is the best-known British expositor of deconstruction; Shlomith Rimmon, anxious and scrupulous, has played an important part in the success of Theory in Israel. Christine Brooke-Rose, then in her early years at Vincennes and needing no theoretical instruction from anybody, has continued to write independent Theory as well as independent fiction. Annette Lavers, author of the best English book on Barthes, is now head of the French Department at UCLA. Jacqueline Rose, an exponent of feminist psycho-analysis in general and of Sylvia Plath in particular, is an academic celebrity on both sides of the Atlantic. So one can say that we had some effect; yet, as I remarked earlier, the whole thing happened fortuitously. It might well have remained what it was to begin with, a routine academic seminar.

I myself had written a book, *The Sense of an Ending*, of a theoretical, or, as it came to seem as time went by, a pre-theoretical character; it consisted of the lectures I'd given at Bryn Mawr in 1965, too early for it to show any effect of the *nouvelle critique*. It tried to sketch a general theory of fictions, with particular reference to the fictions of closure. This book showed an interest in Vaihinger and Nietzsche (who, as it turned out, was on the brink of a big revival) and in the psychology and sociology of apocalyptic thinking, but it was recognisable as literary criticism, with much talk of Spenser, Shakespeare, Sartre, Robbe-Grillet, and Wallace Stevens. It was, in fact, an example of literary theory as it was before it was absorbed into Theory. That change was coming on rapidly in the late years of the decade, but it could be claimed that *The Sense of an Ending* entitled me to a voice in these new theoretical debates. Yet as the others, especially Heath, grew more arcanely adventurous, I had, inevitably, a sense that it was for a younger generation to lead the van. The proceedings of the seminar were no longer wholly under my control. I could provide the space and the time, but without feeling that they were exactly my space and my time; the wine brought by this assortment of guests was more interesting, certainly more intoxicating, than any in my own cellar. I was reverting to a familiar position, that of being involved *ex officio*, but very willingly, in a successful activity which I could claim only to have originated and continued. Still, I am told that the seminar did not long survive my departure for Cambridge in 1974.

THOSE LONDON years were the busiest of my life; I was in that not unpleasing condition of franticness when one can do an extraordinary number of things, though in all probability not as well as they could be done without haste. In the midst of all the excitement I often had the sense that I was again sitting at slightly the wrong table and even sleeping in slightly the wrong bed. Restless in Golders Green or Dulwich, Regent's Park or Battersea, I'd make my way to Bloomsbury and try to believe I really did belong there. More and more involved with the Arts Council, I spent many afternoons in St. James's Square and, after the Council moved, at 105 Piccadilly, chairing the Literature Panel—its budget, though small, hard to spend without annoying this or that pressure group—and also an underfunded and in any case useless Experimental Projects Committee. I passed a good many futile but amusing hours in the company of sceptical William Coldstream and tetchy, hospitable Michael Astor, grubbing about in arts labs or watching populists blowing up balloons and doing open-air theatre in parks. There was never a hope that we could persuade the

Council and its chairman, Lord Goodman, that these activities—and there were others so bizarre that I can't even remember what they were—could properly be described as arts and so deserve their attention, but for some reason we were conscientious. There was never a hope that we could achieve substantial revisions of the Obscene Publications Act, but we formed a committee which met and met, and interviewed everybody we could think of, including the present Bishop of Liverpool, the film censor John Trevelyan, the novelist John Mortimer, and Lord Longford, for whom no single-word description is adequate.

Every month the Council met and I took my seat, almost always silently, among the grandees at yet another foreign table. Much as I enjoyed the fringe benefits (theatre, opera), I gave it up, ostensibly because I could no longer afford the time, truly because, as so often happens with me, I needed to get out of something I was becoming too firmly fixed in for comfort, or perhaps discomfort.

Yet I have memories, perhaps unreliable, of crises and congenial personalities that suggest it was in its way an amusing time. One crisis meeting I remember well concerned a show by a group of artists from Los Angeles at the Hayward Gallery. One of the works exhibited was a tank full of fish, which were electrocuted each day at six or seven o'clock in the evening and then fried and distributed, with chips, among the visitors to the gallery. A vigorous protest developed, with the comedian Spike Milligan its main voice, and the Los Angelenos were asked to cut this item. They replied as one man that if the fish killing was banned they would pack up the whole exhibition and go home. An emergency meeting was called at Lord Goodman's flat to find a way out of all this expense and scandal. The day was saved by Lady Antonia Fraser, who argued that most of the people who objected on principle to the killing of the fish probably had no principled objection to eating them; so the exhibition could be closed at five to six and reopened when the fish were already in the frying pans. This wheeze worked perfectly.

Much might be said, admiringly, of the Council in those days, for it was run with intelligence and spirit, had a superb chairman in Goodman, and the best of arts ministers in Jennie Lee. In defence of the proposition that I gave it all up—the responsibilities it imposed and the pleasures it conferred— because it was taking too much of my time, I should add that I simultaneously had a full-time job at University College, was editing the Modern Masters series for Collins in England and Viking in America, and was also trying to write books and do a lot of reviewing, mostly in those days for *The Listener* and *The New York Review of Books*. For various reasons I was often in America. To get my busyness in perspective, I have only to think of Arnold Goodman, by whose standards I was idle; but I was certainly by my own estimate so busy that rather profound domestic difficulties were pushed aside or reserved for treatment in dreams.

The Modern Masters series, which had such success in the 1970s, was born at a lunch with Mark Collins and Michael Turnbull at the Garrick Club, where talk of business is strictly forbidden but universally practised. They wanted me to edit a huge history of literature; I told them it was a bad idea, or at least a bad moment for such a project, since at the time nobody had any clear notion how to go about writing such a history, and nobody could be sure that even if it got done, anyone would be much interested in it.

I had just had a year off, spent mostly in the United States, where I saw the changes that were convulsing the American universities: students had been shot on campus; there were risings and strikes everywhere. On the day of the Cambodian invasion I had flown from the East Coast to Santa Cruz to give a talk. I arrived to find the place closed down except for perpetual protest meetings. I did not regret the trip, because it enabled me to make the acquaintance of Norman O. Brown, to whose post-Freudian exhortations some traced the marked psychic changes that were apparently overtaking American youth. Returning to Connecticut, I discovered that the students, having cut off their long hair and shaved their beards, were knocking on doors and preaching to the householders, who had never before had any contact with them, the wickedness of President Nixon. On beautiful summer lawns young people lay together all night, recovering from their daytime exertions and listening to a troupe of Balinese musicians. Under their blankets or in their sleeping bags they would chat drowsily about the gurus of the time, Marcuse, Guevara, Fanon, Chomsky, Lévi-Strauss. What they repeated was largely hearsay; hence my lunchtime suggestion, quite impromptu, for a series of short, very cheap books offering authoritative but intelligible introductions to such figures. It was accepted and acted upon with such alacrity that the first volumes appeared less than a year after I made this proposal. In Britain they sold for 30p. or 40p., and young people bought them by the handful. Some, Wollheim's *Freud*, for instance, are still in print after almost a quarter of a century, and the series goes on, though the books have grown, like their general editor, heavier and much more expensive.

I suppose there would have been no question of my being entrusted with such an enterprise had I not become known as the author of respectably academic books who was nevertheless a frequent writer in the journals. As I've already remarked, this *deuxième carrière* had been developing for years, and by the 1960s I was writing for papers on both sides of the ocean. For some years I'd been doing pieces for *Encounter* and knew its editors quite well. In 1965, when Stephen Spender retired from the co-editorship and went to America, Melvin Lasky, the other editor, had asked me to take his place.

This was an unexpected and in some ways barely credible invitation, and my decision to accept it was delayed and uneasy; such delay and unease is a familiar prelude to my doing things I shouldn't. It may be difficult for those who do not remember *Encounter* in the 1950s and 1960s, having perhaps seen it only during its long half-life between 1967 and its closure in 1991, to understand its influence. It was started in 1953 with the backing of the Congress for Cultural Freedom, a gentlemanly Cold War organisation supported by American foundations, some of which later turned out to be merely "fronts" for the CIA. The congress so lavishly endowed conferences in pleasant places that it became a well-known gravy train, and some who later admitted or boasted that they had always known of its covert connections took full advantage of the congress's open hand.

Although there was a good deal of gossipy conjecture about it, the funding of *Encounter* and its sister journals—*Preuves* in France, *Tempo Presente* in Italy, *Cuadernos* in Spain, and *Quadrant* in Australia—was still at this time obscure. Anybody who wanted to call it in any sense disreputable had to accommodate the fact that the editors of these publications were all intellectuals of good standing, for example Nicolo Chiaramonte in Italy and in Australia James McAuley.

I suppose McAuley was a typical choice for a congress-funded editorship. As a young man he had achieved a strange celebrity as part-author of the poems of Ern Malley, and could therefore be said to have been the prime mover in one of the most successful hoaxes in literary history. As it happened, I had known him in Sydney in the last year of the war and had a close-up view of the whole Ern Malley affair. The bogus poems were accepted by an avant-garde editor of whom McAuley and his associate, Harold Stewart, disapproved; the victim was comprehensively taken in, and the poems were cried up as the work of a sort of Australian Keats, dead in his twenties. A fictitious sister was said to have discovered the exiguous but complete works among Malley's posthumous papers and sent them to the editor with a letter asking for an opinion. He thought they were wonderful. There followed a great fuss, especially when the newspapers were told of the fraud. The story is complicated by the fact that some of the poems weren't rubbish; the editor was not altogether stupid to accept them. They reached England and were praised by Herbert Read; in the U.S.A. they charmed the youthful John Ashbery and the youthful Kenneth Koch. They were vigorously defended by the Australian painter Sydney Nolan, who for the rest of his increasingly distinguished career never wavered in his view, and to this day there are those who strongly defend Malley's reputation. Paradoxically, it has probably outlasted McAuley's own.

The hoax and its exposure were in my view rather sadistically managed, but the whole affair left one in no doubt about the toughness of McAuley's character and the extent of his talent. When writing under his own name, he was a serious poet and a potent though very conservative influence on Australian intellectual life. In later years he moved steadily to the right, converted to Roman Catholicism, and became an exceptionally committed anti-Communist: hence his editorship of a journal sponsored by the Congress for Cultural Freedom.

Of course all these editors were, in different degrees, anti-Communist, and some, though not necessarily all, knew from the beginning the truth about the foundations which supported their magazines. Irving Kristol and Stephen Spender, the first co-editors of *Encounter*, have consistently and plausibly denied such knowledge. In any case, the work of the Congress could be represented as highly respectable, necessary to political health, and even, up to a point, disinterested. *Encounter* parties were distinguished by the presence of politicians from the left of the right and the right of the left; the magazine was anti-Communist, certainly, an exponent of Cold War politics without doubt, but allowing for the pressure this adherence necessarily placed on editorial policy, still defensible as an organ of judicious and well-informed commentary. Most readers, asked to place it politically, would have opted for the moderate left.

Melvin Lasky, who succeeded Kristol, was a man of similar formation, the product of City College of New York in the late 1930s, its political and largely Marxist heyday. While still attached to the U.S. Army in Berlin, he had edited *Der Monat*, an official publication dedicated to putting the American case in the tense, divided postwar city, and played a part in the establishment of the congress—or, as Neil Berry puts it, perhaps a shade too strongly, in his study of the whole affair, he was "charged with masterminding the ideological offensive against the Soviet Union." His colleague, possibly boss, at the congress, operating from Geneva, was Michael Josselson, now known to have been a CIA agent. Josselson always took a paternal if not censorious interest in the contents of *Encounter* and was often in London, as was the secretary of the congress, the elegant Nicolas Nabokov, cousin of Vladimir, composer and peripatetic agent of Cold War culture. Berry gives a formidable list of the celebrities involved; they included Malcolm Muggeridge, a representative of the congress in Britain who "took part in the money-laundering that launched *Encounter*."

The office in Panton Street was not at all grand, but there was always the feeling, encouraged by most of the operations of the congress, that there was plenty of money around for travel, lunches, and parties. My entry into the office and the peculiar congress atmosphere occurred in 1965. Lasky was always the true boss of the magazine; Spender, who did not love him, allowed that this was so, and even submitted to be called "Steefen," which was Lasky's spelling pronunciation, or perhaps a sort of quiet reproach to the poet for not spelling his name, American fashion, with a *v*.

As I say, the invitation was a great surprise to me, though

perhaps if I'd been wilier it need not have been. I was so far from being known as a political commentator that I could well have been thought a political innocent. I made this point, but it was dismissed as irrelevant. After all, Lasky spent his whole life looking after the politics. What he wanted was a co-editor to handle the literary component. But this was hardly a reason to choose me; numerous writers and journalists in London could have done the job at least as well as I; and then there was the disadvantage (or benefit, depending how you looked at it) that I was living in Gloucestershire, had a job in Bristol, and most weeks couldn't spend more than a day, or at most two, in the office. No matter how hard I might try, I couldn't have much influence on the principal content of the magazine. But what I took to be a handicap was in fact my chief quali-fication. Somewhere in my mind or heart, mixed in with mere vanity, and that disability of which I have spoken, my reluc-tance to disregard the wrong road, I knew I was being set up.

Of course I persuaded myself that I had fully considered all the snags before accepting the job. This process included imperfect investigation of those rumours floating around Lon-don about the past funding of *Encounter*. They were constantly repeated but never with anything like certainty, and in any case, there was no secret about who was at present picking up the tab: it was Cecil King at the *Daily Mirror*. Neil Berry alleges that this slightly odd relationship was the result of a deal encouraged by Josselson, who was beginning to be anx-ious about all the leaks and therefore instructed his little fleet of monthlies to put what looked like clear water between them-selves and the fake foundations that financed them through the congress.

My attempted enquiries were everywhere met with cau-tion, and I found out nothing substantial enough to be weighed against undisputed professions of purity. So I joined, uneasily, but with some hope of enjoying my editorial role, minor though it was. Lasky was anxious to exaggerate my contribution, putting my name, on the ground that K comes before L, ahead of his on the masthead, but I did succeed in having this changed. Even when installed in my office I found that the whole *Encounter* operation remained somehow mysterious. I could never discover the circulation of the journal, or anything substantial about its finances, and I suspected, rightly as it turned out, that the young women who worked in the office were better informed than I. I took no part in the makeup of the issues and, as with my sojourn in the navy, it would have made very little difference if I'd never turned up at all.

My reaction to this unsatisfying situation should have been to get out; in fact, it was to seek to have more control. Lasky agreed that if either of us wanted to argue strongly for an article, the other would not veto its inclusion even if he didn't like it. This pact was tested when the congress organised at a Brighton hotel a huge conference on Europe. The State Department, the Congress for Cultural Freedom, and nearly all the British who were invited were strong advocates of Britain's entry into the Common Market. The speakers were great folks from all over and included the large Bavarian Franz-Josef Strauss. There was, as I remember, only one eloquent dissentient speaker, a journalist named Leonard Beaton from *The Manchester Guardian*.

Beaton argued that Britain's entry into Europe would be very bad for Commonwealth relations; for example, the agriculture of New Zealand had been tailored to British requirements and might be fatally distorted if the system of Commonwealth preference had to be discontinued, as it would. ("How many New Zealanders are there? Three million?" said my co-editor, derisively echoing Stalin's remark about the Pope's divisions.) More remarkably, Beaton contested many of the dismal predictions produced by marketeers who represented entry as the only possible cure for the British economic malaise. He claimed, giving what sounded like plausible reasons, that these sages had deliberately undervalued the postwar performance of the British economy. The occasion being what it was, his speech was not received with acclaim, indeed few took any notice of it; but it seemed to me good that somebody had produced arguments that could leaven the lump of a conference which was otherwise as dull as it was grand because it was committed to a preordained consensus.

When the talking was over, I drove back to London with Beaton and asked him to write up his speech for *Encounter*. Surprised and amused, he asked me what made me think there was the slightest chance of such an article getting into the journal. Remembering the co-editorial pact, I said I thought there was every chance. As soon as possible I spoke to my co-editor, fazing him for once. After reflection he said that it could be done only if a counter-argument were given equal space in the same issue. This extra piece, a specific refutation of Beaton's, would of course be additional to all the other pro-Europe reports of the conference. In the end, of course, nothing was done, and I relapsed into my usual useless activity, writing this and that myself, reading dozens of hopeless unsolicited contributions, and commissioning reviews, some of these by writers soon to be celebrated, like David Lodge and A. S. Byatt. But I can't delude myself into thinking that I revitalised the non-political part of the magazine.

This side of it didn't much interest Lasky, though he looked it over benignly. He was, as I wasn't, a journalist. Whether they belonged to the front or the back, he liked articles that could cause a bit of a stir, like the one about U and non-U language, or John Sparrow's demonstration that the prosecution in the trial of *Lady Chatterley's Lover* had missed the buggery episode; he took pains to ensure that such pieces got a great deal of advance publicity. *Encounter* was always in his thoughts. He scanned the press of England, Europe, and the United States for the revealing one-liners or ten-liners he gathered into the small inset boxes that enlivened the pages. He talked tirelessly to foreign journalists and politicians. In rare moments of leisure he worked at his book on revolutions. He was never anybody's simple mouthpiece, and if his politics closely resembled the politics of the State Department, that was because he believed the State Department had on the whole, and conveniently, got things right.

I'd been at *Encounter* for less than two years when the great crisis developed. It was in part a reflection of the larger turmoil of American politics, the war in Vietnam and the civil-rights movement, subjects on which *Encounter* had tended to be reticent. Conor Cruise O'Brien had already by 1963 been questioning its disinterestedness, and in 1966 he gave a lecture in New York which explicitly accused the magazine of being an agent of some very sophisticated and covert American operations. The charge, quite memorably expressed, amounted to saying that as a forum of opinion it "was not quite an open forum" and that "its political acoustics were a little odd." It had not escaped O'Brien's notice that certain topics elsewhere regarded as pressing were neglected or avoided in a journal that professed to be keeping an intelligent eye on the world, at least until somebody in Washington said, probably via Geneva, that it was time to give them a judicious airing.

It might just have been possible to let O'Brien's remarks pass without notice. A report in *The New York Times* questioning the source of the fake foundation funds had been disconcerting but not particularly damaging, and despite his persistence and persuasiveness, O'Brien's remarks might have been similarly ignored. But there was now an unexpected and intemperate intervention by Goronwy Rees. This strangely celebrated man, once Bursar of All Souls, Oxford, and then the principal of the Aberystwyth branch of the University of Wales, wrote a regular *Encounter* column signed simply "R."

The column, occasionally quite pungent but normally unexciting, well enough though sometimes stodgily written, was the justification for his spending several hours a day at the office. The sale of review copies, it was said, brought in just about enough to keep Goronwy in Scotch.

He had been famous in his youth, as brilliant, as a great lover, and as the original of the character of Eddy in Elizabeth Bowen's novel *The Death of the Heart*. Amazingly well known to many important people in London, he had fairly recently become more generally notorious because of a newspaper article he wrote about his friends the spies Burgess and MacLean. This cost him his job in Wales. Now he made a not very good living writing the official histories of department stores and the like, and doing this column for *Encounter*. He once said to me (this was about 1966), "You can live decently in London on £7,000 a year, but it's bloody well impossible to make £7,000 a year." Nevertheless, he was always in a sense looked after. I often wondered why we were so faithful to his sometimes tedious column, but Lasky clearly regarded it as sacrosanct. After his death it began to appear that Rees had probably been more closely and more professionally associated with his spy friends than he had allowed the world to think. People die off, but at this time there were many survivors of wartime secret service agencies, some well known, and it seemed that the indiscreet Goronwy had a special place in their affections.

They didn't find it necessary to talk about this and other allegiances, for of course they all knew the story already, but equally of course I had no real understanding of this network of ex-agents and wartime old boys. And though much less of a Candide now than I was then, I still don't quite understand Rees's response to Conor Cruise O'Brien, nor how it was got into print. This column was a violent attack on O'Brien, which might have passed had he used it for a routine rebuttal of the charge that *Encounter* was under the control of the CIA; but he added certain allegations about the Irish writer's conduct when he was a highly placed UN representative in the Congo only a few years before, at the time of its decolonisation.

It was arranged, or happened, that I did not see this article until it was in print, or I would surely have questioned its wisdom, accuracy, and propriety. Not surprisingly, O'Brien did. I suppose, in the ordinary way, Lasky would have dealt with this affair, but he had gone off on his long trip to South America. There now began the transatlantic telephone negotiations I referred to earlier in my account of Donald Gordon. Bob Silvers, editor of *The New York Review*, conveyed to me O'Brien's determination to sue for libel unless we published a retraction.

We ran up very large phone bills, but in the end I declined to do as Silvers suggested, and for two reasons. First, Rees assured me that he could produce respectable witnesses to the truth of his account, and indeed, he did introduce me to two journalists who said they were willing to present themselves in that role; but I decided they were not credible. Second, I sought counsel from a barrister reputed to be the best libel lawyer in London. He gave me an exquisite little seminar on the law (I can still see him counting off the main points on his fingers), at the end of which he declared that we had a defence of qualified privilege and advised us to use it.

I don't remember the fine legal points, though I know that this defence, involving a measure of retaliation, depends on one believing that the retaliatory remarks complained of are believed to be true. My position was that I had been given explicit and quite solemn assurances that O'Brien's criticisms of *Encounter* were false, and had decided that if I was to go on working for the magazine I must behave as if I fully accepted those assurances. Everything I heard from Silvers tended to shake my faith in them, but I couldn't yet bring myself to resign, and if I didn't do that, then it seemed I had to defend the case. Here was another instance of my deplorable record in the matter of ethical choices, for, when given a clearly defined alternative—choose between this and that course of conduct—I have almost always, for what seemed at the time powerful or virtuous reasons, chosen wrongly. So the writ for libel was served on me.

My libel expert had not predicted that the case would be tried in a Dublin court, though, as the plaintiff later remarked, it seemed a natural enough consequence, since he was Irish; and since the fact that he was Irish was well known, it should surely not have been difficult for the defendants to foresee the choice of venue. There was, it appeared, no defence of qualified privilege in Irish law; so, in effect, I had no defence to offer. The expert was reasonably cheerful about this development, pointing out that since *Encounter* had no property in Ireland, it didn't matter what damages the Irish court awarded: they couldn't be collected anyway.

However, by the time the case came to trial, the whole matter had begun to look different. In March 1967 two American journals published credible articles about the activities of the CIA in financing, via the front foundations and the congress, such magazines as *Encounter*. Funds had also been used to infiltrate left-wing organisations. I was now sure that the rumours had been true and that *Encounter* was, or rather had been, covertly and politically financed. Of course I knew that the sponsorship of Cecil King was perfectly licit; my reasons for resentment were that I had been told many lies about the past and that *Encounter* was still in rather devious ways under the control (however delicately channelled) of the CIA. For these reasons I felt I could no longer contemplate a continuing relationship with my co-editor and his associates. I had the memorably solemn word of Josselson: lunching at the Garrick, his London club, he had said in reply to my direct questions that there was no truth whatever in O'Brien's accusations, adding impressively, "I am old enough to be your father, and I would no more lie to you than I would to my son." I disliked finding out for sure that I was, as I had suspected, a dupe. And I was naïve enough, when I found it out, to be shocked by this particular lie.

I now wrote to Melvin Lasky, setting out in detail my complaints and explaining that in the absence of very persuasive explanations I couldn't go on working with him. He didn't answer the letter but came out to Gloucestershire to talk it over. As we walked, hour after hour, round the garden and paddock, he gave me the fullest account that could have been expected of his relation to the congress and of the history of *Encounter*. I was never able to dislike this man, so vivid, so New York, so convinced, so clever; and I knew that when it came to a contest which it didn't matter much to me whether I won, but which was, for him, only a skirmish, though quite a serious one, in a war for survival, I was not a considerable opponent. But I was past the point where I could agree that certain compromises, certain changes in *Encounter*, would enable us to carry on together; and I was also sure that it was less a desire that I should stay on than that I shouldn't, at just this point, resign, that made him appear so pliable. I was now sure that I couldn't continue to work with him.

Round about this time there was a meeting of the trustees of *Encounter*. They were Sir William Hayter, former British ambassador in Moscow; Andrew Shonfield, of the London School of Economics; Edward Shils, as potent in Chicago as in Cambridge; and Arthur Schlesinger, Jr. Stephen Spender had also flown in. The trustees had never before, so far as I know, been convened or consulted about anything, and were before this moment only grand names on the writing paper.

But they turned up, two of them straight off the plane from New York, at a lunch in a private room at Scott's restaurant, which was still in its old premises in Piccadilly, commanding a view of the Haymarket, which grew very familiar as the day wore on.

The meeting solved nothing; all I remember is that Spender became very agitated and announced that he was going off to look at some picture in the National Gallery to calm himself. When reminded of this years later, he warmly denied having done so, but I have a clear memory of the moment, no doubt because it seemed an odd yet not uncharacteristic thing for him to do in the midst of such a nerve-racked meeting; which only goes to show you shouldn't put too much trust in memoirs. However, I am sure this happened, whether or not Spender ever reached Trafalgar Square. I knew how passionate he was about what he regarded as the treachery of the congress. During the previous summer I had stayed with him at his house in Provence, and heard him on the telephone to Julius Fleishmann, whose Farfield Foundation was one of the congress's supporters, angrily but unavailingly demanding the truth. Spender and I, with a good deal of support from other people, including Isaiah Berlin and Stuart Hampshire, thought we could run *Encounter* honestly, and decided that if that course wasn't open we would resign and start a rival monthly, temporarily entitled *Counter-Encounter*.

We were all very excited. At the height of the fuss my mother died. A more sensible, a better, man would have called an indefinite time-out at this point; instead, I rushed to the Isle of Man, saw to everything that concerned me, and within four days returned to the crisis. I daresay it made me feel I was doing something important, and in a way I was: to defer mourning is an important mistake, a mistake of the kind that later exacts its price; the reflection that the mistake was made out of vanity increases that cost.

Cecil King now called a meeting in his office, his ostensible purpose being to reconcile the co-editors. Meanwhile, I talked to Rees, who was very bitter against Lasky—a day or two earlier I had heard him screaming abuse at the editor in his office. He kindly promised his full support. But on the day before the meeting in King's office at the *Daily Mirror* I telephoned Rees, by arrangement, at some country house where he was spending the weekend, and he announced peremptorily, almost contemptuously, and certainly without explanation or apology, that he had changed his mind and was now against me. What had occurred in the interim to convince him that his bread was buttered on the other side is a mystery, like so many of Goronwy's doings. Of course I had never supposed that his original decision to take my part had anything to do with simple good will toward me; he must for a time have miscalculated his personal advantage, as he had so often done before. And although his tone made me cross, I didn't suppose his defection made much difference to the balance of forces. It now occurs to me that I might have been wrong about this.

On the day of Cecil King's meeting, Lasky, to my naïve surprise, did not appear in the *Encounter* office, though James McAuley was, somewhat inexplicably, there. I was pleased to see him, so unexpectedly, after so many years; but he can only have come to see Lasky. However, he seemed unperturbed by Mel's absence. Perhaps he had already seen him, for any row about *Encounter* would be bound to have repercussions on *Quadrant* and the other journals in the congress stable.

I went off to the meeting with Spender's letter of resignation in my pocket, as well as my own; and Lord Goodman, who knew a lot about the newspaper world and feared for the innocent thrown into what he regarded as a very dangerous arena, came along too. So did the English trustees, Sir William Hayter and Andrew Shonfield. Mr. King was supported by Hugh Cudlipp. I was outclassed and had already been out-

manoeuvred. Lasky simply didn't appear; the whole matter
had presumably been settled in advance. I explained why it
was no longer possible for me to collaborate with my co-editor;
it was simply that although I had no complaint about the
present funding arrangements of *Encounter* I couldn't accept
responsibility for what was done behind my back, or work
happily with anybody who concealed from me the truth about
the magazine's covert allegiances, especially its formative past
allegiances.

In his reply King made two points only. First, he had
great admiration for Lasky as an editor. He was a journalist
of rare quality. Moreover, as one who controlled more than
two hundred periodical publications he, King, knew all too
well that once a paper began to decline it was almost impossible
to rescue it. Since I agreed with what he said about Lasky's
abilities and couldn't possibly argue that mine equalled them,
I was unable to contest the implication that if I was left in sole
charge the fortunes of the paper would inevitably and irreversibly decline. So it was clear within minutes that I should
have to hand over my letter of resignation and Spender's also.
But King's second point was that he did not wish me to resign;
indeed, he put this so strongly that it amounted to an attempt
at prohibition. He said he thought Lasky and I had worked
well together and should continue to do so. Why he thought
that I don't know; virtually all my time on the paper had been
spent in one struggle or another, with little effect on the contents. I expressed my gratitude for this expression of confidence
but affirmed that it could make no difference to my decision,
and I handed him the two letters. Sir William then said quietly
that he would resign his trusteeship but not until the inevitable
fuss died down. I understood this to be the correct diplomatic
stance, but also felt that if Hayter's resignation had coincided
with mine and Spender's, the outcome might have been
different.

King then got me to promise that I'd say nothing to the press until I had word that both sides might do so simultaneously. I agreed; there seemed from my point of view nothing to be gained at this moment by making a fuss, though later, if we should ever get funds to start the *Counter-Encounter*, the position might change. Outside the *Mirror* building Lord Goodman, who had said nothing during the meeting, told me that I had behaved dangerously in crossing Cecil King, who could prevent my ever getting a job in London again. Although I wasn't in a position to deny this if what was meant was a job in journalism, I felt confident that even if King should have thought it worthwhile to persecute me, my academic employment was securely beyond his range. I remain sure of that, and still wonder how so wise a man as Goodman could have shared the popular overestimate of King's powers.

It would now be generally agreed that it was an overestimate. Soon after these events King was wrongly persuaded that he could topple the Prime Minister, Harold Wilson, and replace him with Lord Mountbatten. Ben Pimlott, recording this extraordinary episode in his biography of Wilson, remarks that "one absolutely certain way to ensure the job security of a Labour leader is for a press baron to demand his removal." Strangely enough, the chair to which I had been invited at University College, London, was originally endowed by King's uncle, Alfred Harmsworth, Lord Northcliffe; but, to compare small things with great, I dare say that attempts to unseat me would have been equally unsuccessful. The truth is probably that the degree of irritation I caused him was far too slight to engage the interest of the great man for more than half an hour or so. Not so long afterwards, he was himself toppled by the board of the International Publishing Corporation, the real owners of those two hundred and more papers. According to Peter Wright's *Spycatcher*, King had expressed a willingness to help MI5 in a "dirty tricks" campaign against the Wilson government; he was, according to Wright, a "long-term contact" of M15, an association which would have disposed him to be sympathetic to the covert cultural operations of the CIA.

After the meeting I went to Lord Goodman's flat. Less than an hour after our arrival there, Anthony Lewis of *The New York Times* was on the telephone asking for my version of the events at the *Mirror*. I suppose King extracted my vow of silence in order to get his version published first. If so the plot misfired, for the Sunday papers were full of the story, and told it in a manner that, without being particularly accurate, was not biased in favour of my opponents.

The reactions of *Encounter*'s contributors to these goings-on were various. Some had known or strongly suspected the truth already and saw no reason to stop writing for a journal that offered them space and a measure of celebrity, especially if they saw little harm in the funding of a virtuously anti-Communist publication by the CIA. Roy Jenkins smoothly remarked, "We had all known that it had been heavily subsidised from American sources, and it did not seem to me to be worse that these should turn out to be a U.S. government agency rather than, as I had vaguely understood, a Cincinnati gin distiller"—the reference is to Fleishmann and the bogus Farfield Foundation. Not everybody took the matter so calmly. The need to choose sides might force amicable division in families: Lionel Trilling withdrew an article, Diana Trilling did not. My friend John Wain valued his association with *Encounter*, not least because he was a freelance writer who needed a journal where he could write at more length than the weeklies allowed, because he needed the fees, and because he approved of its politics; on the other hand, he felt that to continue working for the magazine would be disloyal to me, and he wrote to say that he had had to take a very long walk to make up his mind. He revoked his contract and dropped out of *Encounter*, though a few years later he was back. I felt that this compromise left me nothing to complain of; it wasn't my intention that he and his family should suffer out of fidelity to a cause that was not theirs but mine, and one I should probably never have put myself, let alone a friend, in the position of having to defend.

For some time efforts to start another monthly with pure financial support continued, and I remember waiting in several City anterooms with Stuart Hampshire, with no result; we had not even Dr. Johnson's satisfaction, for no moment came when we could reproach anybody for offering interest when we no longer needed it. There never was a *Counter-Encounter*, though it might be said that *The London Review of Books*, a fortnightly that began at my instigation to appear in 1979— with the enthusiastic and financial support of Bob Silvers and his friends at *The New York Review*—more than filled the gap. *Encounter* itself struggled on, indefatigably soliciting American support, until, already almost forgotten, it expired in 1991.

Writers of memoirs cannot wholly avoid the appearance of self-absorption, and I have dwelt selfishly on this inglorious episode. Neil Berry quotes John Gross's opinion that nobody came out of it with much credit. Gross had worked on *Encounter*—indeed, his name still appeared on the masthead at the time of my joining, though he was no longer active. He was one of the people I consulted when I was trying to decide whether to take the job. He was carefully but not decisively discouraging. I now accept his judgement. As on other occasions before and since, I allowed myself to be involved in an enterprise of which I was too ignorant, persuading myself, against all the available (though admittedly doubtful) evidence, that it was honest enough, and discounting the fact that here, whether honest or not, was a world in which I was unqualified to play a part. The worst of it was that while I did not know that I was invited to play the part largely because I was thought to be safely inadequate to it, I could wake in the night and suspect that it was so.

That was a reasonable conjecture; looking the part while not being quite equal to it seems to be something I do rather well. It accounts for my failures or half-failures as husband and parent, for some fairly stately academic *dégringolades*, for much time and spirit wasted in epochs of unease. The *Encounter* affair was characteristic, for I refused to see what was throughout growing more and more obvious. I had, at the critical moment, the power to avoid the O'Brien lawsuit and didn't do so; and I could not make myself walk out of the problem until, at the worst moment, the moment of maximum equivocal exposure, events compelled me to do so. I have never quite understood the mixture of timidity and—a word that comes strangely to mind in the context—*jemenfoutisme* that I exhibit in those existential crises which the outside observer can reduce to simple stereotypes but which may in truth be the central, most profound, most idiosyncratic, and most instructive moments of a life, or at any rate a life considered as subject to a narrative accounting. In my case this blend of impulses—improbable, since there is nothing intrepid in my character, no conscious love of risk, no physical courage—this inappropriate, improper though idiosyncratic blend of impulses has shown itself capable of being explosive. The explosion is likely to be magnified by outbursts of rage and disappointment arising from another grave condition, which is an incapacity to mistrust amiable people. That failing has caused me much trouble and I know it cannot be wholly eradicated. It may be the beginning of useful self-knowledge to know for sure one disgraceful fact about oneself.

WHEREVER you go you find the world divided into clubs. You can easily see that that is what they are: clubs of officers, of academics, of doctors, of lawyers, of confident men, of potentially lovable women. You know you can never be a member, though the privileges are sometimes offered on a

temporary basis. As a guest or temporary member you bring
out the best in your temporary hosts, though you are always
aware that their perfect manners are of a special kind kept for
non-members who will soon be leaving. Things are altogether
easier within the circle of privilege: people inside them know
where they stand, and what makes them other than the tran-
sients they wish for one reason or another to entertain. All this
you know, but always remain susceptible to cordiality. It is
false but not viciously false, it is offered on the understanding
that you will take it for truth but soon depart, that you will
give whatever small thing it may be that they want of you and
then, as you choose, shake hands or simply flounce out.

One such club, an amorphous body admittedly, is the
Press, at whose club I have been a guest, though only very
intermittently, for a good many years. By the time of the *Encounter* business I should already have known enough about
journalists and newspapers to mistrust the spontaneous friendship, the easy welcome extended to an alien. I failed to absorb
a fairly early lesson, offered sometime in the 1950s, trivial by
comparison with what are now everyday enormities. A young
sister-in-law was to be married to a man who had been reading
law at Oxford. For some reason I had to call, early on the
morning of the wedding, at her flat in Notting Hill. Outside
the front door there was a group of journalists, who cheerily
asked me if I was the lucky man. It seemed they worked for
a Sunday newspaper which featured a Wedding of the Week,
and this wedding had been selected. Surprised but with no
special reason to be bothered by what seemed no more than a
piece of tabloid silliness, I went in and found the bride in
distress. She had wanted no fuss, especially since, as I now
discovered, she was already secretly married to her young man.
They had concealed this truth because he had some Oxford
scholarship or bursary the continuance of which was dependent
on his not marrying during its tenure. Now he was free of that

constraint and they were to be properly married, with veils, top hats, flowers, and photographers, giving away of the bride, and all the rest of it. She was a little distressed by the farcical aspect of all this, but more upset by the consideration that her father, a very conventional figure, might feel humiliated, and also annoyed at having to pay for these redundant celebrations.

The reason why this unimportant wedding had been chosen was precisely that it was redundant, and so slightly romantic—these nice young people were virtuously sealing their contract, making everything public and legitimate. Their best man had sold the piquant secret story to the paper for £25, a fair sum in those days. What the newshounds did not know was that the bride's father had no idea of the truth. I went out and talked to them. When the pub opened we went there and I bought them several rounds. We grew very friendly. I explained that there must be a thousand more glamorous weddings that day in London and that they needn't waste their time on this modest event. They looked interested and agreeable. I told them the worst effect of their persisting would be one that had nothing to do with romance: they would be inflicting a totally unnecessary hurt on the girl's father. They agreed. Since they were here they would come to the wedding, have a drink afterwards, and depart. They promised not to take photographs. We parted friends. I was too thick to see that I had given them a story they valued much more highly than the simple one they had come for, still not knowing of the father's ignorance. They did not take photographs but suborned the photographer hired for the occasion and used his instead. Next day they published a picture, not of the wedding or the bride and bridegroom, but of the old man in his tailcoat and top hat, under a vast headline: SHOCK FOR DAD! A friend of his rushed up to him with a copy as, on Sunday morning, he stood, his paternal duty supposedly discharged, on the first tee.

In a sense everybody had been cheating: the young people

themselves, but innocently enough; the best man, an Oxford
Judas; the hired photographer; and of course the journalists.
Sent in to control the affair, I had actually believed I had done
very well, and killed the story; in fact, I'd managed to replace
it with a better one. Notionally I knew from then on that the
club of journalists has its own rules. It also has its own failings,
which may be explained as professional deformation possibly
aggravated by a fondness for drink. For when you read in the
press reports of activities or opinions of which you happen to
have firsthand knowledge, there is almost always something
amiss, often absurdly so, in the reporting. These deviations
from fact occur even when there is apparently nothing to be
gained by them. So there is in journalism an unavoidable tendency to error, as there is in navigational dead reckoning. The
one certainty about a position calculated by dead reckoning is
that it will be inaccurate; it may have its uses but they are not
the uses of the truth, only of serviceable approximation. Of
course truth is in any case a lot to expect from working people
with deadlines. But I know from dealings with journals which
aren't in such a hurry, and can employ armies of checkers to
question every date and quote, that there is, somehow, in
ephemeral journalism, a natural drift from veracity; no editor
is quite capable of the celestial observations needed to correct it.

My last lowering experience of journalistic approximate-
ness so far (and it seems unlikely that there will be ever be
occasion for another) coincided with my abandonment of what
passed for an orthodox academic career—my decision, in 1982,
to vacate the grandly named King Edward VII Professorship
of English Literature at Cambridge. Whether this event can
now be expected to have as much interest as it seems to have
had at the time (front page in the "quality" newspapers) is at
least doubtful, but so far as my own life is concerned, it was
pretty decisive; signalled by a characteristically overdecisive

gesture, it ended one period of discontent and inaugurated another.

IN 1973 and despite continuing turbulence in my private life I was, as I've suggested, working with much satisfaction at University College, London. Nobody could have thought very well of the conditions under which we did our modestly successful business—a dirty old warehouse off Torrington Place, overlooking other dull buildings and next to a zoology department stocked with noisy animals. But, starting from a rather low point, and amid much dissension (some of it quite vicious), we had done a good deal to make sure that the subject was sensibly taught, and along the corridors there were many interesting and cooperative colleagues. London also affords many happily non-academic friendships. It is a city in which friends may meet only two or three times a year, and removal from the capital could mean that one might never see them at all. So it was a worry rather than a pleasure to receive a letter from the Prime Minister offering to suggest to the Queen that I be appointed to the Cambridge chair. Common sense told me to decline the offer with thanks; vanity hinted that I should regret doing so. I was almost ashamed to admit it, but some miniature version of the log-cabin-to-White-House myth was working in me. My partner of the time had no wish to leave London, nor in truth had I. I liked my job, I liked my London friends. I knew very little about Cambridge, and what I knew was not all that appealing. One practical consideration, not inconsiderable to a man with obligations of alimony, also weighed against acceptance: I should have to manage on a much lower salary.

I went, as invited, to Downing Street, fortifying myself with half an hour in Inigo Jones's Banqueting House before accosting the policeman outside Number 10. The patronage secretary was genial but clearly found it hard to understand

why anybody should hesitate to accept such an offer. We talked
at some length, he calling Cambridge from time to time to
check the facts and request some small modifications of the
offer. I asked for time to think, and he gave me a month. I
consulted people who knew both me and the customary arrangements at Cambridge. L. C. Knights, the incumbent,
made it plain that he had not had much satisfaction in the job.
"Ah, for the road not taken," he said. Noel Annan, my boss
at University College, a devoted Cambridge man and former
provost of King's, was strong against the move, adding only
that if I were foolish enough to make it I must somehow be
got into King's, his own and the only college he thought I
could bear. I went off to New England for the summer, determined to walk by the ocean and allow vanity and common
sense to fight it out while I enjoyed myself.

We stayed with friends in a large house on the shore at
Manchester, Massachusetts, a fairly complicated but at that
time still a happy home. The owner was a rich young man
whom my partner had known at Harvard and whose wife had
been her classmate at Radcliffe. The marriage was soon to
collapse when the man went off his head. He would sit under
the glass dome of this house and imagine he was running the
universe. I was among the many subordinates whom he regarded as having helped him to do this, and he expressed his
gratitude by sending to each of them a cheque for a million
dollars. I understand he also sent one to President Nixon. (The
milieu of Manchester was distinctly Republican.) His mother
wrote worried letters urging the beneficiaries not to try to cash
their cheques. However, in that summer of 1973 everything
was still lovely; the chef at the country club could slice Virginia
ham so thin that it was not unknown for a breeze off the ocean
to blow the slices away. In these unusually luxurious surroundings we discussed the Cambridge offer, to the acceptance of
which my partner was still sensibly opposed. Our American

friends couldn't understand why there was need for argument: like the patronage secretary, they felt you simply didn't turn down offers like this one.

On the last day of the month granted me for deliberation I telephoned the man in Downing Street and said I would do it. That night there was a great storm and people arrived for dinner deafened by thunder and dazzled by lightning. The lights went on and off and there was much civilized hilarity. John Updike crawled under an interesting table on the pretence of looking for evidence of its maker's identity, but really to ask in private who all these extraordinary people were.

Next morning I slipped a disc as I got out of bed, and I spent the next six weeks on my back, reading Racine because the school editions of his plays were the only books in the house light enough to be held at arm's length above the head. At the time I was writing a fortnightly column about books for a London newspaper; always patient, its editor still showed some bafflement when he saw that I expected him to lay before his weekend readership of bored and indignant Tories my morose meditations on *Phèdre* and *Britannicus*. The local hospital doctors soon proved that they had no more idea than their British colleagues how to treat this condition, though all rightly related it to stress. Despite the comfort of my surroundings I had some right to be stressed. Sometimes I was painfully and uselessly conveyed to a sauna, where I could sit and sweat and think stressfully about Cambridge.

TO CAMBRIDGE then I came, where a cauldron of unholy hates hissed all about me. Well, not immediately. At first Cambridge was just chilly. I discovered that certain undertakings given me via the patronage secretary were not being honoured. When I complained of this, I was told on the highest authority that no such undertakings had ever been given. I must be a fantasist or a liar. I telephoned Downing Street and was told that the man I wanted had retired. This sounded like the end of the matter. I was starting out with an irritating defeat, a snub; even—I allowed myself an angry exaggeration—a cold lie. There was no doubt of its being cold. However, I was given the private number of the retired secretary, now living in the country. I asked him whether he remembered our interview, and whether he could or couldn't confirm that this and that had been agreed. Not only did he remember the occasion, he said, he had full notes on it. He called Cambridge and the whole thing was instantly, though as far as the Cambridge bureaucracy was concerned, silently, put right, for the error was never admitted to me. From this moment I date my awed respect for mandarin civil servants; this man, having shed his burden of bishoprics and Regius chairs, was still in his retirement on top of his old job. My respect for and confidence in the university administrators was not similarly enhanced. As time went by, I saw enough of their doings to erode it altogether.

It wasn't the warmest possible welcome, but it was, well, an honest introduction to Cambridge. I discovered that although in a vague way it seemed that much was expected of me, there was really very little I could do. I could announce lectures if I chose, though no provision had been made in the year's programmes for my doing so. By clever work on the part of Lord Annan and Edmund Leach, his successor as provost of the college, I had been got into King's, despite its already having more than its professorial quota. I had rooms there but, to my naïve astonishment, no office at the Faculty and no secretarial help; throughout my time at Cambridge I typed and filed or tried to file my own correspondence, which was all the heavier because people other than Cambridge people took my titular authority seriously. I was forbidden to supervise, which is, in Cambridge, to give tutorials, the most important form of teaching (this ban was later partially lifted).

The government of the Faculty was by an elected board with a revolving chairmanship; when, intermittently, I achieved membership of that board, I had my one vote, an instrument quite inadequate to the reformation of spirit and syllabus that seemed somehow vaguely expected of me.

All this I perhaps should have foreseen. In its own peculiar way the Faculty got its ramshackle courses taught and examined, and to most of its members there seemed no reason why my presence should make any difference. Most of them were quite well suited by the current arrangements, from which they derived certain benefits. To my alien eye the faults in its system were obvious and even scandalous; to most of the my new colleagues, my complaints arose out of mere disaffection, presumption, or ignorance of Cambridge ways. Some of my irritation was perhaps selfish; I had come from a well-ordered department of which I had been the permanent head to a job generally supposed to be of higher, indeed of the highest available, dignity, only to discover that I had become a sort of nobody, yet a nobody with a title, with a carnival crown. I was expected to do great things. I had responsibility and no power, so to apply it to me you had to invert the old description of a whore.

There had been from the start some covert hostility; Clive James, who lived in Cambridge, warned me (not, I think, entirely without malice) that this would be so, and he named names. These were of no great importance. I had some experience in that line, and with more significant opponents, and although I had never shed the old weakness of liking too much to believe I was liked, I was not especially troubled. What bothered me was the present condition of what after all had been the most celebrated English school in the country, and the evidence that although some of its teachers were conscious that all was not well, no change that might halt its decline was likely to be accepted by the Faculty and its board.

The preeminence of Oxbridge is such that unless admission procedures are very faulty, or are interfered with by other considerations—for instance, loyalties that might merge with nepotism—the students should all be very good. Some indeed are so bright that one feels that university teaching hardly touches them; they would as well become whatever it is in them to become without it, though they would miss some fun. Even if they were lazily or badly taught—and this fate must, in the circumstances, have befallen some—it would make very little difference to the outcome; they would dazzle the examiners and pocket their Firsts, which, I was surprised to discover, were distributed more lavishly than at other institutions. No doubt the superior quality of the intake justified this largesse. And it was always possible for ordinarily clever, extraordinarily industrious students to beat the examination system. Nevertheless, in a very large school like ours, there would always be a majority that needed to be more or less systematically instructed and guided towards second-class degrees. And these were the students who were, in my view, least well served.

In 1976 an unofficial working party, chaired by me, wasted months trying to agree on sensible proposals for a new teaching and examination programme. A lot of the teaching was done by people who weren't employed by the university. Cambridge is unique in this respect: it has teachers who are paid by the university, teachers who have not become University Teaching Officers and are paid by their colleges, and freelancers who are paid for supervisions at piecework rates (with cash provided directly to the colleges by local education authorities). You need to do a great deal of exhaustingly repetitive supervision to exist on the piecework income, but the arrangement appeals to research students on inadequate grants, and to various others, perhaps former teachers or their widows. Some of these part-timers are well qualified to do the job, but there is no guarantee that all of them are, and at least in my time there was no central register of approved part-time teachers. Indeed, no one had ever supposed there could be such a thing, since it would have been inconsistent with the doctrine of the autonomy of the colleges, which could make their own pedagogical dispositions; they sent pupils to whomever they chose. One college professed itself proud never to have employed an English fellow, but it still admitted students to read English, either supposing that anybody in their fellowship could turn his hand to teaching literature or farming out their teaching to other colleges or to part-timers. In the course of our enquiries we found it was quite possible for a student to spend three years in Cambridge without ever having been supervised by a teacher directly employed by the university or even (in some extreme cases) by a college lecturer. This can hardly have been what the students expected when, glistening with youth, they first offered themselves to our care.

The discovery of this situation rather shocked me, but it was not generally thought to be of much interest. The assembled Faculty refused to allow discussion of the report or the recommendations it contained—admittedly weakened by dissension within the working party itself—and even voted to exclude consideration of such tiresome and time-wasting issues for some years to come.

It was easy to point out that the university teachers, though inaccessible to some students who hoped to benefit from the privileged arrangements for tête-à-tête tutorial attention, gave a great many lectures from which all could benefit. Lectures were provided in extraordinary numbers. The sole contractual requirement imposed on lecturers was that they should give a minimum number of lectures each year—forty was the usual figure. (I am told it has been *increased*.) This benevolence had farcical results. One could plead with authority that English was grossly understaffed (as it was underhoused) by comparison with other faculties; yet of a new appointment the only necessary consequence was that forty more lectures would be added to a lecture list already absurdly and bewilderingly long.

As to the means by which this list was compiled, I will only say that it further shook one's faith in democracy, for it was an ochlocratic competition between what needed to be done and what autonomous agents were willing to do. Very often this was what they had already been doing for years and they did not intend to change it in the interests of coordination. There would be a worried annual meeting at which efforts were made to sort out the gross gaps and duplications in the lecture list. It rarely succeeded. There were indefensible gaps and preposterous duplications. I once found myself lecturing on Wallace Stevens while at the same hour and in the same building Graham Hough was also lecturing on Wallace Stevens. Most of the lectures were badly attended; students shopped around in the early days of a term and selected the courses they meant to follow. Some courses simply expired after one or two lectures. Directors of Studies in the colleges would sometimes forbid their charges to attend X's lectures while strongly recommending Y's; some lecturers were valued as entertainers, others disparaged as bores. Nobody who had worked in a reasonably sane department elsewhere could have failed to be astonished at the complacency with which these chaotic arrangements were regarded; but they suited the indigenous members of the teaching staff quite well, and so attempts to alter them were easily resisted.

I've had to put in this rather tedious detail because my impotent discontent at the state of affairs here sketched was partly responsible for great rows in 1981, when the press again took a hand in my life. But there was an agreeable intermission, for I was invited to give the Charles Eliot Norton lectures at Harvard, and so took leave during the academic year 1977–

78. The Massachusetts Cambridge offered total relief from the pains of Cambridge, England. It was a winter of great storms, and from a seventh-floor flat one could watch them and next day see the citizens skiing to work down the frozen Charles River. Here was a more convivial, more contented, less vain, yet not less valuable Cambridge. Of course it also had its great men, and between some of the great men there were coolnesses, even enmities. I discovered later that the Harvard English department had its own problems of this sort, and for a while I returned there regularly to assist, without great success, in sorting them out, but at the time they were of so little concern to me that I barely knew they existed. Few people thought it necessary or worth the trouble to dislike me. Some became friends; I would often meet the amiable Roman Jakobson, with his wildly rolling eye, for a coffee-shop lunch, and perhaps an hour later in the Harvard Yard he would pass me quite without recognition. I was not being snubbed, as might have been the case in the old Cambridge, but was merely the victim of his infirmities. I was on good terms with people from many different departments, whereas in the English Cambridge you tend to know only people from your own college and your own faculty. My lectures seemed to go well enough and made a nice little book called *The Genesis of Secrecy*. It was a good year; I almost felt at home. But it ended, and I went back to my own Cambridge, where I almost felt abroad.

Some younger colleagues felt discontent not only at the administrative muddle I've described but at what they took to be the narrow notions of literary scholarship that prevailed. As I've remarked earlier, a row about literary theory was already brewing in the 1970s. The Cambridge English Faculty had staged notable quarrels in the past, some the result of wide and rancorously expressed differences of view concerning the proper nature of literary criticism. Dr. Leavis was always likely to be a combatant; but some disputes had nothing directly to do with him, and it sometimes appeared that a disposition to row was inherent in the very personality of the Faculty, taking opportunities to erupt in every decade since its foundation in the 1920s.

This time the *casus belli* was a young man at that time a stranger to fame. The most convenient ground for a fight in university departments is, or was, the granting or withholding of tenure. At Cambridge the usual practice was to give somebody an assistant lectureship and allow him or her to apply for a lectureship after five years. Whoever did not succeed in this application was chucked out, so discussions about tenure (or rather about appointments, since the word "tenure" was sedulously avoided) were often tense. Now this candidate was a convinced structuralist, or rather post-structuralist, holding opinions abominated by some of his seniors, who therefore attended far more critically to his performance than they did to those of other candidates. His lectures, assiduously inspected over two years, had in the end to be judged satisfactory. But he had published a book, which, in a manner quite contrary to normal practice, was savagely studied by his enemies and attacked on all possible occasions. There were those who had sworn at the time of his original appointment to be rid of him, come what may, at this, the first opportunity.

It seemed to me plain that this man was being dealt with unjustly; against my will I got involved in a fight with opponents more determined than I. Useless to recount all the complex manoeuvres, the dirty tricks, the calculated rhetorical performances. In the end my side lost, as I might have predicted. It was not at all a matter of victory or defeat in a lofty intellectual debate about rival literary theories, which is how some students took it, and how the Sunday papers mockingly reported it. It was certainly related to the whole question of how literature should be taught, especially in Cambridge; but intellectually the disputation was feeble and rather disreputable, and the argument ruthlessly *ad hominem*.

I remember in particular three moments in the campaign,

which went on for months. One was a meeting for which undergraduates, excited by this squabble among their teachers, packed a large hall and were addressed by Raymond Williams, agreed to be the most influential and possibly the most judicious of the professors. As chairman Raymond had demonstrated during contentious, five-hour faculty meetings that he was quite good at keeping his head below the parapet, waiting for turbulence to subside. In the present case, however, he was certainly committed to the cause of the young man, so we probably expected something rather fiery. He spoke, and by the time he had finished, the excitement in the hall, so evident when he began, was extinct. It was a truly sedative performance.

I was never on close enough terms with Williams to ask him whether it had been by accident or design that he had so damped the spirits of his audience; perhaps he had considered the possible consequences of a more rabble-rousing oration and, summoning memories of the late sixties, decided that this wasn't quite the moment to seize a flambeau with zeal to destroy. Even the lively Lisa Jardine, who followed him, was unable to revive the spirit of rebellion. It was entirely typical that I myself chose not to say anything whatever; I like large audiences, but only when I am on a platform addressing them. I find it difficult, however powerful the incentive, to rise from a seat in the midst of a large audience and speak to the speaker.

The second memorable moment was a Discussion in the Senate House on the state of the English Faculty. Anybody who can muster four signatures can call for such a Discussion; usually they are sparsely attended, but this time the Senate House was full of people, come out of real interest or simply to watch the fun. Many people spoke, and every word they said is recorded in the relevant issue of the *Reporter*, the official gazette of the university. Since one had to stand on a platform to do it, I made a speech. Looking at it now I do not care for it, since it makes me see that in the course of the controversy I had unwittingly acquired the polemical manners of the opposition. I have it before me, since it occurred to me to reprint it here, but I haven't the heart. Many true and many false things were said from that platform, the vice-chancellor sitting impassively by; but none of them was profound, and none of them made the slightest difference. It was agreed to set up an enquiry into the state of the English Faculty, but even I knew from the outset that this decision was intended only to restore quiet. *Rusé* at last, I sat and listened to my superiors saying earnestly that it would happen, and even as they spoke knew perfectly well it wouldn't—and it didn't.

I became quite seriously depressed by this apparently endless dispute, which tainted friendships, damaged more casual relationships, and made it impossible to do any real work. What should have been at most a minor irritant was the apparent impossibility of explaining to an attentive press what the row was really about, and my third recollection is of lunch in a pizza house with a well-known Sunday journalist, a man perfectly capable of following my patient, perhaps laboured, exposition if he'd wanted to; but he chose only to be amusedly baffled, and his long report was the usual string of misrepresentations. Of course I ought to have expected this, having claimed to have known about that professional deformation, that simple inability of most journalists to tell things as they are, or even, one suspects, as they know them to be. They may have been right to regard this as a local fuss about very little; but after all, it was they who made it more than that by filling columns of newsprint with angry interviews and satirical commentary. One result of their activities was a potentially ruinous libel action, which cost me and others unwelcome exertions to kill off.

So the press made its contribution to my academic as it had to my editorial demise. I suppose I have rarely been so miserable as during that long row. If it was typical of Cambridge, or at any rate of the English Faculty, I could only feel that I had brought a curse on myself for choosing to join it. I began to have quite serious eye troubles, which persisted for some years more; and I would wake in the morning to be at once invaded by the thought that another day of wretchedness had dawned. But one morning I woke with the different thought that after all I didn't have to suffer it, that I could resign, with reasonable assurance that I could make a living in other ways. And so I did, and so I have.

I continue to live in Cambridge and am happy to have an honorary fellowship at King's, to extend into the future the pleasing connection long ago so cleverly arranged for me. But I have not taught or examined in the Faculty in thirteen years, though I gather it is now at peace with itself, possibly because most of the professors are now women, possibly because the depredations of government have forced them into alliances against an external enemy, possibly because there is now not thought to be anything worth fighting for. In my day it seemed there was, but more ruthless politicians were at work then, and I should have known that I'd let myself be drawn into a losing fight. Some natural tears I dropped, but wiped them soon. The world was all before me where to choose.

The long-term effect of the so-called structuralist controversy was happier than might have been expected. The reactionaries got what they wanted, their young victim suddenly became famous and thrived as he would never have done at Cambridge, while I got on, after a while in reasonable calm of mind, with the rest of my life.

The Flight

Then shall the fall further the flight in me.

—GEORGE HERBERT

IT SEEMS TO BE REQUIRED that when one commits the fault of parting irrevocably from a career, whether it was a profession or a marriage, a sentence must be served: a year or two of despondency, with the possibility of remissions for sensible behaviour. Nothing can alter the fact that much of the interest of life has gone for good, that between such moments and the final farewells it is unlikely that very many of the old pleasures and satisfactions will recur. But neither will the old pains, the old sense of being, too painfully, where one is not entitled to be, doing what one is not entitled to do. Slowly it becomes clear that solitude is a boon, though only if it is interrupted from time to time by good friends, men and women, and reasonably attentive children. There are new cares, largely domestic; but with practice these turn out to be far less terrifying than they seemed at first. After a lifetime of having somebody else to do the cooking, it can be agreeable to learn the rudiments, to bake good bread and make acceptable omelettes. And once again I recall Tristram Shandy's father and his conviction that it is a luxury to sleep diagonally in one's bed. Professionally also, it is a luxury to do as one pleases, as it were, to write diagonally on one's page. There are after-dinner and weekend longueurs, it must be said. But given some luck—and this is probably more important than it seems to the person who has it—and given good health and too many invitations to go here or there, do this or that—it is almost possible to regard old age as a good time to live in.

Of course it would be imprudent to suppose it will always be so. I found myself at dinner in King's the other night with three distinguished men, two of them younger than I, who all depended heavily on sticks. I reminded myself that I had that very morning played squash, more cumbersomely than of old, but without pain and with no retributory stiffness. Will there, next year, be more sticks, or possibly fewer men? I earlier quoted Prospero's remark that when he got back to Milan, every third thought would be his grave; he was probably under fifty at the time, but his mood, if not his resolution, is one that can recur at any age after forty. To succumb to it may, at earlier ages, attract the charge of morbidity, but hardly at seventy-five. I have often written about imagined or fictive endings and said they are all images of the real one. Fall and cease. The third thought is much less alarming than it was: it makes sense of everything, even if one would prefer a different kind of sense.

Because there was a time when I dabbled in biblical schol-arship it has been supposed by some that I am a religious man, but this is a *non sequitur*; such scholarship is often practised by the religious, but what most interests even them, I think, is its technical complexity, and what interested me was its bearing on the theory of fiction. I was provided with the means to be religious, sang Mattins and Evensong every Sunday (sometimes with a difference, for we occasionally sang them in Manx), and identified holiness with the activities of the Anglican Church until I was at least fourteen. I was first married in a Unitarian church, where the address was given by a locally famous preacher who cried passionately, "On such sacrifices . . . the gods themselves throw incense." Well, impressive as he was, he was wrong. The incense reserved for my sacrifices, if any of my losses deserve that name, has been figurative; it has been poetry. I turned out not to be a poet, but that disappointment faded, because after all there was plenty of it to be had elsewhere.

From poetry and music I derive the little I know about holiness. They continue to inform me. I am well aware that there are other kinds of holiness, kinds that I can hopelessly admire, that impel people into action, tending AIDS patients or children dying in poverty; also other kinds that call for silence, a sacrifice almost unimaginable to unholy talkers. Knowing of them I am persuaded of the reality of vocations, other people's vocations, and I know that holiness of this sort has nothing to do with bishops promulgating, on suitable occasions, ideas that were shocking in the 1860s yet still get excited reports, no doubt garbled, in the quality press. But I know also that these holinesses normally have little to do with the kind I have attributed to poetry and music. I can faintly sense a rare coming together of these disparate holinesses in certain Bach cantatas, especially the one known as the *Actus Tragicus*, which begins by assuring us that God's time is the best, and then urges us to set our houses in order, for we must die and not remain among the living. God is serenely invited to incline us to consider that our days are numbered. What seems to me an especially luminous junction of holinesses occurs in a performance of this cantata in which the soprano, Teresa Stich-Randall, seems to have known, as she sang, not only what the words and the music but what holiness meant.

OR SO IT STRIKES ME, who know so little about it. Possibly it would have been helpful to seek holiness by staying in one dear perpetual place instead of being a sort of one-man diaspora. The Manx, as I suggested at the outset, like to stay at home, but they have not always been able to. This man has not returned to Man in order to finish his book. I am writing these closing words in Houston, Texas, where, as I gather from the telephone book, there are three people of my name, though one family spells it "Kermmoade," which shows they've come a long way from home.

There was a big Manx emigration to America in the nineteenth century, and for some reason many exiles gathered at Cleveland, Ohio, where you must go if you want to visit the headquarters of the World Manx Association. Back in the twenties and early thirties the American Manx used to charter a liner and sail back home. I remember the big ships in Douglas bay—their draught such that they couldn't berth at the pier —and the crowd waiting for the homecomers, as they were known, to disembark by lighter. Those were moving occasions, but they happen no longer—the Depression, the war, the jetliner, all conspired to put an end to those sentimental journeys. Now, no doubt, the American Manx of the third and fourth generations no longer have any interest in going "home." For myself, I have, in a single generation, lost the piety to do so.

So I have lacked a place to be nostalgic about, but I've gone on hoping to find one. For many years now I have lived in a house with a long garden. In it there is the head of a fierce lion, broken off from the south wall of King's Chapel during restoration work. Possession of that beast represents a piety of sorts, but it was not enough. I had long vaguely known that the garden also needed, not what Yeats called "indifferent garden deities," but a deity to command the perspective, to appear each morning out of the dark or the mist, and invite me to feel, as it were, presided over: a household god or goddess to assure me that I was at home. I have sometimes said to visitors, in the way of idle conversation as I showed them the garden, that the little grove at the end of it needed some statue, perhaps of a nymph. To my delight some generous friends listened to this chatter and sensed that it was, in its way, serious. By their kindness Diana now stands there, an arrow in one hand, a bow in the other, and over her shoulder a quiver. Though a virgin she has discreetly bared her left breast. She leans a little to the left and has a look that is both seductive and demanding. From my bedroom window she looks tall, much taller than she really is, which must be an effect of the *numen*. As she emerges from the dark or the mist, I am inclined to begin my day by drawing the curtains and looking at her. On some winter mornings she has a diadem of frost. Henceforth she will preside over this garden and the commonplace house in it, and as long as she belongs there, I will belong there also, or be as close to belonging as I am entitled to be, for as long as I am entitled to be.

Alan Sillitoe

Life Without Armour

The autobiography of the early years of one of the greatest English writers of the twentieth century.

'A marvellous escape story. Throughout the book, Sillitoe is in a state of constant excitement and impatience for life to begin.'   *New Statesman & Society*

'A modest, unassuming and decent book, best where it tells self-mockingly of Sillitoe's early literary efforts, but chilling also in its brief account of his childhood.'

ROBERT NYE, *Scotsman*

'Few writers have come quite so far on such unpromising fuel. An absorbing book, not only for its portrait of a pre-Welfare State slum childhood, but for its angle on the position of working-class writers.'   D J TAYLOR, *Independent*

'Sillitoe's autobiography is the more impressive for being told in a simple, almost biblical voice: the voice he was in search of all those years, trimmed to the essence and peculiarly his own.'   *Observer*

'A cheery story, something rare in any sort of biographical writing nowadays.'   *Sunday Times*

'*Life Without Armour* is indeed an extraordinary book.'
Mail on Sunday

ISBN: 0 00 638430 7

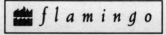